Imitating God in Christ

RECAPTURING A BIBLICAL PATTERN

JASON B. HOOD

IVP Academic

An imprint of InterVarsity Press
Downers Grove, Illinois

InterVarsity Press
P.O. Box 1400, Downers Grove, IL 60515-1426
World Wide Web: www.ivpress.com
Email: email@ivpress.com

InterVarsity Press® is the book-publishing division of InterVarsity Christian Fellowship/USA®, a movement of students and faculty active on campus at hundreds of universities, colleges and schools of nursing in the United States of America, and a member movement of the International Fellowship of Evangelical Students. For information about local and regional activities, write Public Relations Dept., InterVarsity Christian Fellowship/USA, 6400 Schroeder Rd., P.O. Box 7895, Madison, WI 53707-7895, or visit the IVCF website at <www.intervarsity.org>.

While all stories in this book are true, some names and identifying information in this book have been changed to protect the privacy of the individuals involved.

Cover design: Cindy Kiple
Interior design: Beth Hagenberg
Images: foot washing: Foot Washing by Sally Elliot. Private Collection/The Bridgeman Art Library.
     foot print: ©sureyya akin/iStockphoto

ISBN 978-0-8308-2710-7

Printed in the United States of America ∞

Library of Congress Cataloging-in-Publication Data
A catalog record for this book is available from the Library of Congress.

P	21	20	19	18	17	16	15	14	13	12	11	10	9	8	7	6	5	4	3	2	1
Y	31	30	29	28	27	26	25	24	23	22	21	20	19	18	17	16	15	14	13

Contents

Acknowledgments.   7

Introduction: *What Paul Taught Everywhere*   9

PART ONE: Imitating God

1 Idols of God   19

2 Imitators of God   27

3 Priests of God   41

4 Participating in the Work of God.   49

PART TWO: Imitating Jesus

5 The True Human, the Gospel and the Gospels   61

6 Ambassadors, Apprentices and Agents.   71

7 Family Resemblance and Paternity Tests   83

8 Resurrection and Imitation   95

9 The Holy Spirit 107

10 The Apostle of Imitation. 117

11 The Jesus Mirrors. 137

PART THREE: Imitating the Saints

12 A Community of Imitation 155

13 Objections, Obstacles and Presuppositions for Interpretation . . 163

PART FOUR: Imitation Yesterday and Today

14 Imitation for Today's Left, Right and Center 183

15 A History of Imitation 193

Conclusion 209

Author and Subject Index 221

Scripture Index 225

Acknowledgments

Many of the ideas expressed in this book came to me from teachers, of whom I should name and thank Brian Lewis, Robby Holt and Richard Pratt. I hope that in this work I have not strayed far from their wisdom. I also wish to acknowledge an ongoing debt to my doctoral supervisors, Michael Bird and Howard Marshall. I still strive to follow their example, not least in taking primary sources for a mistress.

In one sense the writing of this book began with the publication of three exploratory articles in 2009. I remain grateful for encouraging comments from readers (including Paul E. Miller and Kelly Kapic) of those early attempts to parse some important biblical themes in light of contemporary conversations. I also thank Bryan Chapell for pointing out my erroneous interpretation of his work in a few sentences in one of those articles, and for graciously accepting my apology.

In recent years God has richly blessed me with a number of colleagues who left an imprint in these pages and on my heart, including Robbyn Abedi, Nathan Brasfield, Mark Booker, Justin Borger, Chuck Colson, Scott Lees, Mitchell Moore, Ryan O'Dowd, Abbye Pates, Joshua Smith, the fellows and mentors of the Society for the Advancement of Ecclesial Theology (particularly Gerald Hiestand, Matthew Mason, Doug Sweeney and Kevin Vanhoozer) and The Paideia Centre for Public Theology (especially Craig Bartholomew, Aubrey Spears, Heath Thomas and Al Wolters). And if there is a friend who sticks closer than a colleague, it is Matt Terhune. These conduits of insouciance, prayer, argument, quotations and citations are gifts from God.

Many thanks to the team at IVP, particularly my editor Dan Reid, who helped locate the pulse of this book when I wasn't certain there was one. Dan had me hooked at a preproposal comment on the importance of "union with Christ" for imitation. Thankfully he didn't live up to his reputation by insisting on alphabetized chapters (let the reader understand).

Despite these and other debts, the deficiencies and errors in this book are mine alone.

Mrs. Hood and I wish to acknowledge the importance of our parents in building our faith in Jesus, our love for the Bible, and many others grooves and patterns, almost all of them for the good. It is a privilege to dedicate this book to them.

I write these words next to the bed of my father-in-law in hospice. The recent overflow of praise from his friends and colleagues testifies richly to his standing as a flawed yet faithful hero. We have shared a house for a decade, and with firsthand knowledge of his faith, his habits and his bank account, I could testify far longer. But a dedication shared with three other wonderful exemplars will have to suffice for now.

In any event, he'll soon have a far greater reward.

Introduction

What Paul Taught Everywhere

When I was in seminary, a friend of mine asked a question about the Bible that changed my life. I'm not much for trivia, but this question struck home: "What does Paul explicitly say that he teaches 'everywhere in every church'?"

Paul taught a number of things "everywhere in every church": Jesus as the Son of David, the atoning death of Jesus on a cross, his resurrection and enthronement as Lord, justification by faith, the gift of the Holy Spirit, the unity of the family of God across racial and social lines, the law of love, future judgment at the feet of Jesus. Paul taught these things with enough consistency that we can safely say he never failed to communicate them to his congregations.

Yet none of these things is the correct answer. Since my seminary days I've asked this question of many students and colleagues, but I've never gotten the correct answer from an evangelical.[1] The answer is that Paul teaches his own "ways in Christ . . . everywhere in every church" (1 Cor 4:17).[2] This statement concludes a paragraph in which Paul describes these "ways in Christ" and contrasts them with the mindset the Corinthians have inherited from the world around them:

---

[1]For those keeping score at home, "the cross of Christ" is the most popular answer, with 1 Cor 2:2 often cited. See language similar to "everywhere in every church" in 1 Cor 7:17; 14:33-34.
[2]The NIV's translation is misleading: "my way of life in Christ Jesus, which *agrees with what* I teach everywhere in every church." The italicized words are added to the Greek; they open up the possibility that it is not Paul's "ways in Christ" that are taught "everywhere in every church," but some other teaching with which his "ways" merely agree.

We are fools for the sake of Christ, but you are wise in Christ. We are weak, but you are strong. You are held in honor, but we in disrepute. To the present hour we are hungry and thirsty, we are poorly clothed and beaten and homeless, and we grow weary from the work of our own hands. When reviled, we bless; when persecuted, we endure; when slandered, we speak kindly. We have become like the rubbish of the world, the dregs of all things, to this very day. (1 Cor 4:10-13)

By both ancient and contemporary social standards, many of the characteristics Paul presents here are anything but exemplary. In his day (as in our own), working with one's hands was a shameful, second-class activity to be reserved for slaves if at all possible. What kind of mindset or self-understanding would lead someone to choose to suffer the things Paul describes here?

Earlier in this passage Paul states, "I think that God has exhibited us apostles as last of all, as though sentenced to death, because we have become a spectacle to the world, to angels and to mortals" (1 Cor 4:9). Paul is perhaps describing the apostolic mission here as a march of the condemned, a post-victory parade of captive rebels being marched off to a life of slavery or to be fed to beasts or killed in mock battles. Whatever the imagery behind this sentence, it is clear that Paul sees himself and his disciples as part of a grisly display before humanity and the supernatural world alike.

Any psychologist worth his or her salt can confirm that this sort of martyr complex is unhealthy. But it gets worse. Paul is attempting to instill this framework of death in others. He insists that his approach must be duplicated in the lives of Joe and Jane Christian in Corinth: "Indeed, in Christ Jesus I became your father through the gospel. I appeal to you, then, be imitators of me" (1 Cor 4:15-16). As an example, Paul offers Timothy. "For this reason I sent you Timothy, who is my beloved and faithful child in the Lord" (1 Cor 4:17). Timothy is a flesh-and-blood model who knows and lives the ways of his spiritual father, Paul.[3] He displays for the Corinthians what they should have been putting into practice: a sacrificial, cross-shaped life that reflects Paul's

---

[3]This label for Timothy should remind the Corinthians of the expectation to become faithful "children" in 1 Cor 4:16 and the faithfulness of stewards required in 1 Cor 4:2.

"ways in Christ, as I teach them everywhere in every church."

That's the answer to our pop quiz: Paul taught his sacrificial, cross-shaped life "everywhere in every church."

Now if Paul's cross-shaped life doesn't come to mind as a likely answer to our question, perhaps it's simply because this passage is obscure. But while this question may be the stuff of Bible trivia, there's nothing trivial about the answer. This passage cannot be written off as an obscure thought, tucked away off the beaten path of passages that are more memorable and theologically significant. Paul repeats his cross-shaped résumé throughout his letters to Corinth. Moreover, he insists that he is simply imitating Messiah (1 Cor 11:1), in line with what Jesus repeatedly taught: "If any want to become my followers, let them deny themselves and take up their cross daily and follow me" (Lk 9:23).

DEFINING IMITATION

When we think of imitation, we typically think of a process that involves precise copying. And there is a good bit of rote mimicry in the Bible. God's people rehearsed creeds, prayers, songs, proverbs, stories, rituals and laws with precision. But because there is very little precise copying of Jesus in the Bible, we sometimes downplay the importance of imitation, pointing out how little we can duplicate the actions of Jesus or other biblical characters with precision.

But that is a mistake. In the Bible imitation is rarely about precise copying.[4] Consider how Paul uses imitation. He does not imitate the Messiah by fishing, wearing his hair in a particular fashion, fasting forty days in the wilderness or collecting precisely a dozen disciples. He rarely speaks Jesus' native language, Aramaic. Even when he recommends celibacy (1 Cor 7), Paul does not appeal to Jesus' celibate lifestyle as a model. And in turn, when Paul tells the Corinthians to "imitate me as I imitate the Messiah," he does not mean that they should duplicate his sufferings and sacrifice. Successful imitation of

---

[4]"Mimēsis is not about making exact copies. . . . The Christian vocation is rather that of *creative imitation*." Kevin Vanhoozer, *The Drama of Doctrine: A Canonical-Linguistic Approach to Christian Theology* (Louisville, KY: Westminster John Knox, 2005), p. 401.

Jesus does not depend on literal crucifixion, and the Corinthians are not failures if they are never shipwrecked like the apostle they have been instructed to imitate.

So apparently Paul does not think that *imitate* means "copy precisely in every instance" or "copy the specific details of my life." When Paul speaks of imitation, he has in mind the duplication of a pattern, particularly a pattern that conforms to Jesus' self-denial and cross-bearing. He teaches all of his churches to take his cross-shaped mindset and put it to work.

The present book follows Paul's lead, using a flexible and more expansive approach than the word *imitation* usually brings to mind. In this text imitation refers to actions and mindsets that reflect the actions and mindsets of another.[5] Imitation overlaps with (and is ultimately inseparable from) large theological categories of sanctification and discipleship, and incorporates example, pattern, paradigm (*typos*), partaking (2 Pet 3) and participation. It encompasses or encroaches on verbs like "putting on" or "clothing" (Rom 13:14). It relates to sharing (Rom 8:17), mirroring, reflecting, conforming and mortifying (KJV for "putting to death"). We'll see that imitation is involved in the Bible's discipleship themes of walking and following. As Richard Hays puts it, "To be Jesus' disciple is to obey his call to bear the cross, thus to be like him. . . . When 'imitation of Christ' is understood in these terms, the often-proposed distinction between discipleship and imitation disappears."[6]

One important implication of this approach is that we are not limited to studying passages where imitation explicitly appears. If such a broad, flexible approach to imitation seems objectionable, it

[5]Jimmy Agan delineates various types of imitation in "Toward a Hermeneutic of Imitation: The Imitation of Christ in the *Didascalia Apostolorum*," *Presbyterion* 37 (2011): 31-48.
[6]Richard Hays, *The Moral Vision of the New Testament: Community, Cross, New Creation; A Contemporary Introduction to New Testament Ethics* (New York: HarperOne, 1996), p. 197. Jeff Dryden, *Theology and Ethics in 1 Peter: Paraenetic Strategies for Christian Character Formation* (Tübingen: Mohr Siebeck, 2006), p. 174 n. 27, cites Hays and notes that the frequently made distinction "between 'imitation' and 'following/discipleship'" is not necessary and in fact can be unhelpful if it leaves readers focusing on only one aspect of the cross, either vicarious or exemplary. See also James Samra, "A Biblical View of Discipleship," *Bibliotheca Sacra* 160, no. 2 (2003): 219-34.

may help to remember that we rarely limit theological concepts to the appearance of one word or word group. The word *disciple* does not appear in the New Testament after Acts 21, but no one would think that discipleship is not present after that point. A number of important theological terms, such as *mission*, are labels that are almost entirely absent from the Bible: *mission* appears once in the NIV and never in the ESV or NRSV.

What's more, imitation is simply inescapable. From birth to adulthood, imitation drives our behavior and beliefs. Peer pressure, the herd mentality, word of mouth and other social factors and processes create fresh plausibility structures that facilitate experimentation with drugs, religion, facial hair, sushi and new television programs. We rarely adopt a child, try a new diet or engage in fasting and prayer unless exemplars model these actions and the mindsets that make the actions possible. We keep up with the Joneses, sometimes with reckless abandon, sometimes almost subconsciously duplicating their patterns of speech, consumption, dress and recreation. We don't often use the word *imitation* to describe these phenomena, perhaps in part because we love to think of ourselves as unique and independent actors. But we are all imitators, shaped in a thousand ways by what we see and hear around us.

The Book and the Thesis

While a number of studies focus on the imitation of Jesus or Paul, the concept of imitation does not start with the New Testament. As a result, there are several aspects of imitation we'll explore in this book. First we'll explore God's original design for humans and the imitation of God (chapters 1-4). Next we'll address the imitation of Jesus, God's true image-bearer (chapters 5-11). Because God's redeemed people are being conformed to the character and conduct of God and his Son, we'll then investigate the imitation of God's people (chapters 12-13). And finally we will consider how imitation was used at key points in church history and how imitation applies to various contemporary audiences (chapters 14-15). The last chapter, anchored in John's letters, will use a question-and-answer format to summarize the book's findings.

The idea is to progress from the imitation of God to the imitation of Jesus to the imitation of the saints. There is a certain narrative shape to our journey, one that follows the course of the canon before concluding with church history and contemporary concerns. This approach creates a sense of flow for those who choose to read straight through the text while simultaneously offering a way for pastors and teachers to dip into a chapter that might address a particular passage or a pressing topic.

These three aspects of imitation—the imitation of God, the imitation of his Son and the imitation of the saints—form the backbone of a biblical theology of imitation. They are an integral part of the biblical tapestry of humanity, discipleship and mission. But contemporary discussions of imitation often fail to consider the connection among these three aspects of imitation, and as a result the church has struggled with imitation down to the present day.

Three Audiences

Generally speaking, there are three distinct contemporary approaches to imitation, each with its own problems. Now there are dangers in categorization and generalization, not the least of which is that many Christians do not fall into these categories. So feel free not to find yourself here, or to see yourself in more than one category.

The latitudinal "left" side of Christianity uses the imitation of Jesus liberally, insisting on, say, embracing the marginalized as Jesus did. But this sphere of Christianity often misses the gospel basis for the imitation of Jesus, along with important aspects of the broader biblical framework. For example, there's a call in Scripture to imitate a holy, righteous God. As Richard Hays puts it, "Jesus is not only friend of sinners but also prophetic nemesis of the wicked."[7]

Then there is the massive "middle" of Christianity, full of WWJD bracelets and "be like" sermons. Here the focus on imitation often seems disconnected from God's work for sinners. In the middle and

---

[7]Richard Hays, "Response to Richard Burridge's *Imitating Jesus,*" *Scottish Journal of Theology* 63, no. 3 (2010): 331-35. Burridge's book, *Imitating Jesus: An Inclusive Approach to New Testament Ethics* (Grand Rapids: Eerdmans, 2007), is representative of this sphere.

the left the use of imitation eclipses salvation and substitutes for the gospel, so that preaching, teaching and discipleship can become exercises in moralism or legalism.[8] As with the latitudinal left, there is a distinct lack of attention to the theological framework for imitation. Healthy approaches to imitation require an emphasis on God's initiative in salvation and God's work for us in the gospel.

We can also discern a reluctant or resistant "right" that is highly suspicious of any significant emphasis on imitation. In the face of the shortcomings of the left and the center, reluctance and suspicion can leave imitation downplayed or overlooked in this segment. Reformed scholar Jimmy Agan states, "The topic of the imitation of Christ—the shaping of Christian character and conduct according to patterns observed in the life of Christ—has largely been neglected among Protestant and Reformed scholars."[9]

Readers will have to determine for themselves whether they fall into the left, middle, right, more than one location, or nowhere. But as I have surveyed the landscape, these three spheres seem real enough and large enough to warrant referring to them from time to time in order to clarify the implications of this study.

All three of these groups have weaknesses, even if all three perhaps have contributions to make when it comes to best practices and critiques. In response to this contemporary confusion and resistance, I suggest that we cannot stay clear of imitation. In short, I offer this text not primarily as a how-to book, but as a book that attempts to answer the question, "What does the Bible say about imitation?"[10] And although from time to time we will explore the contemporary significance of what the Bible teaches, the

---

[8]See in particular critiques leveled by Will Willimon and Michael Horton.

[9]Jimmy Agan, "Toward a Hermeneutic of Imitation: The Imitation of Christ in the *Didascalia Apostolorum*," *Presbyterion* 37 (2011): 31-48. Hays makes the same observation with respect to Protestantism as a whole in "Response to Richard Burridge," p. 331.

[10]This book about the Book employs a number of contested assumptions, including the assumption that the Bible is God's Word, the Christian's standard of belief and practice, and that the New Testament's use of the Old Testament is a crucial guide for contemporary interpretation. The author is aware of hermeneutical issues and contemporary scholarly challenges to such approaches but does not have time to address matters such as the unity of the Bible or the authorship of Ephesians.

primary goal is to understand imitation on the Bible's terms, in its categories and configurations.

Conclusion

It is hard to avoid the impression that the contemporary Christian approach to imitation is a messy battlefield fraught with landmines. And once an area is labeled as a minefield, many believers and pastors no longer tread confidently on that turf. As a result, imitation is often soft-pedaled at best and completely avoided at worst.[11] Tempting as it is to neglect or downplay a difficult concept, we cannot treat imitation like a leper. Healthy, robust Christianity does not happen unless imitation has a prominent place in our teaching, preaching, discipleship, counseling, devotion and self-conception.

In other words, imitation is not a disease to be avoided but an essential aspect of Christianity (in fact, it is an essential aspect of being human) that informs our sense of identity, shapes our disciple-making mission and teaches us about our destiny.

As is often the case with exploring theological concepts, the quest for a biblical approach to imitation begins at the beginning. Imitation starts with God, who went digging in the mud to make a mirror.

---

[11]Michael Green, *Evangelism in the Early Church*, rev. ed. (Grand Rapids: Eerdmans, 2003), p. 191.

PART ONE

Imitating God

1

Idols of God

God repeatedly instructs Israel not to make images. But God does not give this command because he is hostile to religion. There are radical differences between Israel and other nations, and the prohibition of idols is implicitly a critique of the worship practices of Israel's neighbors. Israel does, however, share many concepts and practices with its idolatrous neighbors—circumcision, a temple, sacrifices, hymns, pilgrimages, ritual feasts, a holy calendar, worship on mountains and many other practices are found among at least some of Israel's neighbors. So why the prohibition of idols?

Apart from the obvious problem created by images—images facilitate idolatry and the worship of false gods—the root of the prohibition lies here: God, it turns out, already crafted his own images.

When God created humanity, he made us to be his image-bearing idols. (Elsewhere in the Old Testament the word that is here translated "image" usually refers to idols that represent gods or kings.) Seen in this light, God's prohibition is not about his opposition to images but the creation and worship of a lifeless representation of God or false gods. Instead, God makes image-bearers who reflect his glory.

After he creates them, God gives these royal image-bearers the mission of multiplying and filling the earth with living images of the living God. Genesis 1:26-28 and other ancient data show that humans served as God's image-bearing rulers who would represent God and administer his kingship in his world.[1]

> Then God said, "Let us make humankind in our image, according to our likeness; and let them have dominion over the fish of the sea, and over the birds of the air, and over the cattle, and over all the wild animals of the earth, and over every creeping thing that creeps upon the earth."
>
> So God created humankind in his image,
> in the image of God he created them;
> male and female he created them.
>
> God blessed them, and God said to them, "Be fruitful and multiply, and fill the earth and subdue it; and have dominion over the fish of the sea and over the birds of the air and over every living thing that moves upon the earth."

Every aspect of human identity, destiny and mission finds its genesis here in the Bible's opening chapter: humans are God's royal representatives, imaging the one true God as we rule over the world he created.

The significance of the image of God in humans has many facets that have been addressed by theologians throughout the centuries. But Old Testament scholars think that the most prominent aspect of image-bearing lies in representative rule (note eight uses of the word

---

[1]"God ordained humanity to be the primary instrument by which his kingship will be realized on earth." As God's image-bearers, humans bring "the kingdom of God to fruition," and ours is "the wonderful destiny of sharing in his glory." Richard Pratt, *Designed for Dignity: What God Has Made It Possible for You to Be*, 2nd ed. (Philipsburg, NJ: P&R, 2001), p. 7.

over in Gen 1:26-28). In the ancient world kings were sometimes said to possess the "divine image," which would also be present in statues placed in temples and before altars. Emperors would multiply images of themselves in order to fill the sphere of their rule with their likeness. These images depicted the glory of gods and kings and functioned as emblems of their reign. The images communicated that this territory was under the dominion of a particular deity or king whose laws were to be respected, whose fame was to be proclaimed and who would protect those under his or her care.

In modern times, posters and statues of despots such as Mao, Hitler, Saddam and North Korea's Kim dynasty play a similar role. We could also compare the image-bearing functions of corporate logos, social icons, Hollywood royalty and the Roman goddess Libertas, who is symbolized in the Statue of Liberty. Each of these entities has an empire to defend and expand. Image saturation through replication is an important tool of empire expansion and maintenance.

As image-bearers or family members of the gods, ancient kings used the stamp of divine likeness to rule on the gods' behalf. Consider a letter written to King Esarhaddon of Assyria about seven hundred years before Jesus: "A man is the shadow of the gods; a slave is the shadow of a man; and the king is the mirror of the gods." An Egyptian inscription at Luxor shows deities giving the sign or breath of life to Amen-hotep III, saying, "My Son, receive my likeness in thy nose."

But one great difference between Genesis and much of the ancient world is that in Genesis every human receives the task of image-bearing and ruling, not just a king or a handful of priests. God ties the extension of his kingdom and kingship on earth to the spread of humanity. Scholars and pastors across the theological landscape, from John Piper to Walter Brueggemann, summarize the royal identity of human beings:

> God makes man, so to speak, his ruling deputy, and endows him with God-like rights and capacities to subdue the world—to use it and shape it for good purposes, especially the purpose of magnifying the Creator.[2]

---

[2]John Piper, *Don't Waste Your Life* (Wheaton, IL: Crossway, 2003), p. 139.

God wills his human creatures to live life with all the power and privilege, the authority and responsibility which rightly belongs to a king.[3]

The refrain of this scholarly choir was echoed centuries before by
an ancient meditation on Genesis 1 and the significance of human
beings. In an affirmation sandwiched between two declarations of
God's majesty as Israel's sovereign, the psalmist marvels at God's work
in the creation of royal humans:

When I look at your heavens, the work of your fingers,
    the moon and the stars that you have established;
what are human beings that you are mindful of them,
    mortals that you care for them?

Yet you have made them a little lower than God,
    and crowned them with glory and honor.
You have given them dominion over the works of your hands;
    you have put all things under their feet,
all sheep and oxen,
    and also the beasts of the field,
the birds of the air, and the fish of the sea,
    whatever passes along the paths of the seas. (Ps 8:3-8)

We were made for nothing less than glory, honor and enthronement.
But in Genesis 1 and Psalm 8 we also see that the dominion God
assigns is only a reflection of God's own dominion. Human rule is not
absolute; it has to be exercised under the authority of the Emperor
God. Humans have been lavished with royal dignity and assigned to
royal tasks. But being the image of God is not just about sharing rule;

---

[3]Walter Brueggemann, "From Dust to Kingship," *Zeitschrift für die Alttestamentliche Wissenschaft* 84, no. 1 (1972), p. 13. Eugene H. Merrill, in "Image of God," *Dictionary of the Old Testament: Pentateuch*, ed. T. D. Alexander and D. W. Baker (Downers Grove, IL: InterVarsity Press, 2003), p. 445, summarizes the meaning of the image of God in this way: "Humans have dominion over all God's creation ([Gen] 1:26). Again, following the statement of creation (1:27), God pronounced a blessing over the male and female, a powerful word of effective promise that humanity should fill the earth and dominate all its creatures (1:28). The connection between the notion of image and humanity as sovereign seems most apparent: to be the image of God is at the same time to be God's vice-regent in the exercise of divine lordship." See also Sandra Richter, *Epic of Eden: A Christian Entry into the Old Testament* (Downers Grove, IL: IVP Academic, 2008), p. 107; Meredith Kline, *Images of the Spirit* (Eugene, OR: Wipf and Stock, 1999), p. 29.

it is also about recognizing ourselves as servants, vice regents (number two rulers) who remain under the authority of the Emperor God. That means that we rule his way, for his glory.

ROYAL IMITATORS

The royal task of being God's image-bearers carries at least three implications that contribute to a foundation for biblical imitation. We can briefly mention them here, anticipating fuller explorations in later chapters.

First and foremost, our royal status requires that we share in and imitate many aspects of God's character and action. The next two chapters address the ways humans imitate God as his rulers. Sharing in God's image and mission requires "godlikeness," the older and scarier word for "godliness." In fact, image-bearing is about imitation, whether we focus on the ruling dimension or not. Many scholars and believers have little concept of what church fathers such as Augustine knew well: "From the first the idea of image [bearing] is linked with the idea of imitation. . . . [It] is sometimes overlooked . . . [that] the doctrine of the image is a practical doctrine."[4]

Second, the images rebel against their emperor, failing to imitate God as he intended. God's subjects strive to be like him in ways they should not (Gen 3:5, 22). They imitate many other gods, creating a tension that runs through the heart of Scripture: How will humanity fulfill its destiny as the image of God? We will see that the fall actually creates an important new category of imitation. The drama created by human sin reaches its climax in the perfect human image of God: Jesus the Messiah, the true human. In fact, it is possible to frame the drama of Scripture along these lines: "God created humanity to rule the world in his image, and humanity was dethroned from that rule and will be re-enthroned as kings and queens of creation."[5] The

[4]The observation is from Edmund Hill, translator of Augustine, *On the Trinity*, ed. J. Rotelle, trans. Edmund Hill (Hyde Park, NY: New City, 1991), p. 225 n. 23, commenting on 7.3.5.

[5]Stephen Dempster, *Dominion and Dynasty: A Theology of the Hebrew Bible*, vol. 15, New Studies in Biblical Theology (Downers Grove, IL: IVP Academic, 2003). This sentence is a response given by Dempster when asked to summarize his biblical theology of the Old Testament in one sentence in Andy Naselli, "Interview with Stephen Dempster on Old Testament

chapters that cover the Gospels and Paul will explore Jesus' significance as the human solution to the crisis created by rebellion.

Finally, in the hands of believers, royal status often becomes an
invitation to live a life of self-indulgence and self-importance as "a
child of the king." But God's people do not imitate God the Father
alone; they also imitate the Son. They must wait for royal privileges
and inheritance to be given at the appropriate time and to an appropriate degree, when they are fully adopted children of God.[6] Even
though he was the Son of God, Jesus did not consider "equality with
God as something to be exploited" (Phil 2:6). Rather, he made himself
a poor peasant, a slave and a dead man before receiving glory, honor
and rule over all things. No human had more right to full divine privilege than Jesus. He set that right aside in obedience to the Father, and
he requires that his followers share the same mindset (Phil 2:3-11).

The imitation of God the Son does not look glorious or regal by
earthly standards. The earthly pursuit of glory is marked by the pre-
sumption and rebellion of Adam and Eve, who sought to go beyond
the limits of godlikeness prescribed by God. The sad and ironic result
is that in so doing they become far less godlike, as Augustine notes:

> [Man] was delighted also with the statement, "You will be like gods." In
> fact, they would have been better able to be like gods if they had in
> obedience adhered to the supreme and real ground of their being, if
> they had not in pride made themselves their own ground. For created
> gods are not gods in their own true nature, but by participation in the
> true God.[7]

Humans now grasp for power and glory on their own terms, and
God's Word clamps down on these desires at every turn (Deut
17:14-20; Is 57:15; Mk 10:35-44; 2 Cor 12:1-10). In this world of grasping

Theology," Justin Taylor Between Two Worlds, The Gospel Coalition (August 10, 2010),
thegospelcoalition.org/blogs/justintaylor/2010/08/05/interview-with-stephen-dempster-
on-old-testament-theology. Compare *Apocalypse of Moses* 39:1-3; Dan 7; 1 Cor 15. Note also
the two-volume New Testament theology from Ben Witherington III, *The Indelible Image:
The Theological and Ethical Thought World of the New Testament* (Downers Grove, IL: IVP
Academic, 2010), in which Witherington explores Scripture's testimony to the character and
restoration of God's image.
[6]Romans 8:19-23 teaches that adoption is not complete until humans have resurrection bodies.
[7]Augustine, *City of God* 14.13, trans. H. Bettenson (New York: Penguin, 1972), p. 573.

and godlessness, the imitation of God now requires the imitation of Jesus, the theme of the second section of this book.

THE DANGERS OF THEOLOGY

Beliefs are always dangerous things. One of the hidden dangers in theology is that beliefs often come in pairs, like two sides of a coin, which can lead to error if we focus on one to the exclusion of the other: the divinity and the humanity of the Son of God, divine transcendence and immanence, divine sovereignty and human responsibility, grace and judgment. Throughout its history the church has had to learn and relearn that believers are sinners and saints all at once. We can fall into the pits of lawlessness and legalism; we can find ourselves trapped in the deep caves of hedonism or asceticism. The challenge is holding two notions together at the same time. The moment we get one idea nailed down, we must beware of privileging that idea to the extent that we downplay or ignore a parallel concept that might keep our theology from going off the rails. To paraphrase Chesterton, there are many angles at which one falls, but only one at which one stands upright.

For some of us, one challenging element of theology is the uniqueness and "otherness" of God. It's certainly true that God is not like us.

> "For my thoughts are not your thoughts,
>   nor are your ways my ways," says the LORD.
> "For as the heavens are higher than the earth,
>   so are my ways higher than your ways
>   and my thoughts than your thoughts." (Is 55:8-9)

But like many doctrines, the doctrine of infinite difference between humans and God can take a dangerous turn. If we stress only this aspect of what it means to be human, we may begin to undervalue or even eclipse the positive aspects of the Bible's perspective on humanity. In fact, these verses in Isaiah 55 imply the flip side of the coin, a truth we'll find as we explore the rest of the Scriptures: humans were made to think and act like God. For Isaiah 55 does not accent the difference between humanity and God so much as it evokes the similarity between them. The wicked and unrighteous need to abandon their ways and thoughts because they are not believing and acting as God designed them to believe and act (see Is 55:6-7). Humans were made to think God's thoughts after him (albeit not all of them, and not comprehensively, as the other side of the coin reminds us). And humans were made to walk in his ways.

In other words, to err is not human, but to be less human than God intended.

Conclusion

We can master the otherness of God and miss our godlikeness. We can master our godlikeness and miss the otherness of God. If we're going to talk about imitation, we need to think carefully about how we are—and are not—like the God in whose image we have been fashioned. If we find the exploration of godlikeness disturbing, we're probably on the right track. As Kierkegaard put it, "It is less terrible to fall to the ground when the mountains tremble at the voice of the God, than to sit at table with him as an equal; and yet it is the God's concern precisely to have it so."[8]

Because we are created to rule with our Father, he also made us to imitate the character he shows as he rules and guides creation. Even though some divine activities and attributes belong to God alone, imitation stands at the heart of human identity. God did not leave humans in the mud; he gave us his image and spirit so that human character and work might reflect God's character and work. That gift is the genesis of imitation. The following chapters will explore human godlikeness in Israel's story, where God-breathed dirt struggles—in failures, successes, fits and starts—to display its God-shaped destiny.

---

[8]Søren Kierkegaard, *Philosophical Fragments*, rev. trans. Howard Hong, original trans. David Swenson (Princeton, NJ: Princeton University Press, 1936), p. 27.

2

Imitators of God

"What encouragement is greater than this?" cries Chrysostom,
with his instinctive perception of the motive-springs of the human heart.
"Nothing arouses a great soul to the performance of good works so
much as learning that in this it is likened to God."

B. B. WARFIELD

What would God do? I've never seen a WWGD bracelet, and I wonder if anyone has ever thought of creating such a product. In one sense, the question verges on the absurd. The psalmist asks,

> Who is like the LORD our God,
>   who is seated on high,
> who looks far down
>   on the heavens and the earth? (Ps 113:5-6)

Who indeed! But as we saw in the opening chapter, God created humans to represent him, to be his likeness and to rule in his world. This task requires the imitation of God.[1]

---

[1]In fact, the very next verses in Psalm 113 describe God's care for the poor and barren. And while we cannot precisely imitate his actions, we can respond as he does to the needy and lonely. One has only to note the description of the righteous man in Psalm 112:9, on which see below.

Christopher Wright advises that it is perhaps better to speak of the "reflection of God's character rather than the imitation of God, if the latter can be confused with merely copying the actions of God."[2] I do not have a strong preference for the word *imitation* over related terms like *reflection*; we noted previously that such terms overlap. I do, however, think it is worth reclaiming *imitation*, not least in order to correct the mistaken notion that biblical imitation is merely copying. And *imitation* has at least two things in its favor. First, biblical writers are not afraid to teach readers to imitate God (Mt 5:44-45; Eph 5:1). Second, other terms (including *reflection*) can be taken in a strictly passive sense.

As Wright goes on to show, there is significant overlap between God's work and human work.[3] Unless one is predisposed to avoid or downplay imitation and reflection, it is difficult to read the opening chapters of Genesis and fail to see these concepts at work. In those chapters we see that humans imitate God in a number of ways: ruling, working, resting, subduing, naming and evaluating. God works and then puts Adam in the Garden to work. After the creation of Eve, Adam shares God's own approval of creation (Gen 1:31; 2:18, 23; Prov 8:30-31). God names Adam and in turn leads him to name the animals and Eve (Gen 2:19-20, 23).[4] The establishment of a day of enthronement-rest (Gen 2:2-3) anticipates the human imitation of God's enthronement-rest from labor, a connection that is made explicit by passages such as the Ten Commandments (Ex 20:8-11).[5] These aspects of imitation and many others arise from the

---

[2]Christopher J. H. Wright, *Old Testament Ethics for the People of God* (Downers Grove, IL: InterVarsity Press, 2004), p. 37.

[3]Wright, *Old Testament Ethics*, pp. 37-47. Wright's cautions do not lead him to reject imitation. In addition to the context in *Old Testament Ethics* one can find imitation in a number of places in his corpus. For one valuable passage, see *The Mission of God's People: A Biblical Theology for the Church's Mission* (Grand Rapids: Zondervan, 2010), pp. 105-9.

[4]On Adam naming animals: "Name-giving in the ancient orient was primarily an exercise of sovereignty, of command." G. Von Rad, *Genesis: A Commentary*, trans. J. Marks (Philadelphia: Westminster, 1961), p. 81.

[5]"The reason given in Exodus for the observance of the sabbath is imitation of God, who rested from the work of creation on the seventh day." Gordon Wenham, "Law and the Legal System in the Old Testament," in *Law, Morality and the Bible*, ed. Wenham and Bruce Kaye (Leicester, UK: Inter-Varsity Press, 1978), p. 32.

nature and identity of humanity, for sharing God's rule and bearing his image require the imitation of his character and work.

CREATIVITY, WORK, VOCATION

Ruling involves working in God's world as God worked, and God's work is nothing if not creative. Artist-theologians such as Dorothy Sayers and Andy Crouch describe the significance of image-bearing in terms of the creativity humans share with God. The creative activity of Adam's family—who are constantly "making something" of the world and all it contains—is an exercise of power in imitation of God's creative labors.[6] Our creativity in communication, construction and much more illustrates the imitation of the Creator.

Crouch identifies these image-bearing workers as "co-creators." Some object to this title because it elevates humans too greatly (and perhaps sounds too much like the "God is my co-pilot" bumper sticker). Perhaps J. R. R. Tolkien's concept of humans and artists as "sub-creators" is more helpful.[7]

In fact, labels such as "co-creators" and "sub-creators" are not far from Martin Luther's orphic description of human vocation. In his exposition of Psalm 147 and elsewhere, Luther describes the work done by humans as a mask for God and his work. "God milks the cow through the milkmaid," says Luther baldly. Artists, milkmaids, doctors and merchants—all of these are those in whom and through whom God himself labors. The end result is that "nothing, however insignificant, could be credited to God's creatures without also seeing it as the work of the giving God."[8]

---

[6]*Culture Making: Recovering Our Creative Calling* (Downers Grove, IL: InterVarsity Press, 2008). Sayers, in *The Mind of the Maker* (New York: Harcourt and Brace, 1941), develops the relationship between creativity and image-bearing along trinitarian lines.

[7]J. R. R. Tolkien, "On Fairy-Stories," originally published in *Tree and Leaf* (London: Allen and Unwin, 1964); found in *The Tolkien Reader* (New York: Ballantine, 1966), pp. 33-99. According to Donald E. Glover, *The Art of Enchantment* (Athens: Ohio University Press, 1981), pp. 20, 37, C. S. Lewis valued the sub-creator label and applied it for his own purposes (and recommended "On Fairy-Stories"). I owe this reference to my colleague Joshua Andrew Smith.

[8]K. Kapic and J. Borger, *God So Loved That He Gave* (Grand Rapids: Zondervan, 2010), p. 24. The authors cite Calvin, *Institutes* 1.2.55.

RIGHTEOUSNESS

We also imitate a Creator who made and sustains the world in righteousness.[9] The Old Testament wove this belief into the smallest details of the fabric of Israel's covenant life. For instance, Israelites were required to respect their animals while they worked, not muzzling them to prevent them from eating grain while threshing it (Deut 25:4). Israel was to care for aliens because God cared for them when they were landless and rootless: "The alien who resides with you shall be to you as the citizen among you; you shall love the alien as yourself, for you were aliens in the land of Egypt: I am the LORD your God" (Lev 19:34).

The correspondence between divine and human righteousness isn't perfect, and every aspect of human character is damaged since the fall. But this does not prevent the Old Testament and New Testament from teaching the imitation of God's righteousness. As Gordon Wenham states, "Israel must follow justice in her courts, and protect the weak because this is how God acts."[10]

We also see the association between God's righteousness and human righteousness in the pairing of Psalms 111 and 112. In Psalm 112 we see the ideal righteous man presented as a model of good character, blessing and righteous action. But he does not stand alone. Psalms 111 and 112 are set side by side in order to juxtapose the work and character of God with that of the righteous man. God's "righteousness endures forever" because he cares for his creatures (Ps 111:3), and the righteous man "has scattered abroad his gifts to the poor, his righteousness endures forever" (Ps 112:9 NIV). Many evangelicals have been taught to deny that their righteousness might endure forever. But Paul cites this verse when encouraging the Corinthians to give to the poor (2 Cor 9:9; see also Rev 19:7-8).

Paul's emphasis in the conclusion of 2 Corinthians 9 fits elegantly with the original juxtaposition of God's work and human work in the

---

[9]Christopher J. H. Wright, *The Mission of God: Unlocking the Bible's Grand Narrative* (Downers Grove, IL: InterVarsity Press, 2006), pp. 426-27.
[10]Gordon Wenham, "Grace and Law in the Old Testament," in *Law and Morality* (Leicester, UK: Inter-Varsity Press, 1978), p. 9.

Psalms. God's gift, even if it comes through human hands, benefits the giver and receiver and glorifies God. God's "praise endures forever" (Ps 111:10), while the human giver is "blessed" and "his horn will be lifted high in honor" (Ps 112:1, 9 NIV; see also 2 Cor 9:11-15).

REDEMPTION

Our capacity to imitate a righteous God is irrevocably damaged by sin. But even under the reign of sin and decay, imitation is not done and dusted. Rebels still reflect God's greatness and goodness, holiness and happiness, though imperfectly.

In fact, imitation develops a new dimension after the fall: it involves the imitation of God's redemption and restoration of the lost. Exodus portrays "YHWH as the one who promises to redeem (*ga'al*) his people (Ex 6), and as the one who can be praised for having done so (Ex 15)."[11] The law then gives the task of redemption to Israel, whose obedience is to be inspired and informed by its redemption by God. Its people practice redemption in imitation of God's redemption.[12] Deuteronomy puts the imitation of God's redemption into play as a motivation for the pursuit of righteousness in Israel:

> You shall not deprive a resident alien or an orphan of justice; you shall not take a widow's garment in pledge. Remember that you were a slave in Egypt and the LORD your God redeemed you from there; therefore I command you to do this.
>
> When you reap your harvest in your field and forget a sheaf in the field, you shall not go back to get it; it shall be left for the alien, the orphan, and the widow, so that the LORD your God may bless you in all your undertakings. When you beat your olive trees, do not strip what is left; it shall be for the alien, the orphan, and the widow.
>
> When you gather the grapes of your vineyard, do not glean what is left; it shall be for the alien, the orphan, and the widow. Remember that you were a slave in the land of Egypt; therefore I am commanding you to do this. (Deut 24:17-22)

---

[11]Wright, *Mission of God*, p. 267.

[12]See Wright's comments on "God's Model of Redemption: *The Exodus*," in *Mission of God*, especially pp. 266-67.

God's redemption of Israel from slavery provided the ultimate model for the ongoing redemption of Israel's people who had fallen into slavery and the redemption of ancestral lands lost through famine or error. The point is underscored by the use of the same verb, *redeem*, for God's action and human actions (Deut 15:11-15).

We find an example of this redemption in the life of Ruth, a woman from Moab who marries into a Jewish family. After the death of her father-in-law, husband and brother-in-law, Ruth follows her widowed mother-in-law back to Israel. She courageously renounces her nation and her gods and clings in faith and faithfulness to Naomi, Israel and Israel's God. These vulnerable women are assisted and embraced by a relative, Boaz, who takes Ruth as his wife, brings Naomi into his household and buys back the family land. To use the biblical word, Boaz redeems, restoring a disconnected people and place.

It is increasingly popular for evangelicals to portray Ruth's story as the story of redemption in Jesus. Such an interpretation is important; Ruth's story reminds us of our helpless state and the redemption accomplished by our husband-Messiah. But because of the connection between God's work and human work, this story also requires readers to see Ruth and Boaz as examples who respond faithfully to the God who redeems. These two excellent characters are members of Israel's rescued people, a people redeemed from slavery in Egypt so they might put redemption to work in response. Ruth offers a paradigm of God's redemption of sinners but also models a response to God's redemption.

Israel's story rings with the melody of redemption as a new (and unearned) reality given to God's people. That story is incomplete without the harmony: a redemptive response to redemption, the imitation of God's righteousness in the righteous acts of his image-bearers.

DIVINE GENEROSITY

God's creation, care and redemption are acts of generosity, and many recognize the need to imitate God's goodness in response. But one also finds a backlash against trends to interpret passages such as Jesus' feeding miracles on a purely naturalistic basis as fables about generosity. For instance, one finds among the latitudinal left the teaching that the "miracle" in Jesus' feeding of the thousands is really "generosity overcoming selfishness as everyone follows Jesus' example" of sharing fish and loaves.[13] The backlash against such interpretation sometimes includes a reluctance to draw links between God's unique, supernatural goodness and (natural) human generosity. We can only contrast God's work and human work, we are told; we cannot associate the two forms of work, nor should we use God's work to instruct us or guide us.

But the Bible does not share this sharp dualistic approach. Paul ties God's generosity to human generosity:

> I do not mean that there should be relief for others and pressure on you, but it is a question of a fair balance between your present abundance and their need, so that their abundance may be for your need, in order that there may be a fair balance. As it is written,
> "The one who had much did not have too much,
>   and the one who had little did not have too little." (2 Cor 8:13-15, citing Ex 16:18)

Paul appeals to God's miraculous provision of manna for the Israelites in the wilderness as a framework that directs and inspires human generosity.[14] Moreover, though the cross is a supernatural gift, the Corinthians could imitate this gift with material generosity (2 Cor 8:9).

Gordon McConville explains the "obligation of Israel to imitate God" in Deuteronomy as the outworking of a relationship initiated by God. The book "has a kind of inner unity" shown by the "sustained mirror image relationship" between Yahweh's work for Israel (chapters 1 through 11) and the demands of response in worship and obedience in chapters 12 through 26. "This relationship can be described in terms of specific terminology: a correspondence between Yahweh bringing Israel to a place and Israel bringing offerings to a place; between Yahweh acting before Israel and Israel worshipping before

[13]David Turner, *Matthew*, Baker Exegetical Commentary on the New Testament (Grand Rapids: Baker Academic, 2008), p. 369; see also Colin Gunton, *Christ and Creation* (Grand Rapids: Eerdmans 1992), p. 17.
[14]Pace John R. Schneider, *The Good of Affluence: Seeking God in a Culture of Wealth* (Grand Rapids: Eerdmans, 2002), pp. 208-10.

Yahweh; between Yahweh giving the land and other good things and
Israel giving, in imitation of him, to the needy."[15]

Christopher Wright describes the imitation of God as the echo of
God's grace, even if that grace is supernatural. "The detailed requirements of God on Israel are all founded upon the grace of God manifested in their history." The structural arrangement and vocabulary in
"Israel's response to Yahweh in chapters 12-26 mirrors that of Yahweh's
actions toward Israel in chapters 1-11." Wright argues that Deuteronomy's arrangement shows the "priority of grace and divine action
within the covenant framework."[16]

God's generosity, even when described in spiritual or supernatural
terms, can be imitated by human generosity in physical terms.
Throughout the Old Testament as well as in the New Testament, grace
and divine care are intended to produce a horizontal response.

The priority of grace must be firmly gripped, for imitation is often
regarded as a tool for earning salvation or a substitute for the supernatural meaning of texts. Biblical imitation is never a one-way effort.
Redemption has turned slaves into children and mud-covered ur-
chins into mirrors who begin to look like their father.

DIVINE WISDOM

If our status as God's rulers requires the imitation of his righteousness,
redemptive action, creativity and generosity, it also requires that we
share and implement his wisdom. Throughout Israel's literature God
acts in wisdom. When we live and work in wisdom, we imitate the
wise God (Rom 16:27) who creates and sustains the universe in
wisdom (Ps 104:24-25; Prov 3:12, 19-20; 8:22-32).

Every aspect of life requires wisdom, from artistry to business,
from parenting to royal rule (Prov 8:15). Many aspects of God's
wisdom can be imitated. One illustration displays the vast dimensions of this imitation. "The divine building of the cosmic house by

---

[15]Gordon McConville, *Grace in the End: A Study in Deuteronomistic Theology* (Grand Rapids:
Zondervan, 1993), p. 61, citing his fuller argument in *Law and Theology in Deuteronomy*
(Sheffield, UK: JSOT Press, 1994), pp. 33-36; see also p. 37.
[16]Chris Wright, *Deuteronomy*, vol 4, New International Biblical Commentary (Peabody, MA:
Hendrickson, 1996), p. 3.

wisdom is the model for human house building; human culture is a form of the imitatio dei, especially with reference to God's creation of the cosmos as the house in which all houses are contained."[17]

God worked in wisdom as he crafted, ordered and provisioned his world, and humans can—indeed must—imitate by applying God's wisdom in God's world. Wisdom "offers us the key to interpreting our world: its beginning, its purpose, its shape and direction. She can guide us in walking wisely in this life because she knows the places that God carved out for us."[18] As Kidner says, "You have to be godly to be wise; and this is not because godliness pays, but because the only wisdom by which you can handle everyday things in conformity with their nature is the wisdom by which they were divinely made and ordered."[19]

Lady Wisdom appears in Proverbs 8 as a personified attribute "closely related to God"[20] whose admonitions are echoed by human characters in Proverbs (8:12-19, 31). Those who pursue and teach wisdom put the imitation of God and his cosmic wisdom to work in local settings; "the echoes of eternal cosmic Lady Wisdom are merged with the mundane."[21] Two of the most prominent examples are the wise women of Proverbs 31, who model the imitation of divine wisdom in their settings. "The wise woman builds her house" after the fashion of God in Proverbs 8, "but the foolish tears it down" (Prov 14:1; see also Prov 24:3).[22] The generic "righteous man" and "wise woman" in the

---

[17]Raymond C. Van Leeuwen, "Cosmos, Temple, House: Building and Wisdom in Mesopotamia and Israel," in *Wisdom Literature and Mesopotamia*, ed. R. J. Clifford (Atlanta: SBL Press, 2007), p. 81; cited by Craig C. Bartholomew and Ryan P. O'Dowd, *Old Testament Wisdom Literature: A Theological Introduction* (Downers Grove, IL: IVP Academic, 2011), p. 88.

[18]Bartholomew and O'Dowd, *Old Testament Wisdom*, p. 89.

[19]Derek Kidner, *The Proverbs: An Introduction and Commentary*, Tyndale Old Testament Commentaries (Downers Grove, IL: InterVarsity Press, 1964), p. 32. In context Kidner is teaching that Proverbs is not strictly a health-and-wealth document. Of course, wisdom often does pay, as Proverbs and Kidner make clear, precisely because it is the way God designed the world to work.

[20]Bruce Waltke, *The Book of Proverbs: Chapters 1-15*, New International Commentary on the Old Testament (Grand Rapids: Eerdmans, 2005), p. 85.

[21]Bartholomew and O'Dowd, *Old Testament Wisdom*, p. 99.

[22]Tremper Longman III, in *Proverbs*, Baker Commentary on the Old Testament Wisdom and Psalms (Grand Rapids: Baker, 2006), pp. 59, 222, notes the contrast with Dame Folly, who represents the voice of the gods that surround Israel (and contemporary believers), pulling it away from Yahweh.

Proverbs and the Psalter provide a paradigm for imitation or imple-
mentation. They function as illustrations of life lived walking in the
way of wisdom (Prov 4:11-14; 23:19; Mt 7; Eph 5:15; Jas 3:13).

Outside of the wisdom literature, God gives wisdom (often translated "skill") to craftsmen Oholiab and Bezalel so that they can con-
struct his tabernacle; to Joseph, who interprets dreams and governs a
nation; to Joshua, who leads a nation and takes and parcels out territory; and to Solomon, who rules Israel and constructs a temple.
Daniel's God-given wisdom for statecraft was regarded by his masters
as godlike (Dan 1:4, 17, 20; 4:18; 5:11, 14). All of these individuals and
many others live with the grain of the universe as God created it,
working wisely in agriculture, art, craft, family, education, govern-
ment and other social spheres. In our vocations and spheres, humans
imitate the God who employs wisdom in creating and sustaining the
world. Moreover, they imitate God's affirmation and enjoyment of
the world (Prov 8:31) as they enjoy food, sex, relationships, drink
and other pleasures in creation. Far too often in church history, the
imitation of Jesus only leads to asceticism. Adding the imitation of
God encourages the enjoyment of blessings from a God who called
the world good, hosted the first wedding and threw dinner parties
(Ex 24:9-11).

New Testament wisdom literature urges the imitation of the wisdom
of God, Jesus and wise characters (especially characters in parables;
see Mt 7:24-27; 24:25; 25:1-12). Divine wisdom enables a variety of spiritual and moral tasks: Paul wrote Scripture in wisdom given him from
God (2 Pet 3:15). James exhorts believers to ask for and reflect the
wisdom from above, because "human wisdom is wise to the extent
that it mirrors the divine wisdom."[23] By mirroring God's wisdom,
we imitate divine attributes such as purity, impartiality and lack of
hypocrisy (Jas 3:13-17).

It is popular among some evangelicals to see Jesus in the Old
Testament. And indeed wisdom literature contains valuable christocentric treasures waiting to be mined (see Jn 1:1-18; Col 1:15-20; 3:17, 23);

---

[23]Dan McCartney, *James*, Baker Exegetical Commentary on the New Testament (Grand Rapids: Baker Academic, 2009), p. 176.

this interpretive trend is the welcome recovery of a long-lost aspect of Christian interpretation. The New Testament confesses that the history, characters and holy characteristics of the Old Testament all point to Jesus. With respect to wisdom, he is "greater than Solomon" (Mt 12:42). The wisdom of Jesus is justified by the deeds produced in his ministry as he works with the grain of the universe, bending it back toward the shape of God's original design (Mt 11:19). His unexpected message is that the grain of the universe is not wise according to human standards, for it features a crucified Messiah. Death on a cross looks like folly but becomes part of the very definition of power, kingship and victory (1 Cor 1:23-24).[24]

But a Christ-centered approach is not the only way to employ wisdom. As Bruce Waltke notes, "The apostles generally use Proverbs to teach the church how to live godly lives."[25] A commitment to the use of Proverbs as a moral guide for believers can be seen in Proverbs 3:11-12 and 34, Hebrews 12:5-7, James 4:5 and 1 Peter 5:5. Paul picks up the refrain of Proverbs 25:21-22 in Romans 12:20 and alludes to Proverbs 3:7 in 2 Corinthians 8:12. New Testament writers find both positive moral examples and negative examples in wisdom literature (2 Pet 2:22; Prov 26:11). This use of wisdom is also found in Jesus' teaching in parables, which are also a form of wisdom literature.

Both of these elements of wisdom—pointing to the Messiah and telling us how to live—are vital, and we should follow the New Testament and its best readers in carrying out both interpretive tasks. Augustine argued that in Proverbs we find Jesus, the wisdom of God: "It is the Son who is being introduced to us whenever mention is made of wisdom or description given of her in scripture." But in the

---

[24]There are however hints that foreshadow this message in the Old Testament: see Bruce Waltke's definition of righteousness and wickedness in *An Old Testament Theology: An Exegetical, Canonical and Thematic Approach* (Grand Rapids: Zondervan, 2007), p. 289, which is elsewhere in his writings applied to Proverbs.

[25]Waltke, *Proverbs 1-15*, p. 126. Contrast the narrowly Christ-centered approach of Longman in his introductory discussion of wisdom themes in the New Testament in *Proverbs*, pp. 64-69, although Longman clearly sees the moral implications of the book (see p. 104). For a balanced approach, see Doug O'Donnell, *The Beginning and Ending of Wisdom: Preaching Christ from the First and Last Chapters of Proverbs, Ecclesiastes, and Job* (Wheaton, IL: Crossway, 2011).

very next sentence Augustine says, "Let us copy the example of this divine image, the Son, and not draw away from God. . . . He provides a model for us. . . . We by pressing on imitate him who abides motionless; we follow him who stands still, and by walking with him we move toward him, because for us he became a road or way in time by his humility, while being for us an eternal abode by his divinity."[26] If the New Testament writers and Augustine are models for the church's interpretation, finding Jesus and finding moral instruction are both important tasks.[27]

IMITATING DIVINE LOVE

The imitation of divine love is highlighted in the New Testament, but the theme was not invented by Jesus. In tight sequence Deuteronomy 10 contains three references to love, two of which call Israel to imitate God: "What does the Lord your God require of you? Only to fear the Lord your God, to walk in all his ways, to love him" (Deut 10:12). The motivation to love him follows: "The Lord set his heart in love on your ancestors alone and chose you" (Deut 10:15). Israel loves God in imitation of God's love, because he first loved it. The circle is then completed as Israel imitates the God who "loves the strangers, providing them food and clothing. You shall also love the stranger, for you were strangers in the land of Egypt" (Deut 10:18-19).[28]

God's love was their story, and that story became Israel's script.

---

[26]Augustine, *On the Trinity* 7.3.5, ed. J. Rotelle, trans. Edmund Hill (Hyde Park, NY: New City, 1991), p. 225. See esp. note 23.

[27]Summed up by Jaroslav Pelikan in *The Christian Tradition: A History of the Development of Doctrine*, vol. 1, The Emergence of the Catholic Tradition (100-600) (Chicago: University of Chicago Press, 1971), p. 307: "Augustine sought to be as comprehensive as the Scriptures themselves." I owe this quote to Matthew Mason.

[28]Our love is not identical to God's, and not only because his love is perfect and ours is not. Love in the ancient world was a matter of fidelity and had covenantal and imperial overtones: loving your *suzerain*, your emperor, was a matter of imperial submission. This is particularly important to bear in mind for a covenant text like Deuteronomy where love is reciprocal but hardly identical. See D. J. McCarthy, "Notes on the Love of God in Deuteronomy and the Father-son Relationship between Yahweh and Israel," *Catholic Biblical Quarterly* 27, no. 4 (1965): 144-47, and William Moran, "The Ancient Near Eastern Background of the Love of God in Deuteronomy," *Catholic Biblical Quarterly* 25, no. 1 (1963): 77-87. On the connection between love and law, see Wright, *Deuteronomy*, p. 98.

Waltke notes, "It is often said that the Bible represents God anthropomorphically (i.e., as a human being). More accurately, a human being is theomorphic, made like God so that God can communicate himself to people. He gave people ears to show that he hears the cry of the afflicted and eyes to show that he sees the plight of the pitiful (Ps. 94:9)."[29] And if God sees and hears and acts in love, so must we.

SIN AND RESPONSIBILITY

As we saw above, human sin damages the ability to imitate but does not remove the responsibility to imitate. In Ezekiel 28 Tyre is blessed with wisdom and creative skill, until self-deifying pride (Ezek 28:5-6, 17) and unrighteous practices (Ezek 28:18) lead to its destruction. Throughout church history Christians have been tempted to reject the pursuit of wisdom (skill), creativity and imitation. But sin does not make these things sinful. The solution is not the rejection of imitation but the pursuit of God's holiness and righteousness (Ezek 28:18; Eph 4:17-24), and the practice of imitation in a setting of confession and humility.

Consider again the basic task of ruling. While human dominion and judgment are far from perfect and not yet what they will be, our shortcomings do not eliminate the task of ruling. In fact, at present we can do nothing perfectly: our love, justice, holiness and wisdom are all incomplete and touched by sin. But imperfection does not excuse us from responsibility. Ruling is still necessary: churches, families, businesses, nations and educational institutions all require leadership, judgment and discipline.

Governing officials, whether pagan or not, are God's agents (2 Pet 2:13-14; see also Rom 13). The efforts of believers to imitate God and participate in his work are not a blanket approval of all that is done in the name of imitating God and participating in his work. In the same way, Peter's comments are a general statement that God desires the guilty to be punished and the praiseworthy to be affirmed, not a

---

[29]Bruce Waltke and Cathi Fredericks, *Genesis: A Commentary* (Grand Rapids: Zondervan, 2001), p. 65.

blanket approval of all the means employed in that process.[30] Daniel, serving as God's mouthpiece, called the pagan ruler Nebuchadnezzar to account, informing him that he ruled at God's will and should rule in accordance with God's justice and righteousness (Dan 4:19-32; especially 4:27).

Nor do shortcomings and imperfections remove the need for God-imitating, God-honoring rule in the body of Christ (Mt 16:18-20; 18:15-20; Acts 21:25; Gal 6:1). Elders are judged faithful if they "rule well" (1 Tim 5:17). When Paul mocks the Corinthian Christians' over-estimation of their rule and power (1 Cor 4:7-8), he does not imply that they are to give up all efforts at rule and go everyone for themselves. Instead, he teaches a properly cross- and holiness-shaped approach to personal and corporate rule in the Holy Spirit (1 Cor 3:21-23; 4:21–5:13; 6:1-5; 14:40). One day the saints will more fully share in God's rule and judgment (Dan 7; Mt 12:27, 41; 19:28; 1 Cor 6:2, 3; Rev 20:4). Our rule and judgment in the present anticipate the fuller authority destined to be exercised by those in Messiah in the future, in imitation of the loving discipline of God (Heb 12:7-8).

CONCLUSION: IMITATING THE GOD OF ISRAEL

If we are engaged in God's work, ruling as his image-bearers, we should imitate the character he displays as he works. Divine compassion, beauty, holiness and justice should be mirrored in the labors of God's people. We imitate his knowledge, even if our knowledge is not of the same sort as his. The preaching and teaching of God's work should lead to the imitation of God's faithfulness, forgiveness, generosity and righteousness. We do not imitate perfectly, and however impressive our work is by human standards, it is always a pale imitation of God's magnificence. Our best deeds and desires are tainted by sin. Many of the characteristics possessed perfectly by God and appearing in his people are merely imperfect shadows—but they are God-shaped shadows.

---

[30]See also Paul's respect for a wicked leader in Acts 23:3-5, which is in keeping with Ex 22:28. Note the tendency of that section of Exodus to refer to human judges as *elohim*, "gods," which may point to (among many other things) their imitation of divine rule.

3

Priests of God

*The imitation of God is a theme that unites the
ethics of the Old and New Testaments.*

GORDON WENHAM

It's hard for contemporary people to see themselves as royalty. Our self-conception is distorted by our sin and brokenness, and what little we know of royalty is often negative. We see celebrity figures in entertainment, sports, business, politics and religion treated as royalty, and these figures often portray patterns of self-absorption and power grasping. In our attempt to understand our significance and our mission, such social conceptions of royalty do Christians more harm than good.

But humans are not made just to be royalty. We are kings and queens who serve. Our original mission is also a priestly mission. Of course, if it is hard to picture ourselves as royalty, it is even more difficult for us to imagine ourselves as priests. So in this chapter we'll explore this important role that sheds light on imitation in at least two crucial ways: (1) we were intended to be holy images, and (2) we serve the Creator.[1]

---

[1]See especially Greg Beale, *The Temple and the Church's Mission: A Biblical Theology of the
Dwelling Place of God*, New Studies in Biblical Theology, vol. 17 (Downers Grove, IL: Inter-

GOD'S PRIESTS

Priesthood starts in Genesis. As many interpreters of Scripture point out, the shape and contents of Eden and the Garden anticipate the shape and contents of the tabernacle, the temple and the temple's heavenly counterpart, the New Jerusalem. These biblical holy places shared some characteristics with the arrangement of pagan temples, but there were also important differences. While pagan temples held lifeless images at the center, God put his own holy living image in the middle of his cosmic temple of creation. The holiest place in this cosmic temple was the Garden where God began to dwell with his people, and the Garden is comparable to the holy land of Canaan (Gen 13:10) and the holy places later in Israel's story. The two verbs used to summarize Adam's work in the Garden in Genesis 2:15, sometimes translated "work" and "keep," appear together elsewhere in the Old Testament to describe the service of priests in the tabernacle and temple.

In the Garden, in violation of God's commandment, Adam and Eve fatally attempt to become more like God—and therefore less God-dependent—by eating from the tree of the knowledge of good and evil (Gen 3:5, 22-23).[2] Lamech presumptuously insists on the godlike role of avenger, illustrating the excess that characterizes self-enthronement and self-reliance (Gen 4:15, 19-24). Humanity in these instances does not reject rule itself but rule under God characterized by priestly service and worship.

Our godlike capacities turn demonic and anti-human unless they

---

Varsity Press, 2000). Crispin H. P. Fletcher-Louis, in "God's Image, His Cosmic Temple and the High Priest: Towards an Historical and Theological Account of the Incarnation," in *Heaven on Earth: The Temple in Biblical Theology,* ed. T. Desmond Alexander and Simon J. Gathercole (Carlisle, UK: Paternoster, 2004), pp. 81-99, summarizes the implications of temple-cosmos connections, ancient Near Eastern background and liturgical amplifications in Scripture thus: "The high priest acts *imitatio Dei.*" See also Fletcher-Louis, "The Cosmology of P and the Theological Anthropology in the Wisdom of Jesus ben Sira," in *Of Scribes and Sages: Studies in Early Jewish Interpretation and Transmission of Scripture,* ed. Craig A. Evans, Studies in Scripture in Early Judaism and Christianity, vol. 8 (Sheffield, UK: Sheffield Academic, 2004), pp. 69-113, and Fletcher-Louis, *All The Glory of Adam: Liturgical Anthropology in the Dead Sea Scrolls* (Leiden, Netherlands: Brill, 2002), p. 74.

[2]According to William Wilder in "Illumination and Investiture: The Royal Significance of the Tree of Wisdom in Genesis 3," *Westminster Theological Journal* 68, no. 1 (2006): 51-69, Adam and Eve were in a state of immaturity and would be clothed with glory and knowledge upon maturing as intended by God.

are constrained by humility. There is no better antidote for pride than remembering that we are not gods but images and servant-priests in the service of the one true God. These vocations show us that we must glorify God, living before him in constant service in his world and dependence on his provision. There's a comprehensive term for such activity: *worship*. While we often think of worship as an activity limited to particular times and places, worship involves every moment of life and every area of life.

At first glance, an emphasis on humility, service and worship appears to diminish imitation. Our dependent status points to the heart of the difference between God and his creatures. And this status places helpful limits on our imitation, showing us that our character and work is godlike but not deified. We are reminded that we are vice regents (number two rulers), not kings and queens free from all constraints. But a life of humility in service and worship does not rule out imitation. In fact, it enhances and clarifies imitation, and even enables it, for we become what we worship.

WE BECOME WHAT WE WORSHIP[3]

Michael Jackson won a Grammy for telling us that we need to gaze at ourselves in a mirror and "make that change." It's true that what we gaze upon creates change. But the answer is not to look at ourselves or the world around us. MJ's gaze led to a fortune spent on the fulfillment of personal fantasies and plastic surgery after plastic surgery. Over time he changed from self-centered pop star to self-absorbed human catastrophe.

This problem of self-absorption and catastrophe is not just Michael Jackson's problem; it's a universal human condition that we all share. The solution lies not in gazing at ourselves in a mirror but in looking to the one we are supposed to mirror, the God who created us as his images.

The main idea developed in Greg Beale's book *We Become What*

---

[3]What follows is adapted from Jason Hood, "Idolatry, the Gospel, and the Imitation of God," at *Christianity Today*'s online Theology in the News, March 24, 2011, www.christianitytoday .com/CT/2011/marchweb-only/idolatrygospelimitation.html.

We Worship is that "all humans have been created to be reflecting beings, and they will reflect whatever they are ultimately committed to, whether the true God or some other object in the created order. Thus . . . *we resemble what we revere, either for ruin or restoration.*"[4] This concept appears in verses such as Psalm 115:8: "Those who make [idols] are like them; so are all who trust in them" (compare Ps 135:18). The prophets sometimes taunt Israel's enemies—and often Israel's allies or Israel itself—with this truth: they are just as blind and mute or thoughtless and unknowing as their wooden and metal gods.

Beale concentrates on conformity to idols, but he also notes the possibility of becoming what we worship for good. "All of us are imitators and there is no neutrality," he says. "We are either being conformed to an idol of the world or to God."[5] Beale focuses almost exclusively on becoming like false gods, save for an important stretch in his final chapters. There he begins to tap into an important strand of biblical teaching: those who worship the God of Israel will become like him, increasingly fulfilling their destiny of conforming to the Son who is his perfect human image (Rom 8:29; Eph 4:24).

The most famous statue in the United States is the Statue of Liberty. Many Americans are unaware that the image atop the base is a Roman goddess named Libertas. We may not worship this image in a traditional religious sense, but it is not too much to say that American allegiance to self, freedom and independence often becomes a sort of worship. And if we worship these ideals, we become increasingly enslaved to them and unable to serve a God who calls us to discipline, community and dependence on him. We become undependable, unreliable, radically disconnected and unable to depend on others, just as others cannot depend on us. The same independence that can be a source of blessing can become a god whose worship has horrific effects on the fabric of family, vocation and culture. Libertas offers self-indulgence and freedom, but she is a cruel mistress, providing only isolation, loneliness and self-absorption for the individual who clings

---

[4]Greg Beale, *We Become What We Worship: A Biblical Theology of Idolatry* (Downers Grove, IL: IVP Academic, 2008), p. 22, emphasis original.
[5]Ibid., p. 309.

to independence and rejects the service of God, the constraints of Christian community (*koinonia*) or the intimate ties of marriage and Christian friendship.

In contrast, the believer is called to pursue worship, love and obedient service to Yahweh. The pursuit of imitation is a fundamental expression of worship. And as we worship, we see the God we are destined to reflect (Rom 8:29; 1 Jn 3:2). We understand more and more about his character and identity, and (ironically) we better understand who we are, who we are to be and who we are to become.

Temptation to idolatry is multifaceted and ever-present, and we must fight it without respite. The battle requires shrewd awareness of the ways in which we are seduced by culture and its gods. But the best warfare is the engagement of minds and hearts in a different direction. As Beale reminds us, "There is no neutrality." The main solution to idol worship and becoming like our idols is turning to the true God in worship (Rom 12:1-2). Not for nothing is it said that idle hands (and heads and hearts) are the devil's playground. Thus the essence of repentance is not just being sorry but turning around, turning from and turning toward, changing one's mind and one's direction. In so doing we change ourselves. The prince of pop wasn't entirely wrong: we gaze in a mirror and are changed. But we change in a Godward direction, growing in the likeness of the one true God, only when we look to him rather than idols and self.

HOLINESS AND PURITY

The mission of Adam and Eve and humanity—numerical and geographical expansion, worship in the presence of God, rule over God's world under his authority—is also given to Israel, Abraham's family, as the people through whom the nations of the world would find blessing and the presence of God. The priestly mission of humanity is focused intensely on this one family.[6]

Abraham and his family were given the tasks of keeping covenant in "righteousness and justice" (Gen 18:17-19; compare Gen 26:3-5),

---

[6]Beale, *Temple*, pp. 94-95.

pursuing faithfulness and fruitfulness, and mediating blessing to the nations as God's priests. Abraham's family was characterized as royalty in Genesis and given promises of royal rule in the future.

But the mission was not for this family alone. It was God's intent for this one family to be the means by which God would bless the world (Gen 12:1-3; 26:3-5) and the people through whom the nations would know God.[7] This mission required all Israel to embody God's character and holiness. Israel was forbidden to make or possess images, in part because it had been made to be God's image, God's son (Ex 4:22-23). It was sanctified to be the image of the one true God to the world as a kingdom of priests in the service of Yahweh (Ex 19:6). Personal and corporate holiness in Israel would reflect God and his character to others in Israel and to the world. As a result, Israel's book rings with the missional command to "be holy, for I am holy" (Lev 11:45; 19:2; 22:31-33).

Some scholars have argued that Israel's laws were saturated with this message: "To be holy is to be whole, to be one; holiness is unity, integrity, perfection of the individual and of the kind. The dietary rules merely develop the metaphor of holiness on the same lines."[8] These laws provide a constant opportunity to meditate "on the oneness, purity and completeness of God. By rules of avoidance, holiness was given a physical expression in every encounter with the animal kingdom and at every meal. Observance of the dietary rules would thus have been a meaningful part of the great liturgical act of recognition and worship which culminated in the sacrifice in the Temple."[9] Just as ruling as God's image-bearers shapes every sphere of human life, there is also no area of life that is not shaped by the worship of God.

---

[7]See especially Christopher J. H. Wright, *The Mission of God: Unlocking the Bible's Grand Narrative* (Downers Grove, IL: InterVarsity Press, 2006), and *The Mission of God's People: A Biblical Theology of the Church's Mission* (Grand Rapids: Zondervan, 2010).

[8]Mary Douglas, *Purity and Danger: An Analysis of Concepts of Pollution and Taboo* (London: Routledge, 1966), p. 55. See Gordon Wenham, *A Commentary on the Book of Leviticus*, New International Commentary on the Old Testament (Grand Rapids: Eerdmans, 1979), for interaction with Douglas's work. For further thoughts on Old Testament and ethics see Gordon Wenham, *Story as Torah: Reading Old Testament Narrative Ethically* (Grand Rapids: Baker Academic, 2004).

[9]Douglas, *Purity and Danger*, p. 71. This is generally true even if one accepts modifications of Douglas's view, such as those found in her later work.

Far from being abandoned by the New Testament writers, the pursuit of holiness is rigorously applied: "Pursue . . . the holiness without which no one will see the Lord" (Heb 12:14). In 2 Corinthians 6:14–7:1 Paul describes how the covenant promises made to God's people lead to the requirement of holiness. God promises to make a temple out of his people, to live with them (2 Cor 6:16, citing Lev 26:11-12) and to make them his children (2 Cor 6:18, citing 2 Sam 7:14 and Is 43:6). God's family expands to encompass all nations, so that Jews and Gentiles are built into one dwelling place for God (Eph 2:11-22). The only acceptable response to God's sanctifying work is to "cleanse ourselves from every defilement of body and of spirit, making holiness perfect in the fear of God" (2 Cor 7:1). It is no accident that holiness and purity feature prominently in contexts where temple language is used to describe the church.

The mission of holiness as expressed in the Old and New Testaments always comes from the holiness of the Holy One of Israel; it is intrinsic to God's people only because he is present with and in them and they are designed to reflect his glory and share his holiness. It is no accident that the sweeping call to holiness (the book of Leviticus) follows the moment at the end of Exodus when God takes up residence in the tabernacle to dwell near his people. Peter reprises God's command to "be holy, for I am holy" and ascribes this task to "obedient children" of their "Father" (1 Pet 1:14-17). They reflect the character of their Father as his images.

The goal of spiritual formation (or discipleship) is often expressed in the Old Testament and New Testament alike in terms of holiness (2 Cor 7:1). The charge to imitate and implement Yahweh's holiness yields a traditional theological label for discipleship: *sanctification*. Unfortunately, it seems that *sanctification* and related terms such as *godliness* (godlikeness) and *holiness* are not readily associated with imitation. Such labels should also remind believers that they are engaged in work started by God himself, who sanctifies his people while they are anything but holy.

The beauty of biblical imitation in the Old and New Testament is that it is always a response to God's work of sanctifying his people and giving his presence to them.[10] Holiness is never simply self-initiated action. Of course it involves our action, but our efforts are never the beginning of sanctification (Phil 2:12-13). Instead, God's sanctification of his people is the beginning of their pursuit of holiness. That is why the law ties the pursuit of holiness to God's action in sanctifying his people: "Consecrate yourselves therefore, and be holy; for I am the LORD your God. Keep my statutes, and observe them; I am the LORD; I sanctify you" (Lev 20:7-8). The mission could be summarized in both the Old and New Testaments as, "I have made you holy; now be holy, because I am holy and I am with you."

The order of this sequence teaches us that the imitation of God's holiness is never opposed to grace. In the Old Testament, the pursuit of holiness is not works righteousness or proto-Pelagianism. When a child asked a father for Israel's laws, the first part of the prescribed answer was not that the law was a way to earn blessing and life. Rather, the answer begins by pointing to what God did for Israel in redeeming it and setting it apart (Deut 6:20-24). It is simply a faithful response to God's redemption, his sanctification of his people and the imitation of a Father's character.

CONCLUSION

These opening chapters have made the case that humans are created in God's image as royalty and labor in his service as priests. Both of these aspects of our identity are missional tasks that involve the imitation of God. God's image requires far more than the imitation of God's rule; it requires that in all things we reflect the holiness by which he does all things. Christians who focus on the imitation of the love of Jesus may need to coordinate that imitation with the pursuit of holiness and purity. They are called not just to imitate Jesus; they are designed and destined to imitate God. Imitation of God in the Bible is tied tightly to the imitation of his purity and holiness; these tasks are the mission of God's priestly children.

---

[10]This is often labeled "definitive sanctification," or the gift of a holy, sanctified status; it leads to progressive, ongoing sanctification, or growth in holiness.

4

Participating in the Work of God

Since our existence is never autonomous, but at every moment and in every
respect is dependent upon the action of the Spirit who is the Lord and Giver
of life, then the Spirit is never "outside" in the way that other humans and
things are outside. . . . Our transformation into the image of Christ does
not arise from resources that we possess in some independent fashion,
since we possess no resources whatsoever in anything like an
independent fashion. "Without Me you can do nothing" is
an ontological as well as a soteriological claim.

PETER LEITHART

◆ ❖ ◆

Unless Christians are taught that God's work and human work are compatible, they often believe that in any given thought or action either God is at work or humans are, but never both. This dualistic approach can create confusion and even despair as Christians wrestle with sanctification, discipleship and mission. Many Christians believe that any use of their own mind or strength to accomplish a task means they have not worked in the Lord's strength. As a result, these believers have little vision for living life as God's agents, working for his kingdom and for his glory in their vocations, families, witness and relationships with God.

But the God-given ability to imitate makes humans participants in

God's own mission. Thinking rightly about both our role as participants in God's mission on the one hand and God's role in our efforts on the other encourages us and feeds our fruitfulness. We discover that this message produces postures of restful reliance and radical effort. It simultaneously leads to security and striving, quiet confidence and courageous action.

The relationship between God's work and human work is arguably the most misunderstood aspect of discipleship and sanctification. An explanation of this relationship is eye opening for those who tend to view life with a high impermeable wall erected between God's work and their own.[1]

An Old Testament Pattern: God Uses Humans

God is the primary actor in much of Israel's story. Yet throughout Israel's Scriptures, God seems particularly interested in choosing humans as participants in his drama.

God could have made each person by creative fiat, but instead Genesis shows God's habit of working in and through human effort. Abraham and Sarah have bodies that are as good as dead, but God still uses those bodies, rather than an immaculate conception, to produce Isaac. Rather than dropping a boat from heaven, God puts Noah to work constructing an ark for salvation.

Moses serves as God's prophetic mouthpiece and a priestly representative of God to the people and the people to God (Ex 18:19-20; 32:7-14; Ps 106:23). He can even be said to be "God" to Pharaoh and "as God" to Aaron (Ex 4:17; 7:1; see also Ps 45:6). Yahweh and Pharaoh together harden Pharaoh's heart. Some human judges appear to have godlike identities in Israel's story; the word often translated "God" or "gods" (*elohim*) is applied to human rulers (Gen 3:22-23; Ex 21:6;

---

[1]On the other hand, of course, other readers may find less benefit. As best as I can discern, the contents of this chapter are equally plausible within Arminian and Calvinist theological frameworks. However, in both circles one can find a failure to appreciate the participatory role; sanctification is sometimes expressed in almost monergistic terms in contemporary Reformed circles, so that it is claimed that all that is necessary for sanctification is believing the gospel, and in Arminian circles a passive "let go and let God" approach can be found. Both approaches devalue human effort and fail to incorporate the noncompetitive nature of two compatible concepts: God's work and human effort.

22:8-9; Judg 5:9). In Exodus 22:28 there is a close tie between cursing a ruler and cursing God.[2] Yahweh needs no assistance to redeem Israel, bringing them out of slavery and giving them commandments. But even in those great acts he sometimes works through Moses and the priests, even in simple actions such as holding up a staff, hearing cases and dispensing judgments, carrying stones down a mountain to deliver the law or holding hands in the air. The simplicity of these tasks teaches readers that God does not need human participants. He simply chooses to use them.

In Joshua both Yahweh and Israel are the subject of action during the conquest (Josh 1:11; 8:1-2; 10:8-11, 42). To insist that either God or humans alone wins victories in Canaan is to miss the point that God often works through humans to achieve victory without forgoing his claim to credit and glory. "Because of divine initiative, Joshua's hand becomes the power by which the enemy is defeated. . . . Chapters 10-12 argue that the southern and northern parts of Canaan were given to the nation by its God who fought for it. The key to this success was Joshua [and those with him] who heard God's word and obeyed it, just as God heard Joshua's prayer and answered it (11:12)."[3] On the cusp of the Promised Land and daunting battle, Yahweh promises to be with his people (Josh 1:6). In response he requires not passivity but strength and courage (Josh 1:7), the unity of the people of God (Josh 1:12-15) and covenant fidelity (Josh 23–24).

The theme continues in Judges. God brings salvation through humans, even left-handers, women and depressed people (Judg 6:13) with poor self-esteem (Judg 6:15)—maybe even foreigners (Judg 3:31). Judges 3:15 and 28 claim that redemption is God's work. But God doesn't accomplish redemption apart from humans who get their hands bloody and dirty.[4]

In short, the Bible resists a simple either/or response to the question,

---

[2]Cyrus Gordon, "*Myhla* in its Reputed Meaning of Rulers, Judges," *Journal of Biblical Literature* 54, no. 3 (1935): 134-44; Barnabas Lindars, *Judges 1-5: A New Translation and Commentary,* International Critical Commentary (London: T & T Clark, 1995), pp. 239-40; and New English Translation Bible notes for the relevant passages and translations.

[3]Richard Hess, *Joshua,* Tyndale Old Testament Commentaries (Downers Grove, IL: Inter-Varsity Press, 1996), p. 25.

[4]Even a Christocentric reading of Judges or other Old Testament books should not eclipse the fact that God works in and through fallen leaders and institutions, blessing many by their actions.

who is at work in the world and in our deeds? Examples can be found throughout the Old Testament.[5] Against expectations God seems to prefer gaining glory through humans, not just in spite of them (although there is quite a bit of the latter as well). The takeaway is not always "God doesn't need you." That is true enough, and there are passages where this message clearly appears. But sometimes the message of a text is that the unlimited God is able to use limited humans to accomplish his purposes as they act in faith.

Even pagans contribute to God's kingdom, both in their good deeds and in their bad. Although they are not fully aware of it, Pharaoh, Nebuchadnezzar, Cyrus, the Caesars, Caiaphas and Pilate accomplish God's kingdom purposes. God's use of tyrants does not minimize their responsibility for their sin as they do God's work: they are used by God for his purposes, then judged for the evil of their actions. Even the most wicked act in human history, the death of Jesus, is planned and executed by humans in accordance with God's good purposes (Acts 2:22-23; 4:27-28) so that good is accomplished (Gen 50:20).

WHO BUILDS THE KINGDOM?

On the one hand, the kingdom is established without human hands (Dan 2:34). On the other hand, God takes over the nations of this world, and their glory is brought into his kingdom, the New Jerusalem (Rev 11:15). The ships of Tarshish may be destroyed as instruments of slavery and wickedness (Ezek 27; Ps 48); they may also float into the new creation bearing wealth for the glorification of the New Jerusalem (Is 60:6-22).[6]

On the one hand, God himself is divinely responsible for the development of his kingdom through the numerical and geographical limits of humanity (Gen 8–11; Acts 17). On the other hand, humans are still

[5]See Paul House, *Old Testament Theology* (Downers Grove, IL: InterVarsity Press, 1998), pp. 455-62. In his outline of Ruth, House makes God the subject of each passage, even though humans are the actors. That House's approach is correct can be seen in the fact that both Yahweh and Ruth are "blessed" and praised (Ruth 2:11-12, 20; 4:14, 15).
[6]For an important discussion, see Richard Mouw, *When the Kings Come Marching In: Isaiah and the New Jerusalem*, rev. ed. (Grand Rapids: Eerdmans, 2002), pp. 20-24; cited in Andy Crouch, *Culture Making: Rediscovering Our Creative Calling* (Downers Grove, IL: InterVarsity Press, 2008), pp. 167-68.

privileged to participate in the mandates of Genesis 1 and 2 and Matthew 28:18-20. Paul almost never thanks individuals for what they do for him and the kingdom, preferring to thank the one who authored all things rather than the conduit of his blessings.[7] Luther's approach to vocation begins with a discussion of the very human means used by God to answer the prayer "Give us this day our daily bread."

God did not bring a tabernacle and a temple (his earthly throne rooms) down out of heaven. Instead, he gave Moses a blueprint and human artisans his Spirit to work on wood, linens, metals and gems. With respect to the church, the new creation temple of Jesus' body (Eph 2:11-22), humans empowered by God's Spirit are used to make converts and build disciples (Eph 4). But it is no less true to say that God builds his church (Mt 16:18). It is never either God or humans at work building disciples. God did not give his word apart from poets, prophets, scribes and apostles. He did not create the canon of Scripture apart from human emotion, thought and effort (and human reception of Prophets, Gospels and Letters), but through limited human representatives (1 Cor 1:16) who communicated God's own speech. The God who wrote on Belshazzar's wall did not need humans, but he chose to use Daniel to interpret and proclaim what was written on the wall (Dan 5:17-28).

The Old Testament is loaded with references to God being with his people (2 Chron 20:17). When God is present, he is often fighting for his people in war, and usually through their weapons, not apart from them. Jesus' promise to be with his people always (Mt 28:20) is a promise of victory in kingdom warfare. This promise does not guarantee that their work is identical to his work, nor that they will be victors in every battle, nor that victory does not look like a cross; this warfare is not quite like Old Testament warfare. But it is a promise that his people are not working alone.

While angels would be more efficient and German shepherds, parrots and dolphins less sinful, God seems happy to use the work of human ambassadorial representatives to advance his kingdom

---

[7]The only exception to the pattern "I thank God for you" is 1 Cor 16:4.

(2 Cor 5:17-20). Whether God or humans are at work does not seem to be a question that often plagued biblical authors, nor do we see New Testament authors concerned with who is doing the greater percentage of work in sanctification.[8]

In the New Testament we encounter the application and intensification of the Old Testament message of participation through the empowerment of the Holy Spirit and union with the Messiah. The Holy Spirit does not bypass human minds, hearts, desires and effort. Instead, we see in the New Testament a new covenant work of the Holy Spirit recreating people and empowering them. God's sanctifying work in humans is a part of salvation that is his gift, yet that work creates and sustains our work (1 Cor 15:10; Eph 2:10; Phil 1:6, 8; 2:13; Col 1:29).

Paul describes his preaching as God "making his appeal through us" (2 Cor 5:20) and his apostolic ministry as "work[ing] together with him" (2 Cor 6:1). Paul's sense that he was co-working with God did not encourage him to be passive or take his foot off the gas; on the contrary, it led to strenuous effort (2 Cor 6:2-13). Just as God reconciled the world to himself through a human, Jesus (2 Cor 5:18), so now he works through human ambassadors (2 Cor 5:20). As John Murray puts it, "God's working in us is not suspended because we work, nor our working suspended because God works. Nor is the relationship strictly one of co-operation as if God did His part and we did ours. . . . God works in us and we also work. But the relationship is that because God works, we work."[9] Murray is correct: the key to the relationship is not relative weight, as if God's work in us diminished our labor or striving, and it is even less a matter of either-or. Rather, the key is priority and initiative.

For Paul the belief that God works through him and others for mission and sanctification produces more human effort and desire for sanctification and the growth of God's kingdom, not less. Paul's belief in God's work in him and others led him to give more instruction and

---

[8]Notwithstanding a category of God-only actions such as justifying, regenerating and resurrecting humans.

[9]John Murray, *Redemption Accomplished and Applied* (Grand Rapids: Eerdmans, 1955), pp. 148-49.

exhortation, not less. In the Old Testament the message that God is with his people to fight is a call to strive for victory without fear, not a call to retire from the battlefield. In the same way, the New Testament message that Jesus remains with his believers during their mission (Mt 28:20) leads to more missional labor, not less.

PARTICIPATION: A FEW IMPLICATIONS

There are a number of implications regarding this approach to God's work and our work. First, if we are participating in God's work as we fill the world and rule it, our labors are affirmed and approved by God. Many believers hardly ever ponder their glorious destiny, and many are unaware of the possibility that they can have a foretaste of that destiny in their present work, worship and relationships. It is important to be aware of our fallen condition, but it is possible to focus on shortcomings and brokenness to the exclusion of what humans are still capable of accomplishing. The image of God has been effaced but not erased. Our participation in God's work is corrupted, but it is never completely corroded.

Many Christians do not ponder their status as the likeness of God. For many evangelicals, the only significance of image-bearing is that murder and abortion are wrong. They have lost sight of the dignity God gave their work when he made it (after a fashion) his own work and enabled our thoughts and deeds to reflect his own. As a result, it is very easy to accept God's love for us on a spiritual level and ignore God's involvement and delight in everyday life, laughing or love-making. Many Christians do not believe that their activities—whether parenting or preaching, pastoring or partying—are important, that they have been done "in him" (Acts 17:28) and that God enjoys them. We struggle to affirm the good our unbelieving friends sometimes accomplish, such as great works of art, wise governance and acts of moral goodness. As Luther's comments on vocation suggest, we must learn to see ourselves as God's agents in tasks as humble as milking a cow and labors as spectacular as composing a masterful symphony. As Jack Miller once said, God does not just love us; he likes us. He enjoys our enjoyment of his world, and he labors in our labors.

Second, seeing ourselves as participants clarifies the claim that
God's mission is in some respects our mission and that he is at work
in and through us to build his kingdom. (In some respects the label
imitation tends to emphasize the human side of mission, while *participation* brings human and divine labor together.[10]) Sharing his
kingdom mission clarifies our role as imitators, helping us see that we
are to work for God in a godly way. We can study his work and his
ways and put them into practice. We may be toddler-like in our abil-
ities, but we are still on a path to maturity that makes imitation vital.

Third, understanding that we are participants in God's work
should lead us to humility, dependence and worship. If humans live
and move and have their being in God, they are never independent,
as Leithart's quote at the beginning of this chapter makes clear.
Micah 6:8 strikes the comprehensive note required: What does
Yahweh require of you but (1) to do justice, (2) to love mercy and (3)
to walk humbly with your God? Loving mercy and doing justice are
God work, done in imitation of him according to his standards. But
this verse tells us that God requires not just imitation but "walking
humbly with your God." "Walking with God" is a common Hebrew
metaphor for living in right relationship with God, which means
among other things a relationship of dependence. It is an acknowl-
edgment that while we may imitate God and participate in his work,
we are servants, not gods. "Humbly" describes our mode of life when
we are fully apprised of our inability to do anything at all apart from
God. Dependence also produces humility in our evaluation of others:
God is powerfully at work even in what seems pernicious or puny,
foolish or forlorn (Gen 50:20).

CONCLUDING THE DRAMA

The drama of the Old Testament story does not resolve in its own
pages. It ends as an unfinished stanza with a puzzled question mark.
Despite the high points, despite many instances of the imitation of
God and participation in his work, the Old Testament teaches us of a

---

[10]I owe this way of putting things to Keith Johnson.

gaping hole, a festering wound that will not close and heal. Our rebellion is the reason the story does not end with Exodus, or David, or
return from exile, or Malachi. In the world around us—in art, in relationships, in nature—humans hear whispers of beauty and blessing.
But these whispers are often little more than fleeting echoes to remind
us of a beautiful but unattainable destiny. Our efforts at glory and
goodness are shadows of something that is still on its way. Our drive
for beauty and justice points to a beauty, justice and peace that are
perfect and permanent.

Throughout the Old Testament there are dreams of a glorious
destiny when the world will be as it should be, with the saints enthroned to participate in the glory and rule of God and the Son of
Man (Dan 7). But the universal reality of sin and the trajectory of
failure in Israel reveal a crisis of epic proportions. Humans are mired
in brokenness, condemned to death and enslaved to sin that robs
them of glory. Human nature was once the promise of glory, but now
human nature is the human predicament.

But in God's plan, humanity saves itself. For muddy images mired
in sin and misery, into the depths of humanity's tragedy and Israel's
carnage, God sent a true human, the perfect participant in God's
work and God's story.

Jesus came to share our clay and restore our royalty. He is the
human who brings humanity back to God and the world back to humanity. Those who want a glorious destiny must come to him and
through him, the one who never cracked the image of God and who
participated perfectly in God's work.[11] As the flawless image of God
he perfectly reflected God's glory, the glory of the Father's only Son
(Jn 1:14). Those who know his Father will not be surprised to learn
that this Son turns out to be righteous, holy and wise. And because he
mirrors the Father, humans made to imitate God are now to imitate
the Son.

---

[11]Channeling Scot McKnight's "cracked eikon" label, as found in *Blue Parakeet: Rethinking
How You Read Your Bible* (Grand Rapids: Zondervan, 2008), pp. 65-75.

PART TWO

Imitating Jesus

5

The True Human, the Gospel and the Gospels

A Messiah you cannot imitate is not worth having as a Messiah.

RICHARD PRATT

A disciple is not above the teacher,
but everyone who is fully qualified will be like the teacher.

LUKE 6:40

One notable trend in 1990s American pop culture was the WWJD ("What would Jesus do?") phenomenon. The abbreviation dominated wrist bands, bumper stickers and T-shirts. As with all trends, backlash was probably inevitable, not least given the commercialization and trivialization involved in such sloganeering. In addition, the trend was construed as encouraging the use of Jesus "merely as a model for being good," which "created a backlash among some pastors and theologians, especially in the Reformed community."[1]

On the other hand, Robert Stein gives nuance to the question: "'What

[1]Kelly Kapic, "Evangelical Holiness," in *Life in the Spirit: Spiritual Formation in Theological Perspective*, ed. Jeffrey Greenman and George Kalantzis (Downers Grove, IL: InterVarsity Press, 2010), p. 109.

did/would Jesus do?' *if* answered correctly is the will of God for the Christian. Unlike many of the scribes and the Pharisees, the believer can both say as Jesus said and do as Jesus did (Mt 23:2-3)."[2] Of course, the trick is to answer the question correctly, particularly when the answer is often sweet as syrup and just as amorphous—for instance, "Be nice and do really nice things for people." Then there's the massive challenge of putting a first-century Messiah's life and teaching to work in the twenty-first century.

Whatever we think of the WWJD question, every disciple needs to learn to read the Gospels with eyes open to the message of imitation. This chapter begins our study of the imitation of the Son. Two vocations for Jesus and three vocations for his disciples will serve as foundational elements for imitation through New Testament eyes.

Two Vocations for Jesus

Two foundational Christian beliefs provide a framework for a theology of the imitation of Jesus. These beliefs build on the observations we've made so far—namely, that humans are made to be like God and participate in his work. But they also portray the uniqueness of Jesus' work.

1. Jesus is God's true image, the true human. Because of Jesus' divinity, in shifting our focus from imitation of the Father to imitation of the Son we are not turning our attention away from the imitation of God.[3] On the other hand, Jesus' humanity is often neglected and unexplored when Christians focus exclusively on his divinity.[4] But the Christian faith stands or falls (1 Tim 3:16; 2 Jn 7) on the truth that Jesus "is man as man was meant to be."[5]

If the significance of Jesus' humanity is often not fully appreciated, his status as a human king is also underplayed. Terms like *Messiah* (Christ), *Lord* and *Son of God* tend to be used without regard for the

---

[2]Robert Stein, *The Method and Message of Jesus' Teachings* (Louisville, KY: Westminster John Knox, 1994), p. 114, emphasis added.

[3]See Ignatius of Antioch, *Letter to Romans* 6.3. More precisely, we are imitating a person—the eternal, divine Son—as he lived in his human nature.

[4]As Richard Pratt puts it, "There can be little doubt that while our [Reformed] tradition affirms the full humanity of Christ, it stresses his divinity." "Westminster and Contemporary Reformed Hermeneutics," *Reformed Perspectives Magazine* 8, no. 45 (2006).

[5]Michael D. Williams, *Far As the Curse Is Found: The Covenant Story of Redemption* (Philipsburg, NJ: P&R, 2005), p. 224.

royal status those terms originally carried. But the gospel and the Gospels show us that God has not abandoned his plan to have humans rule the earth. His kingdom now as at the beginning is tied to his plan to fill the earth with his royal image. The great drama in Scripture revolves around the question, when will humans be the rulers God intended them to be?[6] Because of humans' inability, the Messiah is the substitute, the true human and true king.

The arrival of the reign of God is the reinstatement of the originally intended divine order for earth, with man properly situated as God's vice regent (number two ruler). In other words, what is new about God's kingdom when Jesus is enthroned is not that God is on the throne in a new way, but that a human is finally enthroned with him. The "exaltation of Jesus as man" is "the way in which the 'reign of God' has now come where it was not here before."[7] Even if God was not always recognized or honored as king over all, he retained his sovereignty. Through Jesus, however, a human is now enthroned over all according to God's original plan for his world. We can only briefly summarize the case, but it fits with the following important pieces (as well as many other Old Testament passages and concepts):

- God's design for humanity in Genesis 1–2; Psalm 8

- The promises of human enthronement in Psalm 2; 110

- The hope of a king from David's family who would subdue the world (Gen 49:8-11; Is 11:1-10)

- The vision of a glorious "Son of Man" reigning with God in Daniel 7, joined by the saints who share in his rule

The theme of human enthronement is present in Jewish literature and New Testament promises. To cite just two examples, in *Apocalypse of Moses* 39:1-3, "God prophesies to Adam that at the eschaton Adam's

---

[6]Other big-picture questions, such as how humans are made right with God, are vital. But if we describe in detail how someone has been made right with God, yet fail to explain what they will become, we've done them a disservice. Three hours before writing this footnote I received a text from a pastor friend wrestling with this destiny: "Have NEVER seen rightly Romans 5:17 until now. Wow. Adam was to reign but failed. We are now made right to reign."
[7]Dan G. McCartney, "*Ecce Homo*: The Coming of the Kingdom as the Restoration of Human Viceregency," *Westminster Theological Journal* 56, no. 1 (1994): 1-21.

dominion will replace that of Satan, that he will sit on Satan's throne."[8] And in Romans, creation's groaning is not assuaged until resurrected humans inherit her. Humans receive grace, righteousness and resurrection bodies so that they will reign through the enthroned Messiah and inherit all things with him (Mt 19:28-30; 28:16-20; Rom 5:17; 8:15-25; 1 Cor 15; Eph 1:22).

As the new Adam and the true human, Jesus has accomplished what humanity consistently failed to accomplish. Adam and Eve failed to be the royal humans God commanded them to be. Noah and his contemporaries failed. Israel failed. And every human has failed. Jesus alone has earned the full affirmation of God as the true Son who deserves exaltation and a throne to rule the world (Mt 4:1-11; 28:18; Phil 2:5-11). Other humans are incapable of his perfect accomplishments, and on their own they would have no claim to inherit the world. As the true human Jesus submits perfectly to God's will for the benefit of others so that Father and Son together extend forgiveness, healing, restoration, reconciliation and re-enthronement to a broken and rebellious humanity.

2. The Messiah is a representative human. Our theology of Jesus should not stop at describing him as a substitute. By giving the Holy Spirit, Father and Son begin to restore humans to their true godlike humanity. That means that Jesus is also our representative.

If the goal of salvation is not to be less human, it is still less to rid ourselves of bodies. Nor does God leave us eternally sinful, for that is ultimately a subhuman condition. God has no interest in a plan B for humans. Jesus came so that we might be human as God intended, sharing in the character, rule and glory of God, "conformed to the image of his Son" (Rom 8:29).

Those who return to God through Jesus begin to be healed by the benefits of Jesus' mission. Commonly identified benefits include the forgiveness of sins, resurrection and eternal life. These benefits are at the heart of the Christian message, and motivation for imitation should feature these blessings. Jesus' miracles also witness to new creation as he

---

[8]Joel Marcus, *Mark 1-8: A New Translation with Introduction and Commentary*, Anchor Bible, vol. 27 (New York: Doubleday, 2002), p. 174. I owe this reference to Matthew Mason.

rehumanizes those whom he heals.[9] And the benefits of Jesus' ministry include the opportunity to begin to be restored morally and spiritually in the present, following our elder brother and becoming more like him.

The crushing, hellish weight of human sin and shame is Jesus' alone to bear in an atoning sense, reconciling humans to God. But his followers must bear the weight of others' errors, absorbing blows, turning cheeks, forgiving grievances, surrendering bitterness and vengeance. If they wish to follow Jesus, they must bear shame and scorn just like their master. And as they do so, they become more truly human after the pattern of the true human.

THREE VOCATIONS FOR JESUS' DISCIPLES

As a substitute Jesus accomplishes the great tasks necessary for salvation, and his disciples can only be recipients, not participants. But as representative and Lord, Jesus leads his followers into vocations that are like his own. There is some overlap between these tasks, and each metaphor eventually breaks down, but we can see three vocations that illuminate the task of a disciple.

1. Disciples are authorized agents. Jesus' disciples are authorized to serve as agents of his empire. To be authorized is to receive authority and power to do Jesus' work in Jesus' name. Authorized agents preach the good news of the kingdom, shepherd those who need guidance and display God's victory over disease and demonic forces (Mt 10:5-8; 11:3; 28:18-20; Lk 10:18-19). In Luke authorization extends beyond the twelve to the seventy. This authority is derived from Jesus' own God-given authority (Mt 10:1), but it is all the more potent because it derives from God himself. It is so potent that when the disciples return from their first mission, Jesus declares that Satan "fell like lightning" (Lk 10:1-20).

The disciples imitate Jesus as they work, and they become so identifiable with Jesus and his authority that some of their actions are heaven's actions, and their presence is his presence:

---

[9]See chapter 1 of Colin Gunton, *Christ and Creation: The Didsbury Lectures, 1990* (Grand Rapids: Eerdmans, 1992).

Truly I tell you, whatever you bind on earth will be bound in heaven, and whatever you loose on earth will be loosed in heaven. Again, truly I tell you, if two of you agree on earth about anything you ask, it will be done for you by my Father in heaven. For where two or three are gathered in my name, I am there among them. (Mt 18:18-20)

The agents eventually share in the authority of Jesus eternally, reigning with him as he rules over all things (Dan 7; Mt 19:28-30). When they do so they are restored to the position God originally intended for humanity.

2. Disciples are apprentices. Ancient discipleship was essentially a form of apprenticeship. As apprentices, disciples follow an expert and absorb their master's mindsets and practices until they become capable on their own. Jesus' disciples do not graduate from apprenticeship to perfection this side of death, and Jesus never leaves the disciples without his presence. But Jesus works to make his apprentices like their master, not least so that they will be capable of making other apprentices.

Apprenticeship is increasingly a lost art in the contemporary world, and a number of obstacles suggest that this metaphor requires more attention than it normally receives. When we follow a coach or the CEO of our company, that doesn't mean we are authorized to do things they do. As a result, it is not readily apparent to modern disciples that when Jesus calls people to follow him, he means they are to imitate his self-sacrifice and dependence on God. It is not clear that our vocations are similar to his vocations or that following Jesus means doing Jesus-like things.

The notion of a "personal relationship with Jesus" is sometimes presented as a self-styled relationship capable of being tailored to our tendencies and desires rather than being understood in terms of lordship and apprenticeship (which are, of course, personal and relational). We shall have more to say later about apprenticeship in the Gospels, but for now it is enough to note that apprenticing with Jesus requires putting ourselves second, which means putting ourselves on a cross (Mk 10). Apprenticing with Jesus requires the surrender of prized traits of the Western world: independence, comfort, originality and efficiency. Apprenticeship also sometimes involves trading breathless activity and accomplishment for the seemingly unproductive task of sitting quietly at Jesus' feet (Lk 10:38-42).

Vocations require an apprenticeship when their main task involves something unnatural. And the most unnatural thing imaginable—the imitation of Jesus in cross-bearing and self-denial—lies at the heart of Christian apprenticeship. No one, not even Jesus (Mt 26:37-39), hangs on a cross and says, "This is a great fit."[10]

3. Disciples are ambassadors. Disciples represent their king by bringing terms of surrender to rebels and the good news of victory to God's people. They are ambassadors who follow in the footsteps of Jesus and Israel's prophets as messengers of truth and mercy, judgment and forgiveness. These ambassadors share the miracle that the debt, wrath and penalty of the world's errors have been borne by the emperor himself through the death of his Son. They herald his call for rebels to bend the knee and give allegiance to him.

While ambassadorial work in the modern world is considered posh, in the ancient world such work could open one to abuse and derision (2 Cor 5:17-20; see the chart on Mark below). Jesus compares his disciples to Yahweh's prophets, the ambassadors sent to Israel and the nations who were rejected and persecuted (Mt 5:10-12; 21:33-46; 23:34; Lk 11:49). Jesus' disciples are sent as he was sent, to be treated as he was treated (Jn 15:20; 20:21).

These three vocations shed light on Christian discipleship and imitation. The uniqueness of spiritual gifts, offices and apostleship means that not all believers will participate in these vocations in the same way. Whether or not we fully identify with these vocations or find them a "natural fit," it is important to adopt these roles and follow Jesus on the way to being truly human. We'll see more about these three vocations in the coming chapters.

THE GOSPEL AND THE GOSPELS

These three vocations for believers are based on Jesus' identity and his accomplishments in his vocations.[11] His action and identity are God's

---

[10]I owe this phrase to Dan Doriani.
[11]These three vocations are not the only helpful way to put the matter. One could also explore

gospel, the solution to the crisis of humanity. Since the fall we are radically unlike the one whose likeness we are supposed to share, having surrendered the glory of his image (Rom 3:23). Humans are faced with a barrier between us and the God we are supposed to be like. Despite centuries of religious effort of all kinds, humans have not broken this barrier. God broke the barrier created by sin and our corruption of his likeness by sending his Son in our likeness to condemn that sin on the cross (Rom 8:3). God created humans to bear his image, but then he took the image (form) of a servant-human himself.

One could almost say that God, who created humans to imitate him, has now imitated humans in order to make them right with him. As the true human Jesus is a substitute who does what no other human could do, turning the world right-side-up, healing the rift between God and his broken images and restoring humanity to its place as rulers of God's world. Jesus is God coming to us despite—and because of—our inability to come to him. Jesus is humanity obeying God when all other humans failed to do so.

In the short summaries of the gospel in the New Testament, Jesus is God's gospel (Acts 2:22-36; 3:12-26; Rom 1:3-4; 1 Cor 15:1-4; 2 Tim 2:8). The good news is not something done by Jesus' disciples. The good news is what has been done for them in Jesus' incarnation, atoning death, resurrection and enthronement as the Son of David, who rules over all things as the last Adam (1 Cor 15). The good news is the life-renewing gift of the Spirit.[12] The good news speaks of forgiveness, adoption, a saving relationship with God by faith, and the promise of the re-creation of all things.

The good news is that God has gone to work as a true human, from the incarnation to his triumphant return. The blast zone of his work is the church and the whole of the new creation, where God establishes

---

the human roles of prophet, priest and king (which apply to humanity as a whole, Jesus, and his disciples). See the forthcoming article by Keith Johnson, who cites the imitation of these three offices in Ursinus's commentary on the Heidelberg Catechism; more recently Tim Keller and the Redeemer network as well as the Acts 29 network have used the threefold office in an imitative fashion.

[12]On the gift of the Spirit as part of the gospel message, see Darrell Bock, *Recovering the Real Lost Gospel: Reclaiming the Gospel as Good News* (Nashville: Broadman and Holman, 2010). In the New Testament the gift of the Spirit is the result of the enthronement of Jesus.

his kingdom with renewed godlike humans enthroned as royalty according to his original design.

The Gospels and Imitation

Because Jesus is the gospel, the stories of his life and ministry are called *Gospels*. Many New Testament scholars think the Gospels resemble *bioi* (literally "lives"), an ancient genre of biographical texts.[13] *Bioi* were written to tell of great men and their accomplishments and to present the chief character as a model.[14] Whether they are truly *bioi* or not, the Gospels accomplish both of these tasks. They feature Jesus' unique power, authority and accomplishments: the "good news." But all four Gospels also detail Jesus' life and teaching in ways that make him a model.[15] Jesus' life was such a pattern that even events with unique significance are applicable to the lives of believers.

One can contrast the emphasis on imitation in the four Gospels with the so-called Gnostic gospels and texts. In these texts the imitation of Jesus—especially his sacrifice for others—is almost entirely rejected. If imitation is present at all, it is limited to sharing Jesus' secret knowledge. The earliest Christians used the imitation of Jesus' death as a weapon against heretics (particularly those with Gnostic leanings) who rejected the cross and resurrection as salvation and dismissed self-sacrifice and martyrdom as a pattern for the lives of believers. Failure to feature the imitation of Jesus prominently leaves us walking a pattern carved by Gnostics, not the true Gospels.

---

[13]*Bioi* are a subset of ancient biography; David Aune, *The New Testament in Its Literary Environment* (Philadelphia: Westminster, 1987), pp. 17-76. For important cautions, see Larry Hurtado, "Gospel (Genre)," in *Dictionary of Jesus and the Gospels*, ed. Joel Green, Scot McKnight and I. Howard Marshall (Downers Grove, IL: InterVarsity Press, 1993), pp. 276-82.

[14]Usually the character is a model for good rather than ill. On imitation, *bioi* and the Gospels, see Richard Burridge, *Imitating Jesus: An Inclusive Approach to New Testament Ethics* (Grand Rapids: Eerdmans, 2007), as well as Aune, *New Testament*, p. 62: "The Evangelists regarded the story of Jesus as an example" for Christians. Some of the same paradigmatic tendencies are found outside Greco-Roman literature as well. See also Dale Allison Jr., "Structure, Biographical Impulse, and the *Imitatio Christi*," in *Studies in Matthew: Interpretation Past and Present* (Grand Rapids: Baker Academic, 2005), pp. 135-55, and David B. Capes, "Imitatio Christi and the Gospel Genre," *Bulletin for Biblical Research* 13, no. 1 (2003): 1-19.

[15]See careful discussion of the genre and the virtue-formation function of the Gospels in Jonathan Pennington, *Reading the Gospels Wisely: A Narrative and Theological Introduction* (Grand Rapids: Baker Academic, 2012), pp. 18-35, 159-65.

For example, consider one major Gospel event. It might be tempting to take Jesus' temptation as being only about his role as our substitute, doing what all others could not do. It does not, some might say, shed light on our fight against temptation and sin. But that is a false dichotomy. It is not wrong to suggest that Jesus' temptation shows believers how to fight their own temptations.[16] The admirable goal of exalting Jesus in his triumph over temptation and sin should not lead us to avoid noting, say, that Jesus used Scripture and trust in God to fight the tempter. Provided we also feature the uniqueness of Jesus' sinless life and victory over temptation, we do not corrupt or devalue Jesus' temptation by using his trust in God as a model. In his temptations he was "one who in every respect has been tested as we are" (Heb 4:15). The uniqueness of his comprehensive success ("without sin") does not mitigate our need to look to him as an example of faith in God.

Conclusion

Writing more than seventy-five years ago, J. Gresham Machen was deeply troubled by attempts to replace "Jesus as Savior" with "Jesus as example." He famously called this replacement religion "liberalism," and he saw it as the enemy of Christianity. But Machen also insisted that the two themes of Savior and example were not opposed to one another: "Jesus as a matter of fact is a Brother to us as well as a Savior—an elder Brother whose steps we may follow. The imitation of Jesus has a fundamental place in the Christian life; it is perfectly correct to represent Him as our supreme and only perfect example."[17]

Jesus does not save us in order to end imitation, and the Gospels certainly do not tell his story solely to direct us away from imitation. They provide us with the perfect mirror of true humanity: the cross-shaped, God-shaped human, Jesus of Nazareth, who is our substitute and representative and exemplar.

---

[16]See Russ Moore, *Tempted and Tried: Temptation and the Triumph of Christ* (Wheaton, IL: Crossway, 2011).
[17]J. Gresham Machen, *Christianity and Liberalism* (New York: Macmillan, 1923), p. 98.

6

Ambassadors, Apprentices and Agents

*A disciple is not above the teacher, nor a slave above the master; it is enough
for the disciple to be like the teacher, and the slave like the master.*

MATTHEW 10:24-25

You will indeed drink my cup.

MATTHEW 20:23

My friend Matthew is a plumber. In his industry novice workers are
called apprentices. A plumbing apprentice is more of a plumber than
I am but not yet a master plumber, familiar with all the intricacies of
the profession. In fact, at any given work site, the apprentice is
usually under the authority and supervision of a master plumber
who functions as a model of knowledge and skill. In the same way,
the Gospels present Jesus as a master followed by apprentices in the
direction of maturity.

The opening chapters of Matthew and Luke, however, appear to
pose a challenge to imitation. We find an unrepeatable virgin birth, a
royal genealogy not shared by his readers, and the presentation of
Jesus as the fulfillment of Israel's messianic hopes. In fact, there is

much of Jesus' life and significance that is unrepeatable. But as we continue to read the Gospels, patterns and emphases unfold that invite readers into apprenticeship with the master.

IMITATING THE CRUCIFIED MESSIAH: MARK'S GOSPEL

Mark probably had a number of goals when he wrote his Gospel. But it is safe to say that Mark intended to write a book (1) about Jesus and (2) about discipleship.[1] The claim that Mark is about discipleship may at first seem a curious one, for even though other characters are present in many scenes, Jesus is virtually always squarely in the camera's eye. Mark gives particular emphasis to the supernatural power of Jesus. His Gospel is a Gospel of "shock and awe." In the first half Jesus blazes through the text in power. In the second half Mark focuses on the last week of Jesus' life and his death. In light of these characteristics, why do scholars call Mark a Gospel for discipleship?

There are at least three answers to this question, and each of them sheds light on imitation. First, discipleship is never a matter of moving beyond salvation. Disciples need to know more than the basic facts about Jesus and his cross (Heb 5:12–6:3), but their lives are always shaped and guided by the person and work of Jesus. What's more, discipleship always involves Jesus' work for his disciples as much as it involves their work for Jesus. His work brings freedom, forgiveness and new birth by the Spirit, which creates new power. As a result, any text about Jesus is relevant for Christian discipleship, whether or not it instructs disciples how to live.

Second, while Jesus is the main character of Mark and his disciples often look like anything but a collection of leaders who will change the world, the disciples are present almost from the beginning of the book (Mk 1:16). "In the gospels, discipleship (the process of becoming like Christ) was accomplished by being physically with Christ, seeing what He did, hearing what He said, being corrected by Him, and fol-

---

[1]R. T. France, *The Gospel of Mark*, New International Greek Testament Commentary (Grand Rapids: Eerdmans, 2002), pp. 27-29. James Samra, in "A Biblical View of Discipleship," *Bibliotheca Sacra* 160, no. 2 (2003): 222, notes both the paucity of explicit instruction and the importance of discipleship for Mark.

lowing His example."[2] Jesus makes disciple-making a priority, and Mark writes his Gospel accordingly; the disciples are with their teacher in almost every imaginable scenario. Jesus even sends out his disciples as his agents; they imitate his proclamation and his miracles because he has empowered them to do so (Mk 6:7-13).

Jesus selects disciples without regard for their degree of polish. But he does not intend to leave them in ignorance, mediocrity, prejudice and cowardice. When he calls these followers his disciples, his audience and Mark's audience would understand that he was making apprentices (Mk 3:13-15, 31-35; 6:7-13). At times they deploy unimaginable supernatural power, a point that is all the more amazing given their frailty and error on other occasions.

In the ancient world the basic task of a disciple was to follow a master and imitate his beliefs and practices.[3] The disciples' near-constant presence with Jesus and the fact that they call him *rabbi* (teacher) reveals the importance of this theme for Jesus and for his biographers. As the master-teacher, Jesus is almost always a model. And because the notion of master as model was clear in his context, much of his instruction is implicit. Small details such as how he eats (and with whom), how he prays and how he sees the world are not irrelevant but vital for discipleship. "No amount of abstract verbal instruction can produce mastery of a craft without the concrete example of a master to imitate."[4]

Third, while Matthew and Luke address the finer points of discipleship in greater detail, Mark focuses squarely on the imitation of a crucified master. Several literary patterns in Mark's carefully crafted book highlight the resemblance between Jesus and his disciples.[5]

---

[2]Samra, "A Biblical View of Discipleship," p. 222.

[3]The extent of imitation in this relationship could be taken to extremes. There's the infamous story of a Jewish disciple caught under his rabbi's bed; he offers the (not quite acceptable) explanation that to be a true disciple he needed to imitate what the master did with his wife in the bedroom.

[4]Stephen E. Fowl, "Imitation," in *Dictionary of Paul and His Letters*, ed. Gerald F. Hawthorne, Ralph P. Martin and Daniel G. Reid (Downers Grove, IL: InterVarsity Press, 1993), p. 430; cited by Samra, "Biblical View of Discipleship," p. 225.

[5]David Aune, in *The New Testament in Its Literary Environment* (Philadelphia: Westminster, 1987), p. 62, notes that the use of characters as paradigms was often more implicit than explicit, with a tacit understanding between audience and writer. Literary patterns could en-

Three passion predictions, three illustrations of cross-shaped discipleship. As we can see in the table below, all of Jesus' passion predictions in Mark are followed by passages that describe the tasks of Jesus' disciples, who must take on slave status and the practice of self-denial in imitation of Jesus' cross-bearing for others.[6]

Table 6.1

Jesus' cross and self-sacrifice	Mark 8:31-33	Mark 9:30-32	Mark 10:32-34
Disciples' crosses and self-sacrifice	Mark 8:34-38	Mark 9:32-35	Mark 10:35-45

This arrangement reinforces two points concerning imitation. First, as we've discussed previously, in neither the Old Testament nor the New Testament is imitation a matter of identical action or exact duplication. Imitation is a matter of mindset, such as a willingness to forgive and readiness to stoop in humility (Mk 10:35-45) as much as action. The most famous of these verses in Mark, along with its parallels in Matthew and Luke, subtly conveys this idea:

> If any want to become my followers, let them deny themselves and take up their cross and follow me. (Mk 8:34)

Each disciple has a unique mission with a unique cost that is patterned after the gospel template of the Messiah's cross.

Second, because Jesus demands that disciples follow his own pattern of death and resurrection, this arrangement reinforces the foundational nature of the gospel. Jesus is not just a teacher nor merely Lord. He is the redeemer who brings disciples into a relationship created by

---

courage readers to take characters as positive or negative models. For what follows, see also Jason Hood, "Evangelicals and the Imitation of the Cross: Peter Bolt and Mark 13 as Test Case," *Evangelical Quarterly* 81, no. 2 (2009): 116-25.

[6]"In no other Gospel do the three cardinal announcements of forthcoming humiliation have as structured a function as they do in Mark." William L. Lane, *The Gospel According to Mark*, New International Commentaries on the New Testament (Grand Rapids: Eerdmans, 1974), p. 292. We could perhaps add a fourth reference to the cross in Mark 9:12, which is similarly followed by a reference to John the Baptist's suffering (Mk 9:13). These passages lead James Edwards to suggest in *The Gospel According to Mark*, Pillar New Testament Commentary (Grand Rapids: Eerdmans, 2002), p. 7, that Mark was written during a time when Christians were undergoing persecution. This is possible, but such circumstances are not necessary; Christians are called to crosses regardless of whether they actively experience external persecution.

grace and love, and only in the context of that relationship do his demands appear.

The section of Mark containing these three cross-themed passages is framed by two stories of the blind being healed (Mk 8:22-30; 10:46-52). These chapters together unveil the cross-shaped identity of the Messiah, and the two miracles teach that his identity is incomprehensible and invisible to those who expect glory apart from a cross and suffering. Mark's readers have their eyes opened to the trajectory of Jesus' life and ministry: cross, resurrection and enthronement. Peering into the gospel mystery, the disciples gaze at the upside-down, cross-shaped story of Jesus and learn to see their lives as reflections of that story.

Three vocations, three passions. Jesus and his disciples are also linked by their proclamation of the kingdom of God and the consequence of that proclamation:

- John preaches and is arrested (Mk 1:7, 14)
- Jesus preaches and is arrested (Mk 1:14; 9:3; 10:33)
- Christians preach and are arrested (Mk 3:14; 13:9-13)[7]

For Jesus, John and the disciples, the words for "preaching" (*keryssein*) and "betrayal" or being "handed over" or "arrested" (*paradidōmi*) describe their vocation and their destiny.

While the cross-shaped nature of the Christian appears in the other Gospels and in many other New Testament books, Mark's careful literary arrangement gets to the heart of New Testament discipleship by addressing both the necessity of Jesus' death as a ransom for sinners and the cross-shaped life required of every disciple.

A blueprint for the Christian life? There may be another way in which Mark's Gospel subtly points to the imitation of Jesus. As Larry Hurtado says, "The basic shape of the Markan story of Jesus was designed to make it more directly applicable to the lives of readers as

[7]On John as parallel yet subordinate to Jesus, see John P. Meier, "John the Baptist in Matthew's Gospel," *Journal of Biblical Literature* 99, no. 3 (1980): 383-405, especially 388-400; and David Howell, *Matthew's Inclusive Story: A Study in the Narrative Rhetoric of the First Gospel*, Journal for the Study of the New Testament Supplement Series, vol. 42 (Sheffield, UK: JSOT Press, 1990), p. 259.

those who follow Jesus as their sole reliable and authoritative model."[8] Many notable passages in Matthew, Luke and John not found in Mark "involve matters which are not susceptible of imitation, including the virginal conception and the pre-eschatological resurrection. Mark's whole story of Jesus can be read as a blueprint for the Christian life: It begins with baptism, proceeds with the vigorous pursuit of ministry in the face of temptation and opposition, and culminates in suffering and death oriented towards an as-yet unseen vindication." Against those who choose to downplay imitation, "Mark's Jesus demands nothing of his disciples that he does not do himself."[9] Such characteristics make Mark's story of Jesus' earthly life more capable of serving as a model for readers, although the degree to which Mark intended this approach is not fully clear.

Perhaps these patterns in Mark indicate why Jesus is frequently called "teacher" in this Gospel. This title is used by friends, enemies and Jesus himself (Mk 14:14; see also Mk 14:49). Jesus does not appear to teach much in Mark compared with the large blocks of teaching in Matthew, the frequent parables in Luke and the lengthy dialogue in John. But in Mark as in the rest of the ancient world—and in the modern world also, although it is often unrecognized—a master teaches with actions as much as with words.[10]

---

[8]Larry Hurtado, "The Women, the Empty Tomb, and the Ending of Mark," in *Wandering Galilean: Essays in Honour of Sean Freyne*, ed. Zuleika Rodgers and Margaret Daly-Denton (Leiden, Netherlands: Brill, 2009), pp. 427-50. I would favor changing "sole" to "primary" or "ultimate."

[9]Philip G. Davis, "Christology, Discipleship, and Self-Understanding in the Gospel of Mark," in *Self-Definition and Self-Discovery in Early Christianity: A Study in Shifting Horizons, Essays in Appreciation of Ben F. Meyer from His Former Students*, ed. D. J. Hawkin and T. Robinson, Studies in the Bible and Early Christianity, vol. 26 (Lewiston, NY: Mellen, 1990), pp. 101-19. I owe this quote to Larry Hurtado, who offers it as an "elegant hypothesis," fitting the data without strain. It is preferable to alternative explanations for the shape of Mark, i.e., that Mark found the virgin birth and resurrection to be optional or implausible; it may also explain why Jesus' messiahship and Davidic status is stressed less in Mark than in Matthew and Luke. See similarly Hurtado's "Following Jesus in the Gospel of Mark—and Beyond," in *Patterns of Discipleship in the New Testament*, ed. R. N. Longenecker (Grand Rapids: Eerdmans, 1996), pp. 9-29.

[10]Sociologists, linguists and theologians increasingly note the importance of both indirect and direct communication as noted by Kierkegaard, among others, and as put to use by Kevin Vanhoozer, among others; see Vanhoozer's *The Drama of Doctrine: A Canonical-Linguistic Approach to Christian Theology* (Louisville, KY: Westminster John Knox, 2005).

MATTHEW: APPRENTICES OF THE MASTER

As we continue to read the Gospels we find that Matthew and Luke build on Mark's emphasis on the imitation of Jesus, making explicit what was implicit in Mark. "Like Paul, Origen, and other early Christians," the Gospel writers "thought of Jesus as a model to be emulated," not least because of "the multitude of obvious connections between Jesus' words and his deeds."[11] Matthew is particularly saturated with such connections:

- Jesus exhorts others to be meek ("Blessed are the meek" Mt 5:5) and teaches his own character as the paradigm for this trait: "Learn from me, because I am meek and lowly of heart" (Mt 11:29 author's translation; Mt 21:5).

- He requires mercy and humility (Mt 5:7; 9:13; 12:7; 18:4; 23:12), and he is merciful and humble ("Have mercy on us, Son of David!" Mt 9:27; 11:29; 15:22; 18:4; 20:30).[12]

- Jesus serves God alone (Mt 4:10), particularly by coming to serve through death (Mt 20:28); he requires his disciples to take on the role of servant even unto death (Mt 6:24; 10:24-25; 18:23-33; 20:26-28; 24:45-46; 25:14-23).

- Jesus celebrates and blesses those who are unjustly oppressed because of their identification with God and his kingdom ("those who are persecuted for righteousness' sake" Mt 5:10), and he himself suffers and dies innocently ("Then he [Pilate] asked, . . . 'What evil has he done?'" Mt 27:23).

- Jesus demands faithfulness to the law of Moses (Mt 5:17-20; 23:1-2). He faithfully keeps and interprets that law during his ministry (Mt 8:4; 12:1-8; 15:1-20).

- Jesus requires self-denial in the face of evil ("If anyone strikes you

---

[11]W. D. Davies and Dale Allison, *Matthew 19-28*, International Critical Commentar, vol. 3 (London: T & T Clark, 1997), pp. 715-16. (I owe this reference to Patrick Schreiner.) The following list of ways in which Jesus models his teaching includes material from those pages in Davies and Allison, as well as my adaptations and expansions. See also Howell, *Matthew's Inclusive Story*, pp. 249-59.

[12]Note that some translations may obscure the links present in Greek via *tapeinoō* and *praus*.

on the right cheek, turn the other also" Mt 5:39) and does not resist the evils done to him ("They spat in his face and struck him; and some slapped him" Mt 26:67; 27:30).

- He calls for forgoing oaths in favor of simple honesty ("Let your word be 'Yes, Yes' or 'No, No'" Mt 5:37), and when Caiaphas tries to put him under oath to testify whether he is the Messiah, Jesus simply affirms, "You have said so" (Mt 26:64).

- He teaches his disciples not to give pearls to pigs (Mt 7:6; holy truth is not to be given out indiscriminately), and while Jesus responds to challenges to his identity when necessary during his ministry, he maintains a remarkable silence at his trial.

- Jesus requires private prayer ("Whenever you pray, go into your room and shut the door and pray to your Father who is in secret . . . [and] sees in secret" Mt 6:6) in contrast to the Pharisees' ostentatious public prayers (Mt 6:5-15; 23:5). As if to obey his commands, he prays alone ("He went up the mountain by himself to pray" Mt 14:23).

- Jesus teaches his disciples to prioritize the will of God in prayer rather than their own desires ("Your will be done" Mt 6:10). When faced with the cross, he uses those words three times in Gethsemane (Mt 26:37-44).

- He teaches his followers to reject slavery to mammon and the heaping up of earthly wealth ("Do not store up for yourselves treasures on earth" Mt 6:19). Jesus does not store up treasure ("The Son of Man has nowhere to lay his head" Mt 8:20) and denies himself when tempted with the chance to seize ownership of the whole world (Mt 4:8).

- Jesus teaches that the destiny of his disciples is to bring glory to God (Mt 5:13-16); that is the result of his ministry (Mt 9:8; 15:31).

- He commands believers to carry crosses ("If any want to become my followers, let them deny themselves and take up their cross and follow me" Mt 16:24), and he carries his cross (Pilate "handed him over to be crucified" Mt 27:26).

- Jesus teaches that self-sacrifice is greater than life—indeed, greater than gaining the whole world—and that those who follow the Son of Man will be rewarded with rule and authority (Mt 16:24-27; 19:27-30). Therefore, he denies himself the whole world (Mt 4:8) and lays down his life. In so doing he saves himself and the whole world and receives resurrection life and a boundless kingdom as his reward (Mt 25:31-32; 28:18).

The connections between Jesus' tasks and those of his disciples in Matthew are too frequent to be rated accidental, incidental or secondary to the message of the book. Many of the actions and mindsets are facets of self-denial and the cross. As Richard France observes, Matthew repeatedly presses the point because the cross-shaped approach to life modeled by Jesus and required of his disciples is such "a radical challenge to natural human valuation that it needs constant repetition."[13]

Matthew also stresses connections between Jesus and his disciples that further illustrate the links between their tasks. Both Jesus and his followers are linked to the prophets who were persecuted and killed throughout Israel's history (Mt 21:33-46; 23:29-36). The disciples will follow Jesus in being labeled "Beelzebul" (Mt 9:34; 10:25; 12:24). Jesus commands his followers to baptize in the name of the Father, Son and Holy Spirit, the Trinity that was present at his own baptism (Mt 3; 28).

CAVEATS

A few "footnotes" should be kept in mind that will help us maintain balance. First, as the structure of the Gospels makes clear, imitation is based on what God has done and what Jesus has accomplished for sinners. Biblical imitation is not a matter of grasping God but of grasping the grace God provides for sinners—a grace that includes the ability to trust in God for salvation, as well as the ability to work at imitation with renewed strength. Sinners must imitate brokenness, confession and repentance. Like all the saints they pray for the for-

---

[13]R. T. France, *The Gospel of Matthew*, New International Commentary on the New Testament (Grand Rapids: Eerdmans), p. 374.

giveness of sins (Lk 11:4). Like John the Baptist's audience they ask
what repentance requires (Lk 3:7-14). Like Zacchaeus they turn from
sin without ignoring the debris field in their wake, seeking to heal as
they have been healed (Lk 19:8).

Second, because of the differences between the first century and
the twenty-first, there are many ways in which the imitation of Jesus
needs to be adapted. "The changing circumstances of religious and
social culture require wise discernment and moral improvisation;
Jesus lived in a milieu quite different from the twenty-first century, so
many of his actions will be non-transferrable."[14] But even when imitation does not happen "in uniform fashion," we can "incarnate the
same basic 'idea' (i.e., the knowledge of God) and action (i.e., the love
of God) under different conditions."[15] The imitation of Jesus and his
disciples in the rest of the New Testament illustrates the adaptation of
imitation for contemporary purposes.

Third, the Gospels emphasize the cross-shaped identity of Jesus
and his disciples. But they also forecast the resurrection and the glorification of Jesus and all who follow him on the cross-shaped road
(Mk 9:9; 10:30, 34).[16] The first-century Roman writer Quintilian re-
corded the reason why Romans chose crucifixion for rebels and serious criminals: "When we crucify criminals the most frequented
roads are chosen, where the greatest number of people can look and
be seized by this fear. For every punishment is more a matter of exemplary effect than of retribution."[17] Ironically, the exemplary effect had
the opposite effect in the early church. The crucifixion of Jesus included the ironic declaration that Jesus was enthroned in victory on
the cross. And those who joined him in real or metaphorical crosses
would share in glory.

---

[14]Allen, *The Christ's Faith: A Dogmatic Account*, T & T Clark Studies in Systematic Theology
(New York: T & T Clark, 2009), p. 359, and note the footnotes to the same.

[15]Vanhoozer, *Drama of Doctrine*, p. 397.

[16]On the importance of resurrection in addition to crucifixion, see Jimmy Agan, "Toward a
Hermeneutic of Imitation: The Imitation of Christ in the *Didascalia Apostolorum*," *Presbyterion* 37 (2011): 42-43.

[17]Quintilian, *Quintilian: The Lesser Declamations*, Vol. 1, ed. and trans. D. R. S. Bailey, Loeb Classics Library (Cambridge, MA: Harvard University Press, 2006), p. 259; I have modified the last
phrase slightly in line with older English translations. I owe the reference to Michael Bird.

CONCLUSION

Jesus sums up what it means to be a disciple: "A disciple is not above the teacher, nor a slave above the master; it is enough for the disciple to be like the teacher, and the slave like the master" (Mt 10:24-25). When James and John ask to be enthroned at Jesus' right hand and left (Mk 10:37, 40), Jesus tells them that they will drink his cup and be baptized into his suffering and death. To be at the right hand and left hand of the king of the Jews is to hang on a cross (Mk 15:26-27), rejected by the world as a threat to its peace.

Jesus and the Gospel writers knew the degree of difficulty in this task. Surely that is why Matthew concluded his book with the promise of Jesus' unending presence with his disciples.[18] It is one thing to attempt to carry a cross alone. It is another to travel with a friend who has borne a cross for us and secured resurrection and enthronement. He will not bear our crosses for us, but he whispers promises of our own glory and enthronement as we stumble toward our lesser Calvaries.

---

[18]"Such promises are designed to strengthen the hand of disciples who need encouragement along the path of lowly service; for they will find themselves at the mercy of those who show no respect for the divinely ordained nature of this following in the footsteps of a Christ who went to his glory through suffering. The lower disciples are called upon to stoop, the higher they can be expected to be raised in the future kingdom of God." John Nolland, *Luke 18:35–24:53*, Word Biblical Commentary, vol. 35c (Dallas: Word, 1993), p. 1068.

7

Family Resemblance and Paternity Tests

It is not imitation that makes sons; it is adoption that makes imitators.

MARTIN LUTHER

While the Gospels focus on the imitation of Jesus, the imitation of God is never far from view. The New Testament sees the ultimate aim of disciple-making as image-bearing in true righteousness and holiness (Eph 4:13-16, 23-24; 4:31–5:2, 25-31).[1] If this is not well-known among contemporary evangelicals, it was crystal clear at key points in the church's history. "For Athanasius, as for many other Christians, the whole point of God becoming human was that we might be reformed into likeness to God, so that we might become images of God and imitators of Christ."[2] Sixteen hundred years after Athanasius, references to image-bearing and the imitation of God are almost entirely absent in contemporary discussions of the imitation of Jesus.

But as Zack Eswine puts it, the Christian life is about "apprenticing

---

[1] See Westminster Shorter Catechism, question and answer 35.

[2] Graham Tomlin, *Spiritual Fitness: Christian Character in a Consumer Society* (London: Continuum, 2006), pp. 108-10. Tomlin concludes his summary of Athanasius, trinitarian and Christological doctrine, and Christian formation with this line (p. 110). Imitation and image-bearing were part of Athanasius's motivation and strategy for defending the crucial doctrine of *homoousios*.

with Jesus to be human again," living in the direction of God's original
design.[3] Jesus makes disciples who look like him so that God's character will be reflected in his human family. He welcomes his followers
into a substitute household where God is Father (Mt 5:9; 10:25; 12:50).
In the Gospels this new genealogy leads to a spiritually genetic
likeness, displayed in mindsets and behaviors that begin to conform
to the mind and action of God and his Son.

FAMILY RESEMBLANCE

As the perfect child of God, Jesus models the pursuit of God's will
during the temptation (Mt 4) and throughout his ministry, succeeding
in righteousness (Mt 3:15; 27:19) where Adam and Israel have failed
in their role as God's children. For those swept up in God's great
rescue operation, salvation includes adoption into a new family. This
adoption is based on Jesus' true sonship and is unearned, but it carries
with it the freedom and responsibility to seek God's kingdom and
righteousness. God's children must desire and do God's will, just as
their Father and older brother pursue it (Mt 6:9-10, 33).

In Matthew 6, Gentile orphans estranged from their Father are
inevitably anxious and fretful. They babble on and on in prayer, unaware of the quiet confidence that comes from having a Father who
knows and meets their needs. Their compassion and concern is generally restricted to those who are like them. But God's children should
show his character by practicing generosity without the clannish,
cliquish limits on kindness observed by pagans (Mt 5:43-48). Because
they know the goodness of their Father, Jesus' followers should be
liberated from an orphan mentality, and they are then required to be
godlike in their distribution to others, even to the point of being
"perfect, therefore, as [their] heavenly Father is perfect" (Mt 5:48). As
Jesus' disciples make peace and practice God-shaped generosity in
the form of love for enemies and strangers, they are children of God
who reflect their Father's heavenly identity (Mt 5:9, 45). Learning to

---

[3]Zack Eswine quoted by Dane Ortlund, "What's the Message of the Bible in One Sentence?"
Strawberry-Rhubarb Theology (January 12, 2011), dogmadoxa.blogspot.com/2011/01/
whats-message-of-bible-in-one-sentence.html.

see God as Father "is integral to the socialization of the disciples" in a new family, a new kingdom era and a new way of life grounded in a fresh "worldview centered on the gracious God, on dependence on God, and on the imitation of God."[4]

One obstacle to seeing ourselves as children in the shape of the Son on the cross is a common yet faulty view of divine judgment on the cross that pits Father against Son. This view needs to be corrected, for "on the cross Jesus remained the beloved Son, the Son of his Father's good pleasure (Matt. 3:17, 17:5)."[5] We should avoid, then, any notion of a "broken Trinity" where Jesus is pitted against the Father.[6] The obstacles, brokenness and suffering of Jesus' people are not signs that God is judging them; pain in the present is not a sign of divine disapproval. Christian sacrifice is a sign of God's love as he molds them into the shape of Jesus. Jesus' sonship became clearest when he hung on a cross in obedience, clear enough even for pagans to say, "Truly this man was God's Son!" (Mt 27:54).

Those who follow Jesus will also reveal their identity through costly obedience, trusting that their Father will restore far more than is lost (Mt 19:28-30; Lk 18:28-30). Among the possible losses are cherished institutions like family and tribal connections. Luke shows readers how Jesus relativizes or redefines family and cherished cultural assumptions (Lk 9:57-62; 14:25-27; 18:29-30). Not surprisingly, he models this teaching in his own life (Lk 8:19-21; 9:46-48, 58; 10:38-42).

Paternity Test

An important subplot in Matthew and John is the "paternity debate," a clash over the identity of Jesus and his opponents. Given the principle that offspring reflect their parents' character and deeds, who has the spiritual genetic likeness of God? Jesus' opponents in Matthew

---

[4]Joel Green, *The Gospel According to Luke*, New International Commentary on the New Testament (Grand Rapids: Eerdmans, 1997), p. 440.

[5]Herman Bavinck, *Reformed Dogmatics, Volume 3: Sin and Salvation in Christ*, ed. John Bolt, trans. John Vriend (Grand Rapids: Baker Academic, 2006), p. 389. Bavinck goes on to cite John 16:32.

[6]The label and the caution are found in Tom McCall, *Forsaken: The Trinity and the Cross, and Why It Matters* (Downers Grove, IL: IVP Academic, 2012), from whom I received the Bavinck quote.

have their own genealogy described on the basis of likeness or imitation. In three instances (Mt 3:7; 12:34; 23:33) Pharisees and/or Sadducees and scribes are labeled a "brood of vipers." They forfeit their claim to be Abraham's descendants (Mt 3:9) despite genetic and outward resemblance (circumcision, law, Jewish traditions). Jesus also notes the genetic moral resemblance between his opponents and their ancestors who persecuted and killed the prophets (Mt 23:29-36; see also Mt 21:33-46). This identification signifies that he and his disciples are the spiritual descendants of the true prophets, whom they imitate with truth, righteousness and faithfulness, even as the specter of persecution looms (Mt 5:10-12).

When Jesus describes the parental pattern of his opponents in John, he shares the assumption of his contemporaries that sonship means having a share in a father's identity, belief and behavior. "If you were Abraham's children, you would be doing what Abraham did, but now you are trying to kill me. . . . You are indeed doing what your father does" (Jn 8:39-41). "You are from your father the devil, and you choose to do your father's desires. He was a murderer from the beginning and does not stand in the truth, because there is no truth in him. When he lies, he speaks according to his own nature, for he is a liar and the father of lies. But because I tell the truth, you do not believe me" (Jn 8:44-45). Jesus argues that divine parentage requires sharing in God's understanding and character, saying, in essence, "If God were your Father, you would love me, for I came from God and I am here." Jesus' opponents reject his assessment, calling their own spiritual genetic heritage into question as a result. In John 11 and 12, Jesus' opponents sponsor lies and death, reflecting their family traits as they plot to kill Jesus and Lazarus (Jn 11:49-53; 12:9-11). Jesus produces healing, peace and life as a Son who reflects his Father, the Creator.

This debate helpfully pushes back against a caricature of the Pharisees, that they were excessively "holy" people. Although they regarded themselves as such, Jesus did not, and his critique often comes hard as they place limits on generosity, mercy and love (Mt 23:23; Lk 11:42). If they underestimated their need for grace and mercy, they also failed to imitate God's character and showed themselves to be the offspring of snakes and Satan.

SHARING GOD'S CHARACTER: IMITATING DIVINE DISCIPLINE AND MERCY

Discipline and mercy, two aspects of the imitation of God's work, are more closely related than we might suppose. God's Messiah shows mercy and requires the recipients of his mercy to extend the same to others. Matthew's use of Old Testament prophecy is generally Christ-centered, but the only prophetic text cited twice describes both Jesus' salvific mission and what is required of God's people: "I desire mercy, not sacrifice" (Hos 6:6 in Mt 9:13; 12:7).

Because of contemporary Christians' tendency to conclude the Lord's Prayer with "for thine is . . . ," we easily forget the actual conclusion.[7] The second-to-last line in the prayer runs, "Forgive us our debts, as we also have forgiven our debtors" (Mt 6:12), and Jesus follows the prayer with a very serious warning: disciples who fail to imitate the forgiveness of the heavenly Father are rejecting a parent-child relationship (Mt 6:14-15). God gives and forgives on his own initiative, graciously, to those who do not deserve goodness or forgiveness. But Jesus teaches that when we respond to God's grace by giving and forgiving, God in turn gives and forgives. One can almost speak of a spiral of imitation.

One response to such teaching is to erect boundaries for mercy in order to limit its cost. When Peter fishes for limits on the extent of forgiveness (Mt 18:21-22), Jesus responds to Peter's question by insisting on the practice of forgiveness to a perfect or divine degree, "seventy-seven times." He then tells a parable that simultaneously celebrates the remarkable extent of God's generous forgiveness and the tragic consequences of failing to imitate him by forgiving others (Mt 18:23-35). Forgiveness is incredibly costly for God's Son (Mt 26:28), and it will be costly for those who imitate him.

Forgiveness is an indispensible family trait. "Jesus spins human be-

---

[7]Scholars agree that the ending commonly associated with the prayer was not originally part of Matthew.

havior from the cloth of divine behavior. The embodiment of forgiveness in the practices of Jesus' followers is a manifestation and imitation of God's own character."[8] The Son died on the cross and made peace by providing a means for forgiveness, conforming his will to the Father's will at great cost (Mt 26:28; Acts 10:36; Eph 2:14-17; Col 1:20). "The peacemakers . . . will be called children of God" became a prophecy fulfilled: the soldiers at the cross "were terrified and said, 'Truly this man was God's Son!'" (Mt 5:9; 27:54).

The world hears imperfect yet audible echoes of God's judgment, mercy and forgiveness in the actions of his church (Jn 20:23). In a fallen world, discipline and judgment are no less indispensable than forgiveness, and God gives his church a surprising degree of power to exercise on his behalf (Mt 18:15-20). When the church engages in discipline and judgment, the goal is redemption and healing, not vengeance or destruction (Mt 18:15; 1 Cor 5:5; 2 Cor 7; 13:9-11; 2 Thess 3:14-15; Jas 5:19-20; 1 Pet 1:6-9). To strive for restoration is to imitate God's desire for the lost. When Jesus instructs the disciples on conflict and discipline in the church (Mt 18:15-20), his teaching is sandwiched between a passage depicting God as a shepherd who pursues the lost so that they will not perish (Mt 18:10-14) and a parable underscoring the importance of forgiveness in light of God's forgiveness (Mt 18:21-35).[9]

Elsewhere in Matthew, the admonition to "judge not" (Mt 7:1-2) seems to rule out judgments and discipline altogether. But in the context of that command, Jesus clarifies this saying and teaches how to judge rightly. What is needed is not the end of judgment, but the removal of obstacles so that judgments are more godlike (Mt 7:3-6). Log removal in Matthew 7 and the requirement of more than one witness in the Old Testament and Matthew 18 are safeguards to help ensure that our judgments are more godlike.

---

[8]Green, *Gospel According to Luke*, p. 444.
[9]For a study associating divine and human judgment in church discipline, see Eric Bargerhuff, *Love that Rescues: God's Fatherly Love in the Practice of Church Discipline* (Eugene, OR: Wipf and Stock, 2010).

SHARING GOD'S CHARACTER: HOSPITALITY, JOY AND THE IMITATION OF GOD

Luke 14 provides a model for hospitality in response to what God has done in the kingdom:

> [Jesus] said also to the one who had invited him, "When you give a luncheon or a dinner, do not invite your friends or your brothers or your relatives or rich neighbors, in case they may invite you in return, and you would be repaid. But when you give a banquet, invite the poor, the crippled, the lame, and the blind. And you will be blessed, because they cannot repay you, for you will be repaid at the resurrection of the righteous." (Lk 14:12-14)

In the Messiah, God embraces the poor, crippled, lame, blind and other unattractive guests. The recipients of heavenly hospitality must reflect the heavenly kingdom by their earthly embrace of the unwashed and unwanted. God embraces the spiritually and morally dirty, just as he embraces the physically undesirable.

The three parables of Luke 15 address Pharisees and others who grumble as Jesus "welcomes sinners and eats with them" (Lk 15:2). Jesus does not tell these parables to excuse sinners' sins, nor to give warm fuzzy feelings about God. He tells these stories (1) to reveal the heart of God for those lost in sin, (2) to expose the need for redemption in those who presume to be in the right with God and (3) to tear down fences—including religious, racial or rational barriers—that have been erected and carefully maintained as Jesus' opponents and followers resist the imitation of God's radical gospel hospitality.

The final parable in the sequence, Jesus' parable of the father and two lost sons (commonly called the parable of the prodigal son), drives all three points home. Jesus unmasks the lostness of those who fail to see God in his work; they should rejoice at the recovery of a lost brother. Ignorant of his own need for grace, the older brother struggles with the inequity of divine goodness because his younger brother has received grace, not justice. Both sons apply a tragic, ironic label to themselves: "hired hand" (Lk 15:19, 29). This label implies that those who cannot celebrate mercy at the return of prodigal brothers are just as "un-sonned" as the younger brother who rejected his family and ran away to party.[10] Ironically, the older brother sees himself as a servant outside the household rather than a child who is loved and celebrated by his Father.

As older brothers, the religious leaders stand outside the feast where Jesus welcomes sinners (Lk 15:2). They are on the outside looking in at mercy and joy. By some standards they may appear to be good, faithful and religious. But the rejection of the Father's mercy and hospitality leaves them just as disowned as those who run away and squander the family inheritance.

The older brothers fail to take cues for their response from the Father's response (Lk 15:24), an incredibly gracious response open to all. There is no more important part of the family inheritance than forgiveness, mercy and hospitality. In all three parables of Luke 15, finding what is lost produces or even compels joy and rejoicing: "we had to celebrate," the father says (Lk 15:32; similar language is used in Lk 15:5, 7, 10; 10:20-21).

Joy is a note struck throughout Luke and is the note on which the Gospel ends (Lk 24:51-53). It is the appropriate human response to God's gracious action (Lk 2:10; 8:13; 10:20; 19:6) because it reflects heaven's own response. "Joy on the part of the recipient and spectators of God's grace (Lk 13:17) is but an echo of the heavenly joy over the return of repentant sinners to the Father (Lk 15:5, 7, 10, 32). God and man share in joy."[11]

So the celebration of grace and restoration is another opportunity to imitate God. The text challenges readers to see that superiority and hostility rob them of a childlike relationship with their Father. But they can repent and climb over the bastardizing barriers. And as they enter the Father's festal joy as celebrated children, they often drag other unlikely celebrants along with them.

---

[10]Adopting Miroslav Volf's description in *Exclusion and Embrace: A Theological Exploration of Identity, Otherness and Reconciliation* (Nashville: Abingdon, 1996).

[11]I. Howard Marshall, *Luke: Historian and Theologian* (Exeter, UK: Paternoster, 1989), pp. 202-3.

WALKING IN THE WAYS

In the Old Testament perhaps the greatest metaphor for what we now call discipleship is "walking." "The Old Testament often speaks of walking in the ways of another, whether for good or evil."[12] This pattern begins with Yahweh, who connects his identity with his ways:

> The LORD descended in the cloud and stood with him there, and proclaimed the name, "The LORD." The LORD passed before him, and proclaimed,
> "The LORD, the LORD,
>   a God merciful and gracious,
>   slow to anger,
>   and abounding in steadfast love and faithfulness,
>   keeping steadfast love for the thousandth generation,
>   forgiving iniquity and transgression and sin,
>   yet by no means clearing the guilty." (Ex 34:5-7)

God's ways are the ways in which Israel knew its Emperor God.

> He made known his ways to Moses,
>   his acts to the people of Israel.
> The LORD is merciful and gracious,
>   slow to anger and abounding in steadfast love. . . .
> He does not deal with us according to our sins,
>   nor repay us according to our iniquities. . . .
> As a father has compassion for his children,
>   so the LORD has compassion for those who fear him. (Ps 103:7-8, 10, 13)

These saving actions are God's gospel for his people, whom he redeemed by grace.

Many of the characteristics by which God is identified in Exodus 34 and Psalm 103 are required of his people. Abraham and his family were chosen "to keep the way of the LORD by doing righteousness and justice" (Gen 18:18-19; note Gen 26:4-5). The phrase becomes a way of measuring Israel's success or failure in its mission as God's people called to walk in the way of the Lord (Judg 2:17, 22; Ps 81:13; 95:10).

---

[12]James Samra, "A Biblical View of Discipleship," *Bibliotheca Sacra* 160, no. 2 (2003): 226.

As a result, God's ways are not just his own actions. His ways are paths in which his people walk, revealed by God that we might imitate his character: "Make me to know your ways, O Lord; teach me your paths" (Ps 25:4).[13] God's ways shape the character and work he requires of his people on the basis of his identity and his work for their redemption. We study God's character in his ways in order to implement this character in the way we walk.

In the history of Israel David, Asa and others could function as models who were "available for future kings to see and imitate," and successful kings were said to have "walked in the ways" of David or other faithful kings.[14] On the other hand, kings who rejected Yahweh and did not walk in his ways served as models to be avoided (2 Kings 21:22). Some of Israel's kings walked in wickedness, "in the ways of Jeroboam" (1 Kings 16:19, 26; 22:52). Eventually the rejection of the ways of Yahweh led to exile.

Here is the Christian exclamation point on this Old Testament pattern: one king perfectly embodies the ways of the Lord, and because of that perfection he is uniquely the way provided by Yahweh. Jesus is

> the one who identifies himself by saying "I am the way" (Jn. 14:6a) [and] also the one who is "full of grace and truth" (Jn. 1:14), a phrase that many commentators rightly see as an allusion to the *hesed* and *emeth* of Exodus 34:6. The Son alone reveals and makes accessible the Father: "No one comes to the Father except through me" (Jn. 14:6b). All God's "ways" are thus summed up and clarified in him, the "way."[15]

Through his life, death, resurrection and enthronement Jesus becomes the way. Just as God's people responded to God's actions by imitating his ways in the Old Testament, God's people in the New Testament respond to Jesus' actions by imitating the one who is the way. Paul taught the crucified Messiah, the one who is the way (see

---

[13]See Kevin Vanhoozer, *Remythologizing Theology* (Cambridge: Cambridge University Press, 2010), p. 260. We can note the correlation without losing the distinction between God's ways and ours.

[14]Samra, in "A Biblical View of Discipleship," p. 226 n. 26, notes that the pattern is only as good as conformity to Yahweh's ways.

[15]Vanhoozer, *Remythologizing Theology*, p. 260.

Acts 24:14; 1 Cor 2:2), and Paul taught his own Jesus-shaped "ways in the Messiah" everywhere in every church.

The radical nature of grace is the basis for our radical discipleship, as we see his ways and learn to walk in them. In the face of an argument between his disciples over who is great and who is greater, Jesus tells them,

> The kings of the Gentiles lord it over them; and those in authority over them are called benefactors. But not so with you; rather the greatest among you must become like the youngest [little boys who did demeaning, dirty chores], and the leader like one who serves. For who is greater, the one who is at the table or the one who serves? Is it not the one at the table? But I am among you as one who serves. (Lk 22:25-27)

Jesus does not disapprove of benefaction, but he explicitly contrasts "benefactor" and "servant," because they represent two very different approaches to giving and discipleship.[16] One facilitates the development of a great reputation; the other leads to nothingness. That is, it leads to nothingness in the short run. For Jesus does not leave the command to serve as the final word. He strips away the plastic rewards of back-patting, temporary reputations, plaques on buildings, and thank-you form letters. In their place he provides a glorious inheritance for his brothers and sisters, an inheritance secured by his own suffering service: a kingdom, a king's table and a king's throne (Lk 22:28-30).[17] And as we walk in Jesus' ways, we walk in the way of Yahweh, who serves his children at an eternal table (Lk 12:37).

CONCLUSION

When Jesus' followers reject the way of the zealot, when they shun the way of violence, retaliation, retribution and bitterness, when they stand firm in clarity and biblical truth, when they choose the path of

---

[16]Jesus himself received benefaction (Lk 8:1-3). He needs nothing but allows former demon-possessed women to finance the kingdom of God with what God has given them.

[17]"One who takes up a neighbor's burden, one who wishes to benefit someone who is worse off in something in which one is oneself better off, one who provides to those in need things that one has received from God, and thus becomes a god to those who receive them—this one is an imitator of God." *Epistle to Diognetus* 10.6.

forgiveness and death, they share the spiritual genes of the Son of
God. Like the Son, their elder brother, they reflect the likeness of the
Father as they share his moral genetic code.

8

Resurrection and Imitation

*The Christian life in its entirety is to be subsumed
under the category of Resurrection.*

RICHARD GAFFIN

When I was in college I loved the apostle Paul, and I thought I understood him. I loved the message of grace and the gospel. I had a short statement to explain the heart of Christianity according to Paul: "God worked to save me in the cross." That's a powerful equation and a helpful short summary. But over time I discovered that this slogan could be used as a sieve to filter out a great deal of what Paul intends for his readers to know and practice. It failed to address the new creation that God was working in Jesus' resurrection two thousand years ago—and in humans here and now. My failure to see the bigger Pauline picture led to a rather licentious approach to grace and the Bible and left me confused about much of Paul's teaching. I needed to hear the insistence in Calvin's teaching that "free remission of sins cannot be separated from the Spirit of regeneration."[1]

---

[1]Comment on Romans 8:9 found in *Calvin's New Testament Commentaries: The Epistles to the Romans and the Thessalonians*, ed. D. Torrance and T. Torrance, trans. R. MacKenzie (Grand Rapids: Eerdmans, 1995), p. 164.

A Problem and a Solution: Salvation as Renewal

Throughout the Bible we see that human sin has been the fundamental obstacle to imitation. Israel imitated the nations around it rather than the holiness and righteousness of its God. It became like the stone-hearted, deaf and mute idols it worshiped. After the exile, overt idolatry was no longer much of a problem in Israel, yet Jesus challenged the paternity of his opponents on the basis of their failure to imitate the Father. They looked like their father the devil and shared his deeds of lies and murder.

Imitation—or the absence of it—is not the only way to describe the fall and its consequences. But humans were created to imitate, and we see human rebellion clearly in the inability to imitate God according to his original design: loving, relating, ruling, creating and forgiving like God. Paul summarizes the impact of sin in the opening chapters of Romans: God's images have exchanged "the glory of the immortal God" for corruption and destruction (Rom 1:18-27). Humans continually and universally fall short of the glory for which they were designed as God's images (Rom 3:23): "All people fail to exhibit that 'being-like-God' for which they were created."[2]

There are many implications of falling short, but God's solution to sin is also multifaceted, extending "far as the curse is found."[3] In this chapter we will consider not how humans return to God's presence—how they have access to his presence through atonement and forgiveness—but how they come back to being like God as God intended. Other aspects of salvation, particularly the cross, are far from irrelevant for imitation, as we've already seen. But over the next two chapters we will focus on aspects of Paul's teaching that provide an important, oft-neglected framework for understanding imitation: union with Christ, resurrection, regeneration and Holy Spirit. These gospel elements become the engine for Christian sanctification—the process of looking more like the Father and the Son through the

---

[2]Douglas J. Moo, *Romans*, New International Commentary on the New Testament (Grand Rapids: Eerdmans, 1996), p. 226. "Sharing in God's glory involves conformity to the 'image of Christ' (Rom 8:29-30; Phil 3:21). . . . The absence of glory involves a declension from the 'image of God' in which human beings were first made."
[3]See especially Michael Williams's book by this title (Philipsburg, NJ: P&R, 2005).

work of the Holy Spirit in the believer.

What's more, these elements all point to the renewal of God's original plan for humans and the re-creation of all things. The heart of Paul's theology is not the cross alone; it is the cross and a whole host of other elements, all wrapped up together as an eschatological package. Paul believed that in the Messiah and the Spirit, the "last days" had fallen on him and his congregations (Acts 2:17; 1 Cor 10:11; see also Heb 1:2). As a result, Paul's teaching about Jesus and the Christian life is linked to themes like new creation, new covenant, kingdom coming and second Adam.[4] Resurrection and the enthronement of David's Son as the world's true Lord were held by many Jews to be the signposts of the coming new creation. For Paul, the accomplishment of these long-awaited events in Jesus was at the core of his gospel (Rom 1:2-4; 1 Cor 15:1-5; 2 Tim 2:8). They had to be believed and confessed for salvation (Rom 10:9).

OLD PROMISES, NEW SOLUTIONS

A blueprint for the solution to sin was written out long before Paul wrote his letters. The Old Testament depicts the spiritual deadness of the nations and God's people but also insists that "God has the ability to bring Israel and the nations out from their idolatrous darkness and deep sleep by restoring them and recreating them in his living image again, as Isaiah 29 affirms, replanting in them eyes to see and ears to hear his true word." While idol worshipers become like their gods, God reshapes his people like a potter, "transforming them from reflections of earthly idolatrous images and remaking them into his image."[5] Isaiah's potter and clay language reflects the story of the creation of humans from dirt in Genesis.

Paul believed that God's promised redemption was beginning to

---

[4]See especially Greg Beale, who has argued that the in-breaking of the "new creational kingdom" is the center of New Testament and biblical theology; *New Testament Biblical Theology: The Unfolding of the Old Testament in the New* (Grand Rapids: Baker, 2011), which builds on his epochal *The Temple and the Church's Mission: A Biblical Theology of the Dwelling Place of God*, New Studies in Biblical Theology, vol. 17 (Downers Grove, IL: InterVarsity Press, 2000).
[5]Greg Beale, *We Become What We Worship: A Biblical Theology of Idolatry* (Downers Grove, IL: InterVarsity Press, 2008), p. 279; see also pp. 273, 276.

take place. Rescue and renewal were bursting into a world groaning for liberation (Rom 8:18-25). The Creator who had promised resurrection was making alive what was dead by giving the life-giving Spirit.[6] The result in Paul and Isaiah is mission: "Then they will reflect him and his glorious light as they spread throughout the earth as his emissaries and agents through which God shines his light and reforms others into his image (cf. Is 49:6)."[7]

As we saw earlier, God's effort and our own are not as divergent as we sometimes assume. And in passages such as Ezekiel 37, Jeremiah 31 and Deuteronomy 30, God promises to work within his people to restore them. In Paul's day, righteous deeds and radical communities were evidence that God's Spirit was doing end-times work in and through Paul and his congregations. God and humans were at work bearing new creation fruit. The church was evidence of the fulfillment of Old Testament promises that humans would begin to look like God again, restored to God's original design.[8] God's goal was to make resurrected humans who looked like Jesus (Rom 8:23, 29) and thus like God (Eph 4:23-24). All of creation longs for these new humans to be revealed, because their full unveiling as God's image-bearing children will result in the redemption of creation (Rom 8:18-25). For as humanity goes, so goes the whole world: God's entire creation project revolves around the fate of those he designed to be enthroned over the world. They are "heirs of God" (Rom 8:17), and he will give them "all things" (Rom 8:32 NIV).

God's promised redemptive work was not launched by humans. They could seek the kingdom, pray for its coming, experience foretastes of it and long for its establishment as faithful Israelites often did (Lk 2:25, 36-38; Mt 6:9-10, 33). But they could not accomplish this

---

[6]Darrell Bock, in *Recovering the Real Lost Gospel* (Nashville: B&H Academic, 2010), puts the gift of the Holy Spirit squarely into the gospel definition by exegeting Acts; Jer 31; Ezek 11:15-20; 36-37; Deut 9:22-25; 29-30; Joel 2. (These same promises coordinate the Holy Spirit with the forgiveness of sins, new covenant, a Davidic king, the restoration of human community and creation, among other aspects of end-times renewal.)

[7]Beale, *We Become What We Worship*, p. 278.

[8]G. K. Beale, "The Old Testament Background of Paul's Reference to 'the Fruit of the Spirit' in Galatians 5:22," *Bulletin for Biblical Research* 15, no. 1 (2005): 1-38. See also the discussion in chapter 10 on Acts 17.

work on their own. For Paul the cross, resurrection and enthronement of Jesus was God's unilateral solution to the problem of sin and the means of bringing humans back to God, so that men and women in whom death reigned would reign in life (Rom 5:17)—just as God always intended.

Salvation in the Messiah: A New Identity, a New Life

According to Paul, humans are saved by being united to the resurrected Messiah, and the result is that what is true of the true human is becoming true of others as well. The most characteristic phrases in Paul's letters are "in him," "in Christ" and related terms such as "in the beloved." In the New Testament letters ascribed to Paul, these phrases appear more than 160 times. It is difficult to summarize and describe the implications of this union, and not all of the references are to be taken in the same sense.[9] But it is no stretch to say that the believer's connection to the Messiah implied by these phrases "is the foundation of all the blessings of salvation."[10] Many passages in Paul indicate the present and future blessings that come from the connection between Jesus and his body, the church. In Paul's letters we find that aspects of salvation such as adoption, justification, forgiveness, predestination, baptism and re-creation to do good works are all said to occur "in Christ" (see 1 Cor 15:22; Eph 1:4, 7; 2:1-10; Col 2:12-15).[11]

---

[9]These references can be instrumental, mediatorial, communal, mystical, participatory, etc. Constantine Campbell identifies union, participation, identification and incorporation as aspects of the union with Christ metatheme—all four of which carry ethical implications (*Paul and Union with Christ: An Exegetical and Theological Study* [Grand Rapids: Zondervan, 2012], p. 413).

[10]Graham Cole, *God the Peacemaker: How Atonement Brings Shalom*, New Studies in Biblical Theology, vol. 25 (Downers Grove, IL: IVP Academic, 2009), p. 158; compare James S. Stewart, *A Man in Christ* (New York: Harper and Row, 1935), p. 147: "The heart of Paul's religion is union with Christ." John Murray, *Redemption: Accomplished and Applied* (Grand Rapids: Eerdmans, 1955), p. 170: "Union with Christ is the central truth of the whole doctrine of salvation." Todd Billings notes the importance of this theme for Calvin and much of the Reformed tradition, if not its popular reputation and recent popularizers, in *Union with Christ: Reframing Theology and Ministry for the Church* (Grand Rapids: Baker Academic, 2011). For the Wesleyan tradition, see especially E. Stanley Jones, *In Christ* (Nashville: Abingdon, 1980).

[11]On justification: "[God] reckons righteousness to them, not because he accounts them to have kept his law personally (which would be a false judgment), but because he accounts them to be united to one who kept it representatively (and that is a true judgment)." J. I. Packer, "Justification," in *Evangelical Dictionary of Theology*, ed. Walter A. Elwell (Grand

These aspects of salvation and many others are part of the under-lying gospel motivation for imitation and discipleship. But they do not just motivate believers with gratitude; they are a new reality in which disciples are commanded to live, a new self-conception and worldview that require new creation believers to regard themselves no longer in terms of the flesh (the old era to which they have died; 2 Cor 5:14, 16-17). From the cross to enthronement, life in Christ leads to a Christ-shaped life now and in the age to come. Believers begin to become what they already are in Christ: the true humans they were originally destined to be.[12] Recalling the material covered in our first chapter (Gen 1:26-28; Ps 8; Dan 7), believers are "co-raised" and "co-seated" with the Messiah, enthroned in the heavenlies (Eph 2:6). As adopted children, they begin to look like their Father.

Because believers are united to a resurrected Lord, they are given a new life and a new power for living. Both of these pieces are related to the imitation of Jesus, and we will explore each in turn.

Resurrection for the Living: New Creation Life

Believers normally think of resurrection as a hope for life beyond the grave. But resurrection life is not just relevant after death. Because believers are already united to and raised with the resurrected Messiah (Eph 2:6; Col 2:12), they are participating in a new reality that radi-cally changes their life before death even as it will one day change their life after death.

In other words, God has the same solution to the problem of death and to the problem of a sinful life: resurrection. A favorite Christmas hymn puts it well: Jesus is "born to raise the sons of earth, born to give them second birth."

In Ephesians 1 and 2, Paul describes the power at work in believers as resurrection and enthronement power. Paul doesn't say that he is

---

Rapids: Baker, 1984), p. 596; see also pp. 645, 1052. On union with Christ and salvation from a Reformed soteriological perspective, see R. Gaffin, *Resurrection and Redemption: A Study in Paul's Soteriology* (Philipsburg, NJ: P&R, 1987), and Murray, *Redemption: Accom-plished and Applied.*

[12]Michael Bird, *Introducing Paul: The Man, His Mission and His Message* (Downers Grove, IL: IVP Academic, 2009), p. 136.

praying that they will know what God accomplished for them in the cross, although he will soon address the implications of the cross (Eph 2:11-16). Rather, he prays that they will know "what is the immeasurable greatness of his power for us who believe, according to the working of his great power. God put this power to work in Christ when he raised him from the dead and seated him at his right hand in the heavenly places" (Eph 1:19-20). Paul then describes the enthronement of Jesus (Eph 1:21-22) and cites Psalm 8:6, a poem we saw in chapter one on the royal nature of humans.

Paul wants believers to know that the power at work in them is the power that raised Jesus and enthroned him with the Father. This resurrection and enthronement power is fleshed out in Ephesians 2:1-10 as Paul describes the way God moves disciples from death to life. "By nature" humans are zombies, the dead who walk in their sin as "children of wrath" following the ruler of the power of the air in disobedience and unrestrained desire (Eph 2:1-5). But now God has "made us alive together with Christ." Dead humans are brought to life (Eph 2:5), enthroned with the Messiah as royalty (Eph 2:6) and given good work to do (Eph 2:10).

That sequence should sound familiar. The opening chapters of Genesis, which we explored earlier, contain the same pattern. Just as God created Adam, gave him his Spirit, enthroned him and put him to work in his world, so God creates his children anew in Jesus Messiah, enthroning them and putting them to work in his world.

Theologians of all stripes call these renewed people "the new humanity."[13] Paul frequently contrasts Adam and the old humanity— under judgment and wrath (Eph 2), subject to decay (1 Cor 15) and subject to the "reign of sin" (Rom 5)—with the Messiah, the second and last Adam and the true humanity (these also appear in Eph 2;

---

[13]James Montgomery Boice titled one of his expositions on Romans *The New Humanity* (vol. 4 of *Romans* [Grand Rapids: Baker, 1995]), a title he also employed in his exposition of Ephesians. Compare Rudolf Bultmann's title, *The Old Man and the New Man* (Richmond: John Knox, 1967); James S. Stewart, *A Man in Christ* (London: SCM Press, 1935); Ben F. Meyer, *The Early Christians* (Wilmington, DE: M. Glazier, 1986), pp. 18-19, 182-85, 202-7; D. Martyn Lloyd-Jones, *The New Man* (exposition of Romans, vol. 6) (Edinburgh: Banner of Truth, 1972) on Romans 6. This concept is classically tied to the theological label "regeneration."

1 Cor 15; Rom 5). Even where Paul does not explicitly mention the Adam-Messiah contrast, he calls believers united to the resurrected Messiah a "new creation" (2 Cor 5:17; Gal 6:15). And when Paul addresses ethics, he regularly contrasts this new human identity and the behavior that should accompany it with the old human nature and its practices (among many other passages, see Col 3:1-11; Eph 4:17-32).

Although this is an ennobling identity, it should not produce boasting (Eph 2:9). In the original design with Adam and in the new creation renewal of that design, creation and enthronement are God's work. He displayed life-giving power in humans at creation and enthronement, and now he displays that same power in the re-creation of humans after the pattern of the last Adam (Rom 5:14; 1 Cor 15:45). Kings and queens who are totally dependent on another for their existence and their enthronement have no room to boast. Moreover, those in Adam and in the last Adam are not just royalty but priests in the service of the Emperor God.

Paul does not believe that God is done with the human creation project he launched in the beginning. The God who fulfills his purposes still intends to have humans rule as his images. Just as Adam and Eve and their offspring were to fill the world as God's images, so these newly created children in Christ are to fill the world as the church, the body of the one true image of God. The church is his fullness in the world until all things are gathered up "in him" (Eph 1:10). God is uniting believers in the Messiah, baptizing them in a new name (Mt 28:18-20) and growing them together so that they are "the fullness of him who fills all in all" (Eph 1:23; see also 1:10). And as they fill the world, they begin to fulfill the command in Genesis 1:28 that humans fill the world with God's images (Eph 4:13-16, 23-24). In this way God's original design for the world is fulfilled.

CHRISTIANS CHRISTIFIED: A CRUCIFIED AND RESURRECTED PEOPLE

The new creation life in the last Adam is a new, unearned status that produces new action (Eph 2:10). As Paul says, "It is no longer [the old] I who live, but it is Christ who lives in me" (Gal 2:20). He points to this twofold function of our death and resurrection in the Messiah by using the same death (or burial) and resurrection scheme to describe what has happened for us by our union with the Messiah and what should happen in and through us because of a new mindset, new power and new works.[14] "It is a transforming union. By this union believers are changed into the image of Christ according to his human nature. What Christ effects in His people is in a sense a replica or reproduction of what took place in Him. Nor only objectively, but also in a subjective sense they suffer, bear the cross, are crucified, die, and are raised in newness of life, with Christ. They share in a measure the experiences of their Lord (Mt 16:24; Rom 6:5; Gal 2:20; Col 1:24; 2:12; 3:1; 1 Pet 4:13)."[15]

The stooping/death and resurrection pattern appears in each of the Gospels for both Jesus and his disciples. It is prominent throughout Paul's letters and is tied to his theology of baptism: in Paul "the gospel life is one that refracts the dying and rising of Christ as symbolized in a Christian baptism."[16] In Romans 6 Paul unpacks the ethical implications of resurrection identity for baptized believers: they are taken into the death of the Messiah in order to be united with him in resurrection, so that "we too might walk in newness of life" (Rom 6:3-4), in contrast to an old life under slavery to sin.[17] Since death does not rule over Jesus anymore, sin and death should not rule in believers (Rom 6:8-11); "how can we who died to sin go on living in it?" (Rom 6:2). Disciples alive in Messiah must give themselves to righteousness, as those who died to sin and came alive for God when they were united to the resurrected Messiah (Rom 6:12-14). Paul employs the pattern in Romans 12:1-2, calling believers to death ("present your bodies as a

---

[14]Bird has labeled this pattern "cruciformity and anastasisity"; see his *Introducing Paul*, pp. 162-68. See for instance 2 Cor 1:8-10; 4:11, 16; 5:14-17; Gal 2:19-20; 5:24; Phil 3; Col 2:11-13; 3:3-4; 1 Thess 5:10; 2 Tim 2:8-12; Rom 7:4-6; 8:1-11, 13; 12:1-2; 15:1. I. Howard Marshall points out that this pattern appears even where the cross is not explicitly mentioned; *Luke: Historian and Theologian* (Exeter, UK: Paternoster, 1989), pp. 209-10. See also Jas 4:10.

[15]Louis Berkhof, *Systematic Theology*, 4th ed. (Grand Rapids: Eerdmans, 1996), p. 451.

[16]Cole, *God the Peacemaker*, p. 193.

[17]"Baptism, we might say, gives the Christian not simply his form but also his mission." John Webster, "The Imitation of Christ," *Tyndale Bulletin* 37 (1986): 114, citing H. U. von Balthasar, *Prayer*, trans. A. V. Littledale (London: SPCK, 1973), p. 48.

living sacrifice") and resurrection ("be transformed by the renewing of your minds").

Crucifixion and resurrection mold believers into the Messiah's perfect pattern. We might call this process "Christification," since believers are becoming new humans who are "created according to the likeness of God in true righteousness and holiness" (Eph 4:24; compare 2 Cor 3:18). At the end of time, Christification, or conformity, will be fully and finally complete in actual, physical resurrection (Phil 3:10-11). But in the present we live toward our new human destination by imitating and embodying God's perfect image, Jesus. "Sharing in 'the fellowship of his sufferings' is the way believers experience 'the power of his resurrection' (Phil 3:10; cf. 2 Cor 1:5); the condition for those who aspire to be glorified with Christ is that for now 'we suffer with him' (Rom 8:17)."[18]

The goal of sanctification is the renewal of the image of God: god-likeness refreshed and reloaded.[19] In sanctification believers begin to become humanity 2.0, a Christified version of the original image-bearing, God-imitating humans. Because believers have their identity tied up with the resurrected Messiah, that process of renewal begins now in behavior: "To be an image bearer, one must clothe oneself with Christlike behavior and become an image wearer."[20] The reclamation project will not be completed in the present, and restoration does not come in a smooth, straight line. But shortcomings along the way are not a reason to avoid imitation and effort; shortcomings rather are all the more reason for believers to be taught to "put on" the new hu-

---

[18]R. Gaffin, "Glory, Glorification," in *Dictionary of Paul and His Letters*, ed. Gerald F. Hawthorne, Ralph P. Martin and Daniel G. Reid (Downers Grove, IL: InterVarsity Press, 1993), p. 349. Gaffin also states, "The church's glorification takes place specifically as believers are 'conformed to the image of his Son' (Rom 8:29); the glory-image, universally defaced and perverted in Adam, is restored and made consummate in Christ and the church. This conformity is a reality already underway (2 Cor 3:18 in context)." This is by no means an exclusively "reformed" concept. See Ben Witherington III, *The Indelible Image: The Theological and Ethical Thought World of the New Testament*, vol. 1 (Downers Grove, IL: IVP Academic, 2009), p. 241: "A salvation that is no more than *simul justus et peccator* is not the full-orbed salvation about which Paul speaks, not even in Romans." Witherington cites Gordon Fee, *Pauline Christology* (Peabody, MA: Hendrickson, 2007), p. 487: Salvation and new creation are about "restoring humanity back into the divine image."
[19]See Westminster Shorter Catechism, question and answer 35.
[20]Witherington, *Indelible Image*, p. 242.

manity: "Do not lie to one another, seeing that you have stripped off the old self with its practices and have clothed yourselves with the new self, which is being renewed in knowledge according to the image of its creator" (Col 3:9-10). As Calvin commented on this passage, "The goal of our regeneration is that we may be like God, and that his glory may shine forth in us."[21] From a different passage and a different theological tradition, Gordon Fee summarizes Paul's goal for the Galatians: "for 'Christ [to be] formed in you' (4:19), which in Rom 13:14 takes the form of an admonition to 'clothe yourselves with the Lord Jesus Christ.'"[22] The glory of God is now being shown—dimly, sometimes almost imperceptibly, yet always definitively—in true humans as they are Christified. They imitate Jesus and are formed into his image, which is the image of God.

Now for some readers the insistence on renewal and transformation may raise fears of legalism and triumphalism. But these new humans have a new engine and a new identity that changes everything. Like all the benefits of salvation, these benefits come from the life that believers share with their head, the Messiah (Eph 1:22-23). His body has been given new power. To quote Paul's master, they have "power from on high" (Lk 24:49; Acts 1:5, 8). The Spirit of God begins to shape these new creation people just as he shaped creation (Gen 1:2; Gal 6:15; 2 Cor 5:17). He deserves his own chapter.

---

[21]John Calvin, *Commentaries on the Epistles of Paul to the Philippians, Colossians, and Thessalonians*, trans. John Pringle (Edinburgh: Calvin Translation Society, 1847), p. 180. Or again, on 2 Pet 1:4, Calvin comments, "Let us then mark, that the end of the gospel is, to render us eventually conformable to God, and, if we may so speak, to deify us" (*Commentaries on the Catholic Epistles*, trans. J. Owen [Edinburgh: Calvin Translation Society, 1855], p. 371). Calvin goes on to distinguish between the essence and quality of God and glorified humans.
[22]Fee, *Pauline Christology*, p. 487, cited by Witherington, *Indelible Image*, p. 239.

9

The Holy Spirit

The goal of the Spirit's ministry in sanctification is the reproduction of likeness to Christ, and in this sense to produce the imitation of Christ. It therefore involves following Jesus Christ, taking up the cross and denying self. Indeed, the last two elements are really continuing applications and expositions of the first.

SINCLAIR FERGUSON

For various reasons, each of the three audiences identified at the start of this book seems to struggle with the framework for imitation laid out in the previous chapter. In the messy middle of American evangelicalism, imitation is often made practical as sermons teach us how to cope with stress, be better leaders or manage our lives. But when believers are called to imitate Jesus or other biblical characters, gospel motivation and reminders of the power God gives for imitation are sometimes lacking. We'll see that Paul frequently gets practical with imitation. But we don't need practical advice alone. Paul's practical advice is based on the gospel—the death, resurrection and enthronement of Jesus and new life in him. Gospel foundations lead to "a gospel ethic . . . a normative account of how our lives conform to the pattern of the life, death and resurrection of Jesus Christ that is discerned and freely enacted through the power of the Spirit's indwelling presence."[1] When Paul supplies moral instruction, he applies the universal message of God's story to local behavior, challenging the world's competing stories along the way. If our sermons are offering versions of the world's stories (successful leadership, successful quests for comfort, effective time management) with Christian language, Paul's goal of "Christification" is slowly being replaced with "worldification."

In the Reformed right, present-tense implications of union with Christ such as forgiveness and justification of those "in Christ" are standard fare in many theological texts and pulpits. But other vital aspects go missing. I have often made knowledge about Christ my goal in discipleship. But Paul's goal was Christ "formed in you" (Gal 4:19). The goal of theology is not mere knowledge; the goal of theology is to shape the Christian life.[2] And in the young Reformed world, concepts such as resurrection, regeneration and the Holy Spirit, which contribute greatly to Paul's goal, do not receive the attention paid to other theological aspects.[3]

---

[1]Matthew Lee Anderson, *Earthen Vessels: Why Our Bodies Matter to Our Faith* (Grand Rapids: Bethany House, 2011), p. 11, citing Oliver O'Donovan's *Resurrection and Moral Order: An Outline for Evangelical Ethics* (Grand Rapids: Eerdmans, 1986) as the "key text."

[2]"*Every Christian doctrine ultimately directs us to the love of God and directs us in ways of rightly ordered living. . . .* Sound doctrine both proceeds from and leads to theo-drama: to *doing* the truth for the love of God." Kevin Vanhoozer, *The Drama of Doctrine: A Canonical-Linguistic Approach to Christian Theology* (Louisville, KY: Westminster John Knox, 2005), p. 442, emphasis original; see also pp. 25, 268, 400 and elsewhere in his work. See also J. I. Packer, *Growing in Christ* (Wheaton, IL: Crossway, 1994), p. 18; John Frame often repeats the dictum that theology is "the application of God's Word to [all of] life."

[3]From a Reformed perspective, see thoughts on regeneration from Dane Ortlund, "Remember Regeneration," The Gospel Coalition Voices (Jan. 4, 2011), thegospelcoalition.org/blogs/tgc/2011/01/04/remember-regeneration, and J. I. Packer in Mark Driscoll, "J. I. Packer on Young Christian Leaders," Resurgence: A Ministry of Mars Hill Church (July 30, 2008), theresurgence.com/2008/07/30/j-i-packer-on-young-christian-leaders. Driscoll summarizes Packer's comments: "The doctrine of regeneration has not been fully appreciated by many who do not understand that to be born again with a new heart and new nature means that we have at our deepest level a new identity and new passionate desires for God's Word and ways." On resurrection, Justin Taylor writes, "The resurrection of Christ, the resurrection power mediated by the Spirit, and the coming resurrection of the saints—all remain neglected topics of gospel preaching." Justin Taylor, "Neglecting the Resurrection," Justin Taylor Between Two Worlds, The Gospel Coalition (February 11, 2010), thegospelcoalition.org/blogs/justintaylor/2010/02/11/neglecting-the-resurrection. To cite but one symptom of the absence of resurrection, R. C. Sproul's *Essential Truths of the Christian Faith* (Wheaton, IL: Tyndale, 1998) contains one hundred chapters but no chapter on Jesus' resurrection.

We have seen in the previous chapter the centrality of resurrection and new life for Paul's ethics. And Paul's self-conception does not allow for the segregation of the facts of salvation from action: "Paul's apostolic ministry of missionary suffering and his gospel theology of the crucified Christ were an inseparable unity."[4] "Paul's suffering is not an addendum to his preaching;" it is his preaching.[5] He expects others to see this visible sermon in his life and imitate him as he imitates Christ (1 Cor 11:1). His life demonstrates the message proclaimed by his lips.

On the other hand, on the left-hand side of the spectrum, little attention is paid to the fact that every human is fallen, lost, enslaved to sin, under judgment and in desperate need of a new condition. God's solution is not willy-nilly grace but union with Christ, a new status where reborn participants in resurrection life receive the present and future benefits of Jesus' cross and resurrection. They receive these benefits not because of their goodness but by bending the knee to Jesus as Lord and calling to him for redemption. Paul and the rest of the New Testament writers carefully distinguish between two distinct groups of people: those born of God and those who are not. Christianity insists that radical change is required—a new resurrection life, a gift that brings faith in the Messiah. Without that radical change, humans are the walking dead (Eph 2:1). To lose that story is to lose one's life, no matter how much interest one takes in the imitation of Jesus.

The solution for all three spheres is to dig back into Paul and the fountainhead of union with Messiah, regeneration and resurrection. All of these things are true of believers because of the work of the Holy Spirit. Paul says that "anyone united to the Lord becomes one spirit with him" (1 Cor 6:17), and the Lord who is the Spirit has taken up residence in a human temple.[6]

[4]Scott Hafemann, "'Because of Weakness' (Galatians 4:13): The Role of Suffering in the Mission of Paul," in *The Gospel to the Nations: Perspectives on Paul's Mission*, ed. P. Bolt and M. Thompson (Downers Grove, IL: InterVarsity Press, 2000), pp. 140, 165.
[5]Hafemann, "'Because of Weakness,'" p. 184.
[6]Some interpreters who notice the work of the Spirit prefer *conformity* rather than a term such as *imitation*, which involves human work. Again, I have no strong preference for *imitation*, provided we remember that an emphasis on passive conformity alone would fail to do justice to what Scripture describes and what the Spirit is at work in believers to accomplish.

Renewed by the Spirit

Before we look at the Spirit in Paul, let us consider how the Gospels construe the power for discipleship. The disciples are far from ideal. They fail to understand Jesus and his teaching. John highlights Peter's struggles as he attempts to follow a cross-shaped Messiah when much of what Jesus says about himself confuses them (Jn 2:18-22; 12:16). Peter claims he will lay down his life for Jesus, and Jesus agrees that this will happen (Jn 13:36-37). But the Lord adds the caveat "not now" (Jn 13:38), and Peter quickly denies being associated with Jesus in order to save his life (Jn 18:15-27). Only after Jesus restores Peter and commissions him to care for the sheep is he shown "the kind of death by which he would glorify God." With those words Jesus reinstates Peter as a follower on mission and twice tells him, "Follow me" (Jn 21:19, 22).

Now in order for Peter or any other disciple to obey such a command, a radical change has to take place in them. Before his death Jesus is clear that they do not yet have the engine of transformation that will help them proclaim Jesus, understand his teaching and obey his command to live Jesus-shaped lives and deaths. But when Jesus is glorified, he and the Father will send a helper (Jn 7:39; 15:26; 16:7).

When Jesus returns to his disciples after his resurrection, he launches them out into mission: "As the Father has sent me, so I send you." But as he commissions them, he solves the problem of their pitiful state by breathing into them (Jn 20:21-22).[7] John's description reaches back to the original creation account and Old Testament promises of new creation. The verb John uses for "breathing into" is used in Greek translations of Genesis 2:7 in the same form (*enephysēsen*) to describe God's act of breathing life and spirit into Adam. John wants readers to see that in Jesus' action, the promise of new life and new creation in passages such

---

[7]The connection to Genesis is obscured by the tendency to translate the phrase in question "breathed *on* them." This theology was important to the Fathers—for example, Gregory Thamaturgus, *Oration and Panegyric for Origen* 12: "In consequence of our dull and sluggish nature, he has not yet succeeded in making us righteous, and prudent, and temperate, or manly, although he has laboured zealously on us. For we are neither in real possession of any virtue whatsoever, either human or divine, nor have we ever made any near approach to it, but we are still far from it. The virtues are great and lofty, and can only be attained by someone in whom God has breathed his power."

as Ezekiel 37 and John 3 are beginning to come true.[8]

Jesus promises that his followers will participate in resurrection: "Because I live, you also will live" (Jn 14:19). New resurrection life is not just a future possibility; believers receive a foretaste in the present through the new birth. In John 3 new birth from above (being "born again") is the new creation work of the Spirit in humans, and this work begins to fulfill the promises in Israel's story. Jesus breathes into the disciples so that they begin to participate in this new resurrection life (Jn 20:22). And because they now have the Holy Spirit, disciples are sent as Jesus was sent and are able to forgive or retain sins (Jn 20:21-23). Sending out disciples for these tasks without giving resurrection life and the Holy Spirit would be like requiring nuclear fission from a toddler. Disciples are not sinless, but they are remade and given a new ability to follow Jesus to the cross and resurrection.

The power of the end time work of God does not reside in Jesus alone. Disciples are united to the one who loved them, washed their feet, broke his body, gave his blood and made them holy. He breathes his Spirit into them in order to send them as he was sent. They are empowered by the Holy Spirit, motivated by the love of Jesus and guided by the commands of God. They are the light of the world, evidence that the coming new creation is, in part, already here. Disciples connected to Jesus like branches to a vine have the Holy Spirit in them producing the living water that flows out to the world.

SANCTIFICATION, STRIVING AND THE SPIRIT IN PAUL

Paul shares John's vision of renewal, and he shares the view that the Holy Spirit provides a new life and a new power for obedience. The Holy Spirit is God's present-tense guarantee that in due time he will deliver the full restoration for which his people are waiting. Many of the Spirit's blessings are not fully experienced on this side of the new heavens and the new earth, but there are many implications for believers here and now.

---

[8]The Spirit is at work in creation, new life in Messiah and new creation. In first-century Christian literature the word *regeneration* (*palingenesia*, "re-creation" in Mt 19:28; Tit 3:5; *1 Clement* 9:4) can describe the renewal of dead-in-sins humans, the renewal of the cosmos at the end of this present age, and God's re-creation of the world after the flood.

One prominent example of this already-not-yet dimension of the Spirit's work is adoption (Rom 8:14-15). The Spirit is a down payment on full adoption, the comforter who helps us experience freedom from slavery and the privilege of calling God "Father." The pinnacle of adoption (and all salvation) comes when the new humans are given resurrection bodies and fully share in the new creation. Resurrected and glorified like God's son, they live and reign on earth in God's presence according to God's original design. They are fully human at last, sharing in the glory of God. Presently only Christ is fully human and fully adopted. Believers are not adopted in the fullest sense because full adoption requires a resurrection body fit to rule a recreated world (Rom 8:21-23) and display God's glory.[9]

While this is still future, by the Spirit we can call God "Abba, Father" in the present and grow in the likeness of Jesus (Gal 4:19). And as the down payment on full adoption, the Holy Spirit also brings a powerful foretaste of the new Christ-shaped character God's children should possess. The Messiah's character will be fully formed in believers in the future. One sign in the present moment of that future finished work is the fruit that comes from "walking in the Spirit," the fruit of work in the power of the Spirit. In the present, the Spirit helps God's children reflect their Father's likeness in holiness and righteousness (Eph 4:23-24). In our love, joy, peace, patience, kindness, goodness, faithfulness, gentleness and self-control (Gal 5:22-23), God's Spirit is producing new creation fruit. Empowered and guided by the Spirit, we strive to avoid fleshly passions and desires and put away a whole array of sins (Eph 5:20-21). As we do so we grow in godliness (godlikeness), imitating both the Father and the Son.

The present and future dimensions are summed up well by J. I. Packer: "Christians become increasingly Christlike as the moral profile of Jesus (the 'fruit of the Spirit') is progressively formed in them (2 Cor. 3:18; Gal. 4:19; 5:22-25). Then the physical transformation that gives us a body like Christ's, one that will match our totally transformed character and be a perfect means of expressing it, will be glo-

[9]As cited from Irenaeus at the head of chapter 1, "The glory of God is a living human being."

rification completed (Phil. 3:20-21; 1 Cor. 15:49-53)."[10]

The use of the gifts of the Holy Spirit in the church is dedicated to this goal, as Paul's discussion of spiritual gifts in Ephesians 4 reveals: God gives these gifts in order to build up the body of Messiah, "until all of us come to the unity of the faith and of the knowledge of the Son of God, to maturity, to the measure of the full stature of Christ" (Eph 4:13). The goal of spiritual gifts is that the church would be a fitting body for the true human as he fills the world in his people (Eph 1:10, 22-23). The Spirit's goal is to duplicate and distribute God's image-bearers, who fill the world with his glory (1 Cor 11:7).

Paul regularly appeals for Christlikeness in believers, calling them to imitate the perfect human and grow into his likeness. He makes Christlikeness (Messiah-likeness) the goal because he believes the Spirit is at work. He can issue commands like "put on Christ" without any fear of legalism or moralism. Such new creation efforts could never be moralism or "bootstraps religion." They are the work of God himself working in his people (1 Cor 15:10; Eph 2:10; Phil 1:6, 8; 2:13; Col 1:29). These descriptions, coupled with the concept of spiritual gifts and fruit of the Spirit, should remind believers that sanctification is God's work and their work. It is both-and, not either-or.

The Spirit uses Paul's teaching to accomplish this transformation: commands, warnings, threats and promises all have a role to play. Paul's commands and warnings do not die the death of a thousand qualifications and caveats; he does not kill the rhetorical power of his words. He fearlessly speaks of work, effort, striving and imitation. He does not see the new humans as continually locked in a hopeless struggle over their fate and their justification and adequacy.

The task is not easy and the end product is never flawless. Still, Paul teaches that sin's chains are broken, and he expects progress in sanctification because God's Spirit is at work in resurrection power. Granted that he lays aside a pursuit of righteousness apart from the Messiah (Phil 3), Paul has no allergy to human works and righteousness, because he knows that God is at work in him. He believes

---

[10]J. I. Packer, *Concise Theology: A Guide to Historic Christian Beliefs* (Wheaton, IL: Tyndale, 2001), p. 170.

that the reality of new creation life in believers shapes them into the image of Jesus through Spirit-empowered effort. So Paul commands believers to work at their sanctification because God's Spirit is at work in them.

THE GOAL OF IMITATION

In previous chapters we have seen that in the Old Testament and the Gospels, the imitation of a perfect God provides humans a goal for character, virtue, morality and behavior. The goal for our sanctification is to be godlike: godly, holy, glorified. The goal of imitation and discipleship is perfect humanity, disciples who look like Jesus (Gal 4:19).[11] In the New Testament, the imitation of God is "fleshed out" (surely the perfect term) in the imitation of Jesus, for Jesus perfectly fleshes out God's goal for humanity. He hated what God hated, loved what God loved and loved as he was loved by his Father. Because Jesus is the exact human imprint of the Father (Col 1:15), his character becomes our goal.

Believers are predestined to be conformed to the image of the Son in order that he might be the firstborn within a large household full of siblings who think and act like him and like their Father (Rom 8:29). This is a future event, but it also points to believers' present task. Paul provides a clear present-tense goal for imitation in Ephesians 4:13: Believers grow together up to "the full stature of Christ." The goal of imitation is to be mature, complete, blameless and perfect.[12] These words are held out as the goal for disciples in many New Testament passages (Mt 5:48; 19:21;[13] Rom 12:2; 1 Cor 14:20; Eph 4:13; Phil 3:15 [summing up Phil 3:10-15 and chapters 2–4]; Col 1:28; 4:12; 1 Thess 5:23;

---

[11]James Samra, "A Biblical View of Discipleship," *Bibliotheca Sacra* 160, no. 2 (2003): 223: "The goal of the Christian life is to become like Christ." Samra cites many of the passages addressed in this chapter and adds contemporary theologians Wayne Grudem, *Systematic Theology* (Grand Rapids: Zondervan, 2000), pp. 845-46; Millard Erickson, *Christian Theology* (Grand Rapids: Baker 1985), p. 970; and Anthony Hoekema, "Reformed Perspective," in *Five Views on Sanctification*, ed. Melvin Dieter (Grand Rapids: Zondervan, 1987), pp. 66-68.

[12]See Graham Tomlin, *Spiritual Fitness: Christian Character in a Consumer Society* (London: Continuum, 2006), p. 113.

[13]On the basis of the conversation that follows with Peter and the disciples, along with the fact that Jesus has called his disciples to the task of perfection/completion previously, this is not a hypothetical command, as some suppose.

Heb 5:14–6:12; 13:21; Jas 1:4), often with God or Christ held up as an exemplar. Similar language throughout these passages affirms this goal (see 2 Tim 3:16-17; Eph 4:13-16; Jas 1:27).[14]

It is essential to point out a few caveats. The goal of perfection is not a prerequisite to our acceptance by God. Perfection will not be achieved short of resurrection, and our ongoing failure always requires God's gracious forgiveness. And this goal does not mean sinless perfection in the present. David, Job, Simeon, Joseph, Cornelius, Lot and other Old Testament and New Testament characters are labeled "righteous" and "blameless." Such terms do not mean "completely sinless" (see Job 1; Ps 119:2, 10, 34; Lk 1:6; Phil 3:15).

But to point out caveats is not to grant permission to slack off from the pursuit of perfection. Paul is a model both in caveats and in pursuit. He knows that he has in many respects fulfilled the task given to him by God (Phil 4:9-13). Yet he is also aware that he has not yet arrived. Greatly aware of his shortcomings and ever considering himself a debtor to grace, Paul works and strains to the point of death, always targeting completion and maturity (Phil 3:10-15). He believes that God is at work in him (Phil 2:13) and that in the Messiah he has all the resources he needs to strive, to succeed, to sacrifice and to suffer (Phil 4:11-16). Paul would surely agree that we need to repent of false and mixed motives, but I do not find in his letters (or elsewhere in the New Testament) the increasingly common assertion that we need to "repent of our good works."[15] We repent (turn) to good works, not from them.

CONCLUSION

Almost all of Paul's major theological emphases are linked to, and have an impact on, imitation. Imitation and related concepts (discipleship and sanctification) flow from the heart of what Paul believed and taught about salvation, Christology and the renewal of humans as God's image-bearers in Christ. Paul joins the Gospels in seeing the

---

[14]Note the emphasis throughout the New Testament on purity, holiness and godliness. See Tomlin, *Spiritual Fitness*, p. 123 n. 12.
[15]A Google search for the phrase in quotes produces 55,000 hits.

imitation of Jesus' sacrificial death as a template for the Christian life. His heavy emphasis on the Holy Spirit, resurrection and union with Christ also implicate imitation as a fundamental human task.

It should be no surprise, then, that almost all of his letters put imitation into play in significant ways, as we shall see in the next chapter. B. B. Warfield does not exaggerate when he says, "'Be ye imitators of me, even as I also am of Christ Jesus,' is rather the whole burden of the ethical side of Paul's teaching. And in this [Paul] was but the imitator of his Lord, who pleads with us to 'learn of Him because He is meek and lowly in heart.'"[16]

Paul rigorously applies both the benefits and the burden of the life and death of Jesus. That is another way of saying that Paul applies all the blessings of Jesus' life and death, even those blessings that look something like death on a cross.

---

[16]B. B. Warfield, *The Savior of the World: Sermons Preached in the Chapel of Princeton Seminary* (New York: Hodder and Stoughton, 1913), p. 249.

10

The Apostle of Imitation

Brothers and sisters, join in imitating me, and observe those
who live according to the example you have in us.

PHILIPPIANS 3:17

The distinctive shape of obedience to God is disclosed in Jesus
Christ's faithful death on the cross for the sake of God's people. . . . The
fundamental norm of Pauline ethics is the christomorphic life.
To imitate Christ is also to follow the apostolic example of
surrendering one's own prerogatives and interests.

RICHARD HAYS

On a hill overlooking Athens stood the Areopagus, the cradle of
Hellenism and the heartbeat of the city's religious and cultural life.
Like most good Jews in his day, Paul disdained idolatry and its catastrophic consequences. When he encountered the tragic idolatry on
display in Athens, he was so moved that he could not keep from
speaking about God, humanity and salvation in Jesus.

As Paul climbed the hill to speak to philosophers, officials and
merchants, he took with him his "biblical view" of humanity: "Hu-

manity as a whole was created to function, incarnationally, as God's image or idol."[1] Humanity "has the peculiar responsibility for bearing divine presence and carrying out the divine will."[2] God atoned for human error in Jesus' cross and renewed human life through his resurrection. He has enthroned as Lord the true human who perfectly bore the divine presence and carried out the divine will. Now, by the life-giving Spirit, he restores *"our own responsibility to bear divine presence and action."*[3]

As Paul preaches, he puts his Jewish theology to work and (ironically) uses a line from Epimenides originally about Zeus: "In him we live and move and have our being" (Acts 17:28). Paul uses the poet's observation and juxtaposes the service of dead idols with the living God's purpose for humanity. Moreover, "just as children reflect the image of their parents, so God's children should reflect him, which they do by reflecting the glorious attributes of his 'divine nature' (cf. Gen 1:27). Paul's logic is simple: 'If like begets like, it is illogical to suppose that the divine nature that created living human beings is like an image made of an inanimate substance.'"[4] Rather, the true God must be a living, creating, life-giving being. That kind of God wouldn't need humans to serve him. And that kind of God would raise the dead (Acts 17:31).

Athenian pagans are stuck in "ignorance" (Acts 17:30) like the mindless idols they worship. Those who mock the resurrection (Acts 17:32)

---

[1]Crispin H. P. Fletcher-Louis, "God's Image, His Cosmic Temple and the High Priest: Towards an Historical and Theological Account of the Incarnation," in *Heaven on Earth: The Temple in Biblical Theology*, ed. T. Desmond Alexander and Simon J. Gathercole (Carlisle, UK: Paternoster, 2004), p. 99. Noting the concerns of J. Todd Billings, *Union with Christ: Reframing Theology and Ministry for the Church* (Grand Rapids: Baker Academic, 2011), pp. 123-65, I take *incarnationally* in this stretch of Fletcher-Louis's argument in a descriptive sense, that is, meaning "in the flesh" or "embodied," rather than in the classic christological sense.

[2]Fletcher-Louis, "God's Image," p. 84.

[3]Ibid., p. 85 (emphasis original). Fletcher-Louis notes that this truth does not absolve readers of privilege or responsibility: The "resurrection of divine (privilege and) *responsibility* for the one human Jesus Christ must therefore be mindful of the besetting danger at the root of idolatry: a self-absolution from the responsibility given to us at creation of bearing divine presence."

[4]Greg Beale, *We Become What We Worship: A Biblical Theology of Idolatry* (Downers Grove, IL: InterVarsity Press, 2008), p. 197, citing William Larkin, *Acts*, IVP New Testament Commentary (Downers Grove, IL: InterVarsity Press, 1995), p. 259.

reject resurrection and the beginning of re-creation in the image of Messiah, God's perfect image (1 Cor 15:49; Col 1:15; 3:10). But their sad plight makes it all the more dramatic when "new believers turn from their idols to trust in God and be restored to him, and by implication, to be like him, since now they had truly become 'his offspring [family]' (v. 28)."[5]

In this encounter Paul reveals the importance of imitation and imitation-related themes in his theology and in every aspect of his ministry and the Christian life. Paul's letters are dense with the theme of imitation. Many passages address the imitation of the ways this cross-shaped apostle taught "everywhere in every church" (1 Cor 4:8-17) and the application of the character of Father and Son to Christian communities.

IMITATION, PARTICIPATION AND THE SLAUGHTER OF THE ELECT

Paul ties our humanity to Jesus' humanity when he says we cry, "Abba! Father!" by the Spirit (Rom 8:15). "Abba" is important not because it is an affectionate term like "Daddy" or "Pops" but because Jesus used this term in his native Aramaic. God adopts humans, gives them his Spirit and unites them to the Messiah so that they share in his Son's identity. The use of "Abba" is a sign that Jesus' relationship with God is now true of others, who receive the Father's love for Jesus and become "heirs of God and joint heirs with Christ" (Rom 8:17).

Paul moves from adoption straight into imitation, noting that a path of suffering is nonnegotiable: "We are children of God, and if children, then heirs, heirs of God and joint heirs with Christ—if, in fact, we suffer with him so that we may also be glorified with him" (Rom 8:16-17). Later in the same chapter, Paul describes the glorious destiny of believers: they will be truly human, just as Jesus is. But for life in the present time, verse 17 stands as an affront to the easy-believism and the "cheap grace" critiqued by Dietrich Bonhoeffer, a grace that assumes believers may grab the benefits of being a child of God while refusing to bear a cross.[6]

---

[5]Beale, *We Become What We Worship*, p. 281.
[6]The original title of Bonhoeffer's classic work is simply "Discipleship" (*Nachfolge*); "The Cost

But Paul also wants disciples to remember the destiny they share in Jesus: fully human children, resurrected and reigning in God's creation. Creation is longing, Paul says, for God's children to be revealed, to again become the royal stewards they were designed to be. That is why humans are not fully adopted until their bodies are fully redeemed (Rom 8:23). Only then will they be able to inherit—as "heirs of God and joint heirs with Christ" (Rom 8:17)—the whole redeemed world, the cosmos that was promised to Abraham and his descendants (Rom 4:13).

A few verses later Paul wishes that he could be "accursed and cut off from Christ" in order to save his fellow Jews stuck in the consequences of unbelief (Rom 9:1-3). Many note that Paul echoes the willingness of Moses to be cut off for the sake of Israel (Ex 32:32). But what is easily missed is that Paul models the mindset of Jesus, a mindset that often takes him beyond hypothetical impossibilities into actual suffering that leads to the salvation of the lost (Col 1:24). In some instances, Paul's cross-shaped suffering is the means by which his prayers are answered.

Just as imitation does not mean for Paul "Do exactly what I do," following the death and life pattern of Messiah does not always require literal death and resurrection. As seen in the previous chapter, the death and resurrection pattern of the Messiah is used throughout Paul's letters to describe the pattern of life required of believers (e.g., Rom 6). In Romans 12:1-2 Paul echoes the death-resurrection pattern: "Present your bodies as a living sacrifice. . . . Do not be conformed to this world, but be transformed by the renewing of your minds." A "living sacrifice" means that imitating a crucified Messiah does not always lead straight to literal death but that imitation is about obedience with all we are and all we possess in imitation of the sacrificial obedience of Jesus. Believers must develop renewed (resurrection) minds, made new by the rejection of sinful patterns of thought and action—minds appropriately reflecting the status of those who are clothing themselves with the Lord Jesus Christ (Rom 13:13-14).

---

of" is added to English editions. Some attempt to explain Paul's challenging caveat—"if we share in his sufferings"—as merely passive participation in Jesus' suffering for sinners. But Paul is simply repeating the same requirement thrown down by Jesus himself.

Paul works out the commands of Romans 12:1-2 throughout chapters 12 through 15, explicitly mentioning the imitation of Jesus and giving commands that Jesus himself embodied, such as "overcome evil with good." In Romans 15:1-7 Paul draws on the pattern of the servant Messiah in order to guide the life of believers in a socially, racially and theologically mixed community. Jews were expelled from Rome by an edict of the emperor Claudius some years before Paul wrote, but had recently been allowed to return when Claudius's edict expired with his death. Jewish believers in Jesus would return to a church that had been shaped by Gentile believers in their absence. Paul inserts the gospel into this potentially tricky situation and urges the believers to imitate Jesus' hospitality: "Welcome one another, therefore, just as Christ has welcomed you, for the glory of God" (Rom 15:7).

Paul sums up his preceding instruction on Jew-Gentile relationships (Rom 14) as the imitation of the other-centeredness and divine hospitality of God and his servant Messiah. If Jesus became the servant to save Jews (Rom 15:8) and Gentiles (Rom 15:9), they should serve one another in love, not pleasing themselves but imitating Jesus, building up others and working for their good as Jesus did (Rom 15:1-3). "Romans 15:1-17 urges us to seek the blessing of others, and not to please ourselves. Why not? Paul's answer is one of simple but devastating eloquence. Christ did not please himself (15:3). The implication is so powerful it does not need to be spelled out. Do what Christ did; imitate him because you are his and his Spirit indwells you."[7]

Paul's next paragraph demonstrates his own commitment to imitating the Messiah in these matters. He mentions the priority of his crosscultural, cross-racial, cross-denominational (i.e., "strong" and "weak") fundraising efforts for the poor (Rom 15:23-27), a massive effort to create and sustain Christian fellowship (*koinōnia*) that would eventually lead to his arrest and lengthy imprisonment.[8] He warmly

---

[7]Sinclair Ferguson, *The Holy Spirit*, Contours of Christian Theology (Downers Grove, IL: InterVarsity Press, 1997), p. 153.
[8]See Jason Hood, "Theology in Action: Paul, the Poor, and Christian Mission," *Southeastern Theological Review* 2, no. 2 (2011). It might surprise many evangelicals to note that at this juncture Paul's collection took precedence over frontier church planting to an unreached people group.

greets family members across racial lines in Romans 16.

Paul also makes a shocking exegetical move. In Romans 15:21 he quotes from Isaiah's famous "Song of the Suffering Servant" (Isaiah 52:13–53:12) and applies it to his own ministry.[9] He is a servant of Jews and Gentiles, called by God to suffer for their sake. The New Testament writers liberally applied Old Testament messianic passages and concepts to the work of Jesus. But because they believed that God's people were united to the Messiah and empowered by the same Spirit, they could also apply messianic concepts and promises to describe the mission and destiny of those "in Christ." There are important distinctions between Jesus and other humans and between the apostles and other slaves of Messiah, even when they imitate his work or share his tasks. But such distinctions do not keep believers from a mission of suffering that is like Jesus' mission.

Later in the church's history Calvin would adapt this emphasis on Christ's suffering servant as the fulfillment of Old Testament prophecy. He "applies many of the Old Testament prophecies of the rule of the Messiah amongst the nations to the preacher of the Word."[10] Calvin could look at Old Testament prophecy and see himself because he believed that the work of the Spirit made him a preaching participant in the mission of the Messiah.

Such radical associations with the Messiah and his work are not just for apostles such as Paul and preachers such as Calvin. While Paul regards Jesus as the Passover Lamb (1 Cor 5:7) who takes away the penalty of sin and shame, Jesus is not the only sheep to be slaughtered. The followers of Jesus deny themselves, pick up the plug and straps for the electric chair[11] and follow him like lambs meekly to the

---

[9]Luke similarly applies the mission of the Servant to the apostles, who will "suffer with him" (Rom 8:17); see also Acts 13:47; 14:22. Saul/Paul is also probably cast in Suffering Servant terms in Acts 9:13-16. "Paul in his own person takes on the prophetic role of Israel—he is the light to the nations, the bringer of salvation. . . . Paul sees himself as not only proclaiming but also actively bringing about the new age of God's direct rule over the cosmos in both judgment and salvation." B. Rosner and R. Ciampa, *1 Corinthians*, New International Commentary on the New Testament (Grand Rapids: Eerdmans, 2011), p. 12.

[10]Ronald Wallace, *Calvin's Doctrine of Word and Sacrament* (Edinburgh: Oliver and Boyd, 1953), p. 87.

[11]An image borrowed from Michael Bird.

slaughter. After describing the glorious inheritance for the saints and the blessing of being free from condemnation, Paul cites Psalm 44 and applies it to believers.

> Who will separate us from the love of Christ? Will hardship, or distress, or persecution, or famine, or nakedness, or peril, or sword? As it is written,
>> "For your sake we are being killed all day long;
>> we are accounted as sheep to be slaughtered."
> No, in all these things we are more than conquerors through him who loved us. (Rom 8:35-37)

The preposition used to describe the location of Christian conquerors is *in* all these terrible things, not apart from them. The Messiah conquered sin and death in suffering and sacrifice. Our share in that victory will come as we follow his example, not in a single act of sacrifice but in an ongoing action: "We are being killed."

Moreover, each word in the list of tragedies and difficulties in Romans 8:36 is also found in the different versions of Paul's résumé in Corinthians, with one obvious exception: when writing Corinthians, Paul has not yet been put to the sword. On the surface, all of these experiences are tragic and shameful, but for Paul they are opportunities to experience the unfailing love of God and to contribute to the kingdom by suffering, fulfilling Old Testament prophecy.[12]

But the Messiah's people do not just share in Jesus' suffering; they also share in his victory and inheritance (Rom 8:16-17). The prophecy of Genesis 3:15—that the seed of the woman would crush the serpent's head underfoot—is fulfilled in part in Romans 16:20, not by the Messiah alone but by the Christlike (Messiah-like) people he uses to crush their common enemy. "Warfare causes suffering, spiritual warfare being no exception. Those who take up the mission of God's people by simply living, working and witnessing in the public square

---

[12]It is important to note that while all suffering can be part of discipleship, "generic" suffering common to all people (car accidents, cancer) should be distinguished form the "missional" suffering, or cross-bearing, that Paul has in mind when he speaks of imitating Jesus. If I am shipwrecked on a Mediterranean cruise, I am not imitating Paul's Mediterranean shipwreck sufferings.

so dominated by the gods of this world, who choose to live by the distinctive ethical standards that flow from their biblical worldview, who confess Jesus as Lord, and not Caesar or Mammon—such people will suffer in one way or another."[13] The messianic task of co-suffering with Christ is a life of spiritual warfare and sacrificial, cross-shaped living that ends in the victorious inheritance of all things.

A Cross-Shaped Ministry

No texts engage the cross-shaped character of Christian life and ministry more deeply than the letters to Corinth. Paul defends his ministry against some believers who prefer spit and polish, excellence and glory. He rejects the more attractive standards that were preferred by the Corinthians and their culture, insisting on a cross-shaped ministry complete with chains, scars and sacrifice. While many church leaders today build their ministry on personal revelations, "Paul's personal revelations are irrelevant for establishing his apostolic ministry, [but] his suffering plays a strategic role."[14]

As we saw in previous chapters, Paul's way of life is so integral to his message that he responds not by mitigating his way of life, but by reminding the Corinthians of his cross-shaped spiritual résumé on multiple occasions (1 Cor 4:8-17; 2 Cor 1:8-10; 4:7-12; 6:3-10; 11:7–12:10, 14-15; 13:3-4) and sending Timothy as a faithful model to reboot the concept of a cross-shaped Christian. He repeatedly urges them to adopt the cross-shaped life he models (1 Cor 6:5-7; 8:13; 9:1-27; 10:32–11:1; 15:30-35). This life of slavery looks and smells like death to those outside the Messiah (2 Cor 2:14-16). It rarely looks like high salaries and loaded benefit packages. It almost never involves places of power, affirmation and honor from the world around us. We might be reminded of Kierkegaard's biting parable:

We are assembled in a magnificent cathedral. His lordship, the right

---

[13]Christopher J. H. Wright, *The Mission of God's People: A Biblical Theology of the Church's Mission* (Grand Rapids: Zondervan, 2010), p. 239.
[14]Scott Hafemann, "A Call to Pastoral Suffering: The Need for Recovering Paul's Model of Ministry in 2 Corinthians," *Southern Baptist Journal of Theology* 4, no. 2 (2000): 22-36, esp. p. 31.

reverend count preacher, adorned with many titles, the chosen favorite of the highest circles of society, steps forward to preach. Standing before a chosen circle of the elite, he preaches under stress of deep feeling upon a text he himself has selected: "God had chosen the base things that are of the world and the things that are despised" [1 Corinthians 1:27]. And nobody laughs.[15]

And nobody weeps in repentance.

Paul avoids elitism in order to undermine the Corinthians' anti-gospel values, priorities and boasting. With respect to his financial package, Paul has two options for instilling a cross-shaped approach to generosity. He can require the Corinthians to pay him and his associates for their work, thus teaching them to sacrifice. Or he can model sacrifice by refusing to take a salary. I don't know if we must conclude that one strategy is always better than the other, but it is instructive that Paul feels compelled to give them a sacrificial example so that they might "be imitators of me, as I am of Christ" (1 Cor 11:1). Perhaps it was particularly important to model an ethic of service and labor in the face of Greco-Roman values, which prized idleness and looked down on "blue collar" labor (Acts 20:34; 1 Cor 4:12; Eph 4:28; 1 Thess 4:11). At a minimum, Paul's solution kills two birds with one stone: it teaches the imitation of Paul's "ways in Christ," and it undermines appraisals of Christian ministry that fail to tally the cost of discipleship and cross-shaped service.

The importance of cross-shaped models in the flesh in Paul's conception of Christian ministry cannot be underestimated. Paul writes Scripture directly to the Corinthians, yet he still feels constrained to send Timothy to remind them "of [his] ways in Christ Jesus" (1 Cor 4:17).

First Corinthians 2:2 is an underappreciated witness to this strategy. When Paul says, "I decided to know nothing among you except Jesus Christ, and him crucified," he is not talking only about the content of his preaching on the saving benefits of the cross. He is also speaking about the cross-shaped way of life he lived and taught "everywhere in

---

[15]Originally published in *The Fatherland*, August 23, 1855; cited from E. O. Geismar, *Lectures on the Religious Thought of Søren Kierkegaard: Stone Lectures, 1936* (Minneapolis: Augsburg, 1938), p. 85.

every church" (1 Cor 4:17). In the face of deeply embedded cultural standards for success and excellence, Paul insists that he does not follow a Messiah who found glory apart from death and sacrifice.

But this interpretation of 1 Corinthians 2:2 does not mean that we leave behind the Messiah or the gospel. The Greek philosopher Pythagoras claimed that "our souls undergo a change when we enter a temple and behold the images of the gods face to face."[16] Pythagoras is right; his pagan worship leads to the imitation of dead, mute and deaf gods. But according to Paul, believers are granted access to God's presence, the holiest place. There they see the Messiah, God's true image, and they begin to look like him. "All of us, with unveiled faces, seeing the glory of the Lord as though reflected in a mirror, are being transformed into the same image from one degree of glory to another" (2 Cor 3:18). Not only is the veil not lifted without the gospel; when we behold the Messiah we see a cross-shaped king, whose image we are meant to reflect. We cannot know imitation without knowing the crucified Messiah.

CROSS-SHAPED CHRISTIANS

Paul bears a cross in his ministry to display the gospel of the cross, but also in order to guide the Corinthians to take the shape of the cross in their lives. "Paul articulates the primary character of Christian experience to be that of 'always carrying in the body the death of Jesus, so that the life of Jesus may also be manifested in our bodies' (2 Cor. 4:10)." Paul uses *nekrōsis* rather than *thanatos* (the usual term for "death"), perhaps because *nekrōsis* indicates more of a process than a single event.[17]

Because the imitation of Jesus' death is a process, Paul applies the imitation of the sacrificial death of Jesus to a host of areas in the Christian life that, on the surface at least, have nothing to do with the

---

[16]Seneca the Younger, *Moral Epistles* 94.42.

[17]John Webster, "The Imitation of Christ," *Tyndale Bulletin* 37 (1986): 113, citing Rudolf Bultmann, "Ignatius and Paul," in *Existence and Faith* (London: Collins, 1964), p. 328. Webster also critiques Bultmann, who rightly notes that parts of the *imitatio* tradition are excessive and excessively literal. Bultmann "overstates his case when he proposes that *imitatio* is 'completely foreign' to Paul."

cross. Richard Hays describes "the operative norm" in Paul's discussion of idol meat in 1 Corinthians 8:1–11:1: "relinquishment of self-interest for the benefit of others." These three chapters teach the Corinthians to apply

> Paul's willingness to relinquish his own freedom for the sake of the gospel. With a telling self-description he signals that he has not forgotten the idol meat issue: "To the weak I became weak, so that I might gain the weak" (1 Cor 9:22). That is, of course, precisely what he wants the "strong" Corinthians to do: to become weak. He is offering himself as a model for imitation. Because he presents himself as one "not seeking my own advantage, but that of many" (1 Cor 10:33), he can at last articulate the exhortation that undergirds the entire idol meat discussion: "Become imitators of me, as I am of Christ."[18]

Not only does this imitation principle undergird the idol meat discussion; it is "the whole burden of the ethical side of Paul's teaching."[19] In 2 Corinthians 8:1-9 Paul holds out the cross as a model for the Corinthians as they ponder whether to fulfill their commitment to give to impoverished Judeans. He recalls "the generous act [grace] of our Lord Jesus Christ, that though he was rich, yet for your sakes he became poor, so that by his poverty you might become rich" (2 Cor 8:9). The profound unfairness of this exchange serves as the ultimate model for generosity and trumps all arguments against giving. In a more sustained way Paul holds out the Macedonians as a cross-shaped model of Christian generosity: they gave freely and beyond their means, sacrificially participating despite affliction and "extreme poverty" (2 Cor 8:2).

At the moment, following the Messiah looks like a "triumphal procession" of prisoners who smell like death (2 Cor 2:14-16). But for those who are raised to new life in the Messiah, the march of prisoners condemned to death can be seen as it really is: a journey with two destinations, the cross and the resurrection life beyond. Paul does

---

[18]Richard Hays, *The Moral Vision of the New Testament: Community, Cross, New Creation; A Contemporary Introduction to New Testament Ethics* (New York: HarperOne, 1996), pp. 42-43.
[19]B. B. Warfield, *The Savior of the World: Sermons Preached in the Chapel of Princeton Seminary* (New York: Hodder and Stoughton, 1913), p. 249.

not merely call believers to a life of cross-bearing. Just as Jesus was sacrificed only to rise to new life, so our missional suffering can be seen as a "momentary affliction . . . preparing us for an eternal weight of glory beyond all measure" (2 Cor 4:17). Believers are being conformed to Jesus, God's true image. That process begins in sanctification, or growth in holiness in the present (2 Cor 3:18). It culminates in resurrection (1 Cor 15:49).

The most important fact about a cross-shaped approach to ministry is not that it is faithful to Paul's vision for ministry, nor even that it is effective, although (unexpectedly) it sometimes is. The most important motivation for the imitation of Jesus in ministry is that Jesus himself, in his role as Lord, laid down this requirement for everyone and followed that path himself until he arrived at resurrection. Paul practices "creative imitation" of Jesus in obedience to that requirement and calls for the same from his disciples (1 Cor 11:1).[20]

A BIBLICAL APPROACH TO CLONING

In Galatians, Ephesians and Colossians Paul broaches imitation in at least three ways. First, as noted previously, he describes believers' new creation life in Christ. This new life is the resurrection pattern of new humanity, raised from death in sin to newness of life. The death-resurrection pattern of life "in Messiah" is prominent in all three of these books, both to indicate the new reality in which believers live—already "clothed . . . with Christ" (Gal 3:27) and seated/enthroned with him (Eph 2:5-6)—and the moral task of the believer: "Christ . . . formed in you" (Gal 4:19; 5:24; 6:14) and a further "clothing" (Col 3:9-10). As noted in the previous chapter, the Spirit works to remind believers of what they already are in Christ and helps them desire and act so that moral transformation becomes a reality. Seen in this light, the reality described by Paul in Galatians 2:19-21 is about both justifi-

---

[20]Kevin Vanhoozer, *The Drama of Doctrine: A Canonical-Linguistic Approach to Christian Theology* (Louisville, KY: Westminster John Knox, 2005), p. 442. Vanhoozer adds, on p. 397, "This is how we follow the drama of Christ's life: not by repeating it in uniform fashion but by repeating it so as to continue the through line of the Word's communicative action in order to incarnate the same basic 'idea' (i.e., the knowledge of God) and action (i.e., the love of God) under different conditions."

cation and sanctification: a new and unearned righteous status before God and a new way to live by the Spirit after the cross-shaped pattern of the Messiah.

Second, on four occasions in Ephesians Paul goes out of his way to mention his life condition: He is a prisoner (Eph 3:1) who is suffering (Eph 3:13), a slave (Eph 3:7—by grace! How gracious of God to enslave Paul!), an ambassador in chains (Eph 6:19). These brief comments in Ephesians reveal Paul's mode of ministry, mirroring what one finds in the Corinthian letters and elsewhere. Prison or chains are sometimes included as part of Paul's résumé of missional suffering (2 Cor 6:5; 11:23; Col 4:18; Phil 1:7, 13, 14, 17; 2 Tim 2:9; compare Philem 10, 13). The author of one-fourth of the New Testament characterizes himself as an imprisoned slave, bearing "the marks of Jesus branded on my body" (Gal 6:17). He didn't write Colossians from the penthouse headquarters of the International Apostolic Pauline Mission. He wrote from prison, and he did not wish that fact to be lost on his hearers: "Remember my chains. Grace be with you," concludes his letter to Colossae (Col 4:18).

Paul's status is relevant for the Ephesians and other Gentiles because he is suffering for their glory (Eph 3:1, 13). Paul's ministry is an exchange: he gives up his freedom—and eventually his life—so that the nations can participate in glorious inheritance (Col 1:24). By this cross-shaped approach to mission, Paul models the ministry pattern of Jesus, who descended (Eph 4:9) so that he would later be exalted. "When Paul writes autobiographically, he writes paradigmatically."[21] Paul pleads with his readers in Galatians 4:12 to become "like him in his freedom from the 'works of the law' as Israel had encountered them in slavery to this world under the old covenant (Gal 4:1-7; 5:1)" (see also Eph 2:11-22). Of course, this freedom also involved a great deal of suffering, as the context in Galatians makes clear: "Paul's suffering was the instrument by which he 'publicly portrayed' the cru-

---

[21]M. J. Gorman, *Apostle of the Crucified Lord* (Grand Rapids: Eerdmans, 2004), p. 258. See P. T. O'Brien, *Ephesians*, Pillar New Testament Commentary (Grand Rapids: Eerdmans, 1999), p. 274, "The recurrent prison theme seems to have a rhetorical function," citing Dan Reid, "Prison, Prisoner," in *Dictionary of Paul and His Letters*, ed. Gerald F. Hawthorne, Ralph P. Martin and Daniel G. Reid (Downers Grove, IL: InterVarsity Press, 1993), pp. 752-54.

cified Christ 'before (the Galatians') eyes.'"[22]

Third, after reminding the Ephesians of the way in which he is imitating Jesus, Paul teaches these new humans how to enact the imitation of God and Jesus. In so doing Paul highlights the importance of sound theology for imitation (Eph 4:32; 5:1-33): God is forgiving and tenderhearted; the Messiah loved us; the Messiah sacrificed himself for us. The general posture of submission that the church displays toward Jesus must be present in the way believers relate to one another in mutual submission, with wives and their relationship to their husbands singled out as a particularly important sphere for this practice. Jesus' loving sacrifice for his body and bride provides the standard for a husband's love. It is difficult to overestimate just how foreign this depiction of marriage and a husband's role was in the Ephesians' cultural context.[23]

Paternity is one of the subplots running through Ephesians and Galatians. Beloved children of God (Eph 5:1, 20) take on his character, becoming "children of light" (Eph 5:8). They pursue what is good and right and true, partaking in the life of Christ, not the life of death and sin (Eph 5:6-8). God does not adopt human children because they have been reflecting him well. Adoption is a gift, not a payment for services rendered. Ephesian believers were once "children of wrath" (Eph 2:3; 5:5-6), without hope and inheritance, not sharing God's character. Humans are adopted while sinners (Eph 1:5; 2:1) in order that they might become heirs of all things that belong to the Father. That inheritance includes the right to rule over all things with Messiah (Eph 2:6) and new status as God's beloved children (Eph 5:1). And this inheritance and new identity include the responsibility to share the family trait of godlikeness.

But the new identity also includes new ability. The Spirit provides new ability by working to "clone" believers into the image of Jesus in

---

[22]Scott Hafemann, "The Role of Suffering in the Mission of Paul," in *The Mission of the Early Church to Jews and Gentiles*, ed. Jostein Ådna and Hans Kvalbein (Tübingen: Mohr-Siebeck, 2000), pp. 167 and 174, respectively.

[23]Max Turner, "Ephesians," in *New Bible Commentary*, ed. D. A. Carson, R. T. France, J. A. Motyer and G. J. Wenham (Downers Grove, IL: InterVarsity Press, 1994), p. 1241: "Within the hierarchical social order they uphold they were radical and profoundly liberating."

true righteousness and holiness (Gal 5:22; Eph 4:7-24; Col 3:1-17).[24] Spiritual growth is accomplished by walking according to the "spirit of adoption" (Rom 8:15; Gal 4:5-6), who empowers believers to produce the fruit of that Spirit (Gal 5:22-23). "We become God-like when we learn the virtues of love, joy, peace, patience, kindness, goodness, faithfulness, gentleness and self-control (Gal. 5:22-23)."[25] These fruits are the traits of Father and Son and the work of the indwelling Spirit; they are no less the result of humans who imitate their Father in the power of the Spirit.

Some find it more comfortable to speak of this transformation in passive terms, and this is often accompanied by the belief that spiritual growth is more about God's work than human work. But this approach mitigates the fact that humans participate in the work of the Spirit, working for their own growth and that of others. Paul labors (in the childbirth sense of that word) until "Christ is formed in" the Galatians (Gal 4:19). In Ephesians 4 the purpose of spiritual gifts is the active construction of God's family into maturity in Christ. Paul's body metaphor describes the difference between the Messiah (head) and his church (body) but also indicates that the whole point of sanctification is to become like the Messiah corporately, not just personally. Spiritual gifts craft the church into a collective representation of mature humanity, "the measure of the full stature of Christ" (Eph 4:11-13). It is not surprising, then, that Paul features the imitation of Father and Son and image-bearing in what follows (Eph 4:23–5:2, 25-32).

THEOLOGY APPLIED

Theology is not just meant to be known; it must be applied.[26] One of the greatest threats to biblical ethics, including the imitation of God and Jesus, is the tendency to remove theology from its biblical context

[24]As Luther put it, the disciple's "righteousness goes on to complete the first [imputed, alien righteousness] for it ever strives to do away with the old Adam and destroy the body of sin. . . . This righteousness follows the example of Christ in this respect and is transformed into his likeness." *Luther's Works* 31.300.
[25]Graham Tomlin, *Spiritual Fitness: Christian Character in a Consumer Society* (London: Continuum, 2006), p. 84.
[26]Vanhoozer, *Drama of Doctrine*, p. 16: "The purpose of doctrine is to ensure that those who bear Christ's name walk in Christ's way."

without regard for the way theological truth is applied.[27] Accordingly, Paul grounds imitation not in a standard of behavior but in theology and mindset. In Philippians 2:3-11 Paul charges the church to share the sacrificial mindset possessed by Jesus: "Let the same mind[set] be in you that was in Christ Jesus."[28] Jesus himself initiates imitation by becoming like humans. He stoops, becomes a servant and participates in our humanity and its dire condition. He even humbles himself to the point of a humiliating death, in order that we might then participate in him and in his life. The Son plays a human role before the disciples are called to play a role in imitation of the Son. They become participants in the humbling, cross-shaped path to glory only on the basis of his initiative and accomplishments.[29]

Throughout this text we have noted that imitation is not a matter of precise or exact copies of Jesus. Imitation is often a matter of sharing a mindset, direction or pattern rather than literal and precise duplication. Paul sometimes executes his ministry in precisely the opposite way Jesus did: he plants a church and settles for a time while working to support himself (Acts 20) rather than engaging in an itinerant, non-church-planting ministry funded by wealthy women (Lk 8). But what is not optional is the self-sacrificial approach taken by Jesus and a vision of inherited glory for those who lose their lives for his sake, according to his pattern. Gordon Fee's response to those skeptical of the imitation of Jesus is helpful: "These objections are based on a fun-

---

[27]See Jason Hood, "The Cross in the New Testament: Two Theses in Conversation with Recent Studies (2000–2007)," *Westminster Theological Journal* 71, no. 2 (2009): 281-95; the other great threat is to sever ethics from the teaching and theology that drive them. On the spiral of imitation, see Susan Grove Eastman, "Philippians 2:6-11: Incarnation as Mimetic Participation," *Journal for the Study of Paul and His Letters* 1, no. 1 (2010): 1-22; and "Imitating Christ Imitating Us: Paul's Educational Project in Philippians," in *The Word Leaps the Gap: Essays on Scripture and Theology in Honor of Richard B. Hays*, ed. J. Ross Wagner, C. Kavin Rowe and C. Katherine Grieb (Grand Rapids: Eerdmans, 2008), pp. 427-541.

[28]See the history of interpretation in Frank Thielman, *Philippians*, NIV Application Commentary (Grand Rapids: Zondervan, 1995), pp. 123-25, and more fully in S. Fowl, *The Story of Christ in the Ethics of Paul: An Analysis of the Function of the Hymnic Material in the Pauline Corpus*, Journal for the Study of the New Testament Supplement Series, vol. 36 (Sheffield, UK: Sheffield Academic Press, 1990), pp. 77-101. James D. G. Dunn's interpretation, which focuses on Adam-Christ contrast, is incorrect in its opposition to incarnation but helpful in pointing out the relevance of the Adam-Christ connection.

[29]Paul notes important links between our work and divine work elsewhere in this context; Phil 1:6, 8; 2:11-13.

damental misunderstanding of imitation in Paul's thought, which does not mean 'repeat after me' but rather (in the present context) 'have a frame of mind which lives on behalf of others the way Christ did in his becoming incarnate and dying by crucifixion.' One can appreciate the desire not to let this profound passage [Phil 2] lose its power by making it simply an exemplary paradigm, but Paul himself seems to have done that very thing."[30]

When readers come to Philippians 2, Paul has already noted that the Philippians are mimicking Paul's suffering (Phil 1:29-30). But now he calls them into an incarnational and cross-shaped mindset. Bonhoeffer noted the importance of Jesus first calling would-be disciples to a mindset of self-denial before calling them to follow him on the path to the cross. Paul makes a similar observation in the famous key passage in Philippians 2, and the remainder of Philippians requires this mindset. The verb *crucify* can function as a motif for Christian discipleship described in this letter. Paul teaches believers to crucify:

- rivalry (Phil 2:1-3)
- a self-centered, self-glorifying mindset (Phil 2:4-13)
- the right to grumble about their circumstances (Phil 2:14-18)
- the right to a comfortable life (Phil 2:25-30)
- ethical or ethnic pride (Phil 3:3-5)
- righteousness apart from Messiah (Phil 3:7-9)
- passive, status-quo Christianity (Phil 3:10-16)
- a claim to resurrection life apart from the sacrificial imitation of Jesus (Phil 3:9-11)
- the quest for self-satisfaction and self-glorification in Christian mission (Phil 3:17-21)

---

[30]Gordon Fee, *Pauline Christology: An Exegetical-Theological Study*, (Peabody, MA: Hendrickson, 2007), p. 372 n. 6. See also Edouard Cothenet, *Imitating Christ* (St. Meinrad, IN: Abbey, 1974), p. 22: "The imitation referred to is not a matter of reproducing the material gestures of Christ but of conforming to the spiritual attitudes which He revealed." Cothenet notes on p. 16 that the rigid distinctions sometimes made between imitation and related concepts such as participation and following are not distinctions found in the text of the New Testament.

- the right to disagree and hold on to strife (Phil 4:2)
- the right to live and let live while the Christian family around us disintegrates (Phil 4:3)
- anxious self-pity (Phil 4:4-7)
- cultural standards for success and acceptance (Phil 4:8-9)
- comfort, abundance and strength in one's self (Phil 4:10-13)
- the right to cling to resources (Phil 4:14-19).[31]

Christian gymnasiums frequently feature Phil 4:13: "I can do all things through Christ who strengthens me." And recently I saw a bumper sticker proclaiming, "Mission Possible: Phil 4:13." Whatever this means in a Christian gym or on the back of a car, for the Philippians it meant participation in the pattern seen in Jesus and Paul. Christ in Paul has empowered him to win and—especially—to lose. He calls the Philippians to consider the suffering king and imitate his mindset, which led him to take a cross-shaped path to glory.

FROM THE LIPS OF PAGANS

As in Acts 17, Paul's rare references to pagan literature are tied to the theme of imitation. In 1 Corinthians 15:33 he cites Greek dramatist Menander on the capacity of humans to be shaped by their peers: "Do not be deceived: 'Bad company ruins good morals.'"[32] Paul reminds Titus, whom he left in Crete to build up the church, that Epimenides has correctly diagnosed the locals: "Cretans are always liars, vicious brutes, lazy gluttons" (Tit 1:12). Instead of imitating the character of other Cretan unbelievers, Cretan believers in Jesus must learn the character of God, who "never lies" (Tit 1:2). Christian exemplars like Titus will be "a model of good works" (Tit 2:7) in order to show Cretans how to be "lover[s] of goodness" instead of evil, "self-controlled" instead of brutes, and "prudent, upright, devout" rather than lazy or gluttonous (Tit 1:8).[33] Instead of being shaped by their culture

---

[31]To encourage the Philippians along the way, Paul also includes a host of motivations as he teaches on sacrifice: see Phil 1; 2:1, 13, 15, 29; 3:9, 11, 14, 21; 4:7, 9, 13, 17-19.
[32]Menander, *Thais* 218.
[33]For juxtaposition of the pagan quotes and Old Testament emphases, see Greg Beale, "Bibli-

and their gods, they will become renewed humans in Christ in the likeness of God.

FROM CROSS-SHAPED CHRISTIANS TO RESURRECTED CHILDREN

For Paul the character of God and the self-sacrifice of Jesus is the paradigm for disciples, a paradigm he applied to everything from marriage to generosity, from forgiveness to evangelism and pastoral care. The example of Jesus also lies quietly behind much of Paul's teaching. It is not difficult to see Jesus in Paul's description of love in 1 Corinthians 13 or in the ethical commands in Romans 12 and 13. For the mind trained to imitate Jesus, it is impossible not to think of Jesus when Paul says, "Overcome evil with good" (Rom 12:21) or, "Love . . . does not insist on its own way. . . . It endures all things" (1 Cor 13:4-7).

Paul's letters and the rest of the New Testament are saturated with this theme, and in many quarters of the church today, the saturation levels of Jesus imitation must rise. Consider Colossians 1:24: "In my flesh I am completing what is lacking in Christ's afflictions for the sake of his body, that is, the church." Vicarious suffering does not end with Jesus' death on the cross. Paul is not atoning for sins with his suffering, but he is showing that Christians must continually lay down their lives for the sake of Jesus and his kingdom.[34]

The Messiah's suffering did not provide bread and education for Africa's poor, leadership training for Latin American churches, evangelists for pagan North America, companionship for the rejected or families for the orphans and the lonely. Jesus' death and resurrection were God's great Word to us, but they did not do the hard work of translating the Bible into ten thousand languages. The church's suffering and self-sacrifice, with a million crosses modeled after his cross, meet these needs and more as we imitate the infinitely greater sacrifice and suffering of Jesus.

---

cal Faith and Other Religions in New Testament Theology," in *Evangelical Christianity and Other Religions,* ed. David Baker (Grand Rapids: Kregel, 2004), pp. 80-90.

[34]"[Paul's] sufferings were an indispensible link in the chain of their salvation." John Stott, *The Cross of Christ* (Downers Grove, IL: InterVarsity Press, 2006), p. 313; see also 2 Tim 2:10.

11

The Jesus Mirrors

Let us copy the example of this divine image, the Son, and not draw away
from God. . . . He provides a model for us. . . . We by pressing on imitate
him who abides motionless; we follow him who stands still, and by
walking with him we move toward him, because for us he became
a road or way in time by his humility, while being for us
an eternal abode by his divinity.

Christ, the master of the mint, came along to stamp the coins afresh.

AUGUSTINE

◆ ◈ ◆

Who are Christians? What does God do with humans when he
rescues them? While many Christians find this question difficult to
answer, the Bible provides high-octane fuel for our self-conception.
We've seen that we are called images (or idols), rulers, priests, temples
and sacrifices; apprentices, ambassadors and agents; adopted, resurrected, new creation people who are being "clothed with the Messiah."
These pictures of humanity and Christians are not static or passive;
they are dynamic depictions that inform our mission as they unveil
our identity. They show us just how we share God's likeness and character and imitate his work, wisdom, rest and fellowship.

To be sure, the New Testament authors believed that Jesus perfectly fulfilled this original design for humanity. The Son perfectly resembles, reflects and imitates the Father. He is the true human, a substitute who accomplished the mission that Adam, Israel and humanity failed to accomplish. But Jesus' work of fulfillment is not yet complete. He is gathering a people to himself, and through them and with them he will fulfill the dynamic tasks God gave to humanity, empowered by his Spirit.

Because he is the true human, the New Testament writers teach readers to mirror Jesus. One perfect human in God's image achieves atonement and enthronement, and only one will bring God's purposes to completion. But God remains committed to his original plan to fill the world with his images. The New Testament depicts the church's fulfillment of this mission in terms of God's temple and Jesus' body.[1]

BODY AND TEMPLE

These two powerful overlapping metaphors—God's temple and Jesus' body—highlight the church's character and identify one of the chief ways by which God's glory fills the earth (Rom 1:23; 1 Cor 11:7; 1 Pet 4:9-11; Irenaeus: "The glory of God is a human fully alive"). "Whereas in the gospels there are indications that Jesus himself fulfils the new Temple expectations of the Old Testament and various Jewish writings, in Ephesians and 1 Peter [and 1 and 2 Corinthians] *Christians in union with Christ are that Temple* (Eph 2:19-22; Rev 3:12; 1 Cor 6:19)."[2]

Just as stunning is the idea that disciples are the body of the Messiah, the "fullness of him who fills all in all" (Eph 1:23; see also Eph 1:10). Believers grow into maturity, "the full stature of Christ. . . . We must grow up in every way into him who is the head . . . and to clothe [our]selves with the new self, created according to the likeness of God in true righteousness and holiness" (Eph 4:13, 15, 24). Growing

---

[1]The temple and body metaphors are but two sides of the same conceptual coin: Jn 2:21; Eph 2:11-22; 4:13-16.

[2]David Peterson, "The New Temple: Christology and Ecclesiology in Ephesians and 1 Peter," in *Heaven on Earth: The Temple in Biblical Theology*, ed. T. Desmond Alexander and Simon J. Gathercole (Carlisle, UK: Paternoster, 2004), p. 160, emphasis original. See also 1 Cor 6:19; Eph 2:19-22; Rev 3:12.

in quantity and quality, the church fills God's world with his images according to his original plan, so that the whole world becomes God's temple. This project is not complete until heaven fully invades earth, yet God's kingdom is coming now as his name is "hallowed" and his will performed by those baptized into his name and bearing his presence all over the world (Mt 6:8-10; 28:16-20).[3]

The church is Christ's fullness in the world, a worldwide temple that expands until all things are finally gathered up and united "in him" according to God's plan (Eph 1:10, 23). God's temple people are the place where his kingdom reign has broken into the world to establish a beachhead. God's "new creational kingdom" is not just a place but a people, the "end-time new creation temple" filling God's world.[4] The work of the church is to labor—by the Spirit—to build this body-temple in size and maturity until it fills the world. In keeping with these two metaphors, this church is described as God's dwelling place and the body of Jesus, who is the head of the church.

In other words, the church's task is to make more Jesus-people: people united to him who begin to look like him. The new heavenly identity is a gift (Eph 2), but the development of heavenly character is the work of God in and through his people.[5] This new identity leads to the imitation of the character of God and the imitation of the sacrifice of Jesus.

The world encountered God imperfectly in Israel and perfectly in Jesus. The nations now encounter the living God in and through the church where Jesus lives. During his earthly ministry, the Messiah did temple tasks. He judged rightly, forgave his enemies while telling

[3]See especially Greg Beale, *The Temple and the Church's Mission: A Biblical Theology of the Dwelling Place of God,* New Studies in Biblical Theology, vol. 17 (Downers Grove, IL: Inter-Varsity Press, 2000); and Greg Beale, "Eden, the Temple, and the Church's Mission in the New Creation," *Journal of the Evangelical Theology Society* 48, no. 1 (2005): 5-31.
[4]The terms are Beale's (the second is his descriptive term for the church), from "The New Testament and New Creation," in *Biblical Theology: Retrospect and Prospect,* ed. Scott Hafemann and Paul House (Downers Grove: IVP Academic, 2002), pp. 164, 173. See also the overlapping metaphors in Heb 12: images of the place where believers reside include the community of saints, kingdom, city; place, people, presence.
[5]R. C. Sproul summarizes the Reformed view on sanctification as synergistic action in "Climbing Out of the Mire," Ligonier Ministries: The Teaching Fellowship of R. C. Sproul (accessed January 16, 2012), www.ligonier.org/learn/devotionals/climbing-out-mire.

them the truth, spent his life in self-sacrificial worship, embodied holiness and was the dwelling place of the Holy Spirit. Jesus served as the person-place in whom the nations encountered the living God. He respected the temple in Jerusalem, but he trumped it and fulfilled its significance.

Believers reflect Jesus as they practice being the temple: they show God to the world by mediating his presence to the world as a "royal priesthood" (1 Pet 2:9). They are the place where the Holy Spirit resides and where forgiveness becomes realized, continually making sacrifices of praise and self-sacrifice in gratitude. In popular Christian understanding, the replacement of place with people is sometimes paired with the rejection of Old Testament religion and sacrifice. But for Paul the temple status of the church requires the practice of sacrifice in imitation of Jesus' sacrifice. Christians participate in God-pleasing sacrifices and offerings as priests, offered through Jesus the high priest who sacrificed himself (Rom 12:1-2; 15:15-16; Phil 2:17; 4:18; Eph 5:2; 2 Tim 4:6; Heb 13:15-16). Contrary to some popular slogans, we see in the New Testament not the end of religion, temple and sacrifice; rather, we see their transformation.

In the Old Testament holiness characterized God's dwelling places, especially the temple and the tabernacle. The nation of Israel was to reflect God's holiness, a holiness that was to be imitated by the priesthood and all of Israel as God's nation of priests. In the New Testament no less than in the Old Testament, "righteousness and holiness define both the character of God and the intended character of his people."[6] Whenever Paul and Peter address the theme of the church as the temple, "there is an ethical implication to this new Temple ecclesiology."[7] For instance, in 2 Corinthians Paul uses the temple identity to encourage Christians to exhibit their godlike identity, "bringing holiness to completion in the fear of God" (2 Cor 6:16–7:1 ESV; compare 1 Cor 3:16-17; 6:12-20;

---

[6]Ben Witherington III, *The Indelible Image: The Theological and Ethical Thought World of the New Testament*, vol. 1 (Downers Grove, IL: InterVarsity Press, 2009), pp. 241-42.

[7]David Peterson, "The New Temple: Christology and Ecclesiology in Ephesians and 1 Peter," in *Heaven on Earth*, p. 161. Peterson is speaking of Corinthians; but see also Mt 18; Phil 4:2-3; Rev 2–3.

1 Thess 4:3-7; Heb 3–4; 12:14; Rev 2:4-5, 16, 21-23; 3:1-3).[8]

The abandonment of holiness proves fatal, both personally and corporately. Since the church's task is looking like Jesus, the rejection of holiness is not just a personal problem. In a number of places in the Old Testament and the New Testament, the Christian community as a whole is called into action to preserve holiness, because "the temple can be destroyed by false teaching, by divisions based on worldly values, or by giving way to ungodliness in any form."[9]

Of course, the reality is that "the Church is not ideal. It is not, nor was it ever intended to be, a gathering of the nicer people in town. God is not fastidious in the company he keeps. There are sinners aplenty, hypocrites in droves, the ill-mannered and unwashed . . . men and women who are on the way to growing up to the stature of Christ. Not many of them are there yet."[10] But God gifts believers for the purpose of growing together into a holy temple and a mature body. Precisely because the master builder is building his temple, walking off the job is not an option. Christians regard one another as royal priests and build one another in the direction of holiness until the body-temple fills the whole world.

C. S. Lewis said, "Next to the blessed sacrament, your Christian neighbor is the holiest object ever presented to your senses."[11] Lewis is almost right. Because Christ lives in them, because they are his body and he is at work building in his people the holy character of God himself, there is nothing holier than a Christian.

THE ACTS OF JESUS IN AND THROUGH THE APOSTLES

The book of Acts links the sections on the imitation of Jesus and the imitation of the saints. Luke shows us a community that models obedience to Jesus. He believes that Jesus is at work through the apostles, enabling them to imitate him, obey him and do Christlike tasks.

---

[8] Again, Heb 3:6; "We are his house," *if* we hold firm, continuing in belief and obedience (as the rest of Heb 3–4 indicates).

[9] David Peterson, "The New Temple," p. 162.

[10] Eugene Peterson, *The Practice of Resurrection: A Conversation on Growing up in Christ* (Grand Rapids: Eerdmans, 2010), p. 184.

[11] C. S. Lewis, *The Weight of Glory* (New York: HarperOne, 2001), p. 46.

Luke states in Acts 1:1 that his previous volume (Luke's Gospel) addressed "all that Jesus did and taught from the beginning." Commentators often note that this verse suggests that Jesus is not finished
working: in volume 2 (Acts and beyond) Jesus continues to work
through his people by his Spirit. These commentators sometimes
suggest that the title for the book should not be "Acts of the Apostles"
but "Acts of Jesus." The former title ignores Luke's own words, but the
latter tells only half the story. Perhaps the book could be best titled
"The Acts of Jesus Through His Apostles." In the early chapters of Acts,
God's Spirit is poured out as he promised, providing the disciples
with a new engine that recalls the question asked and answered earlier
in this book: Who is working? God or humans? As we saw in the Old
Testament, the answer is often a "both-and," not "either-or." Saul is
busy persecuting Christians, yet he is twice told that he is persecuting
Jesus (Acts 9:4-5; 22:7-8; 26:14-15). The disciples are working and suffering not for their own sake but for the name of Jesus (Lk 24:47; Acts
4:7-10; 5:28; 23:13).

Luke's remarkable perspective on human participation in God's
work extends even to the ungodly and to evil acts. The apostles make
the astonishing claim that God and humans are both responsible for
the death of Jesus (Acts 2:23; 4:27-28). It is not either God or humans
at work in planning the execution of Jesus: God planned what humans
schemed and accomplished, and their work accomplished God's purposes. Humans can be held responsible for what they do even if they
are working out God's purpose. This perspective adds fresh—if con-
founding—layers of meaning to Paul's citation of Epimenides: "In
him we live and move and have our being" (Acts 17:28).

Luke carves out two patterns of imitation and participation in the
work of Jesus in the power of the Spirit.[12] (1) Jesus' disciples do or

---

[12]David Moessner, "'The Christ Must Suffer': New Light on the Jesus—Peter, Stephen, Paul
Parallels in Luke-Acts," *Novum Testamentum* 28, no. 3 (1986): 220-56, especially p. 220.
Charles Talbert, *Literary Patterns, Theological Themes, and the Genre of Luke-Acts* (Missoula,
MT: SBL Press, 1974), pp. 15-23, cites thirty-two parallels, some of which are included here.
See also David Moessner, "'The Christ Must Suffer,' The Church Must Suffer: Rethinking the
Theology of the Cross in Luke-Acts," *Society of Biblical Literature Seminar Papers* 29 (1990):
165-95. According to Robert Tannehill, "Characters in Acts who show qualities and patterns
of behavior similar to Jesus and to scriptural models take on some authority of these

experience things after the pattern of Jesus as agents of Jesus' mission. Luke makes no effort to hide the parallels that highlight this pattern. (2) The disciples in Acts obey commands given by Jesus in Luke and serve as models of obedience for later readers. A few examples (among many) of the first pattern includes the following events:[13]

- Like Jesus, Stephen is accused by false witnesses; like Jesus, he is accused of threatening the temple and law.

- Like Jesus, Stephen cites Daniel 7, asks God to take his spirit and forgives those who are unjustly killing him (Lk 23:34, 46; Acts 7:59-60).

- After prayer, Jesus is empowered by the Holy Spirit for his life of ministry (see especially Lk 3:21; Acts 10:38). After prayer, his disciples are empowered in the same way (Lk 24:45-49; Acts 1:8; 2).

- Jesus launches his ministry with a sermon on his fulfillment of Scripture and the rejection of Jesus; the church's ministry begins in the same way (Lk 4:16-30; Acts 2:14-40).

- Both Luke and Acts contain involuntary healings (Lk 8:44-48; Acts 19:12), the healing of Samaritans (Lk 17:11-16; Acts 8) and restoration to service on the part of those who are healed (Lk 4:38-39; 8:2-3; Acts 28:10).

- Like Jesus, the disciples resuscitate the dead after affirming that the one being healed is not really dead (Lk 8:52; Acts 20:9-12). In both books, those needed by the community are raised (Luke 7:11-16; Acts 9:36-41).

- Like Jesus, the disciples proclaim the "gospel of the kingdom" (Lk 4:43; 9:2), "forgiveness" (Lk 5:20, 24; Acts 2:38; 10:43; 13:38-39) and "the word of grace" (Lk 4:22; Acts 14:3; 20:32).

---

authoritative figures. This is true of Peter, Stephen and Paul, whose missions and sufferings resemble those of Jesus, and Jesus' mission and rejection reflect the experience of Moses with the rebellious Israelites (see Acts 3:22; 7:22-39)." *Narrative Unity of Luke-Acts: A Literary Interpretation, Volume 2, The Acts of the Apostles* (Minneapolis: Augsburg, 1990), p. 75.

[13]See Andrew Jacob Mattill, "The Jesus-Paul Parallels and the Purpose of Luke-Acts. J. H. Evans Reconsidered," *Novum Testamentum* 17 (1975): 45, for a fuller list. In many instances, the events in Luke are not present in the other Gospels, which highlights the connection.

- Witnesses respond to Jesus and the apostles with awe (Lk 5:26; Acts 2:43) and, when the inclusion of the Gentiles is announced, wrath (Lk 4:27-28; Acts 13:47-50; 22:21-22).

As Paul's companion, Luke had ample opportunity to observe his imitation of Jesus firsthand. Luke echoes Paul's self-conception by crafting a story that highlights the many parallels between Jesus and Paul. Among those many parallels we see the following:

- When rejected by humans, both cite Isaiah 6:9-10 to describe this aspect of their ministry (Lk 8:10; Acts 28:26-27).

- Both Jesus and Paul are depicted as law-observant participants in Jewish festivals, firmly ensconced in their Jewish heritage (Lk 2:21-24, 41-42; 22:1-8; Acts 16:3-4; 18:18, 21; 20:6, 16; 22:3; 23:6; 26:4-5; 27:9; 28:1-30). Neither violates the law or customs (Lk 16:17; Acts 6:14; 21:21-24; 28:17), although they are both falsely accused of having done so.

- Paul and Jesus both make a habit of synagogue attendance and preaching (Lk 4:16; 6:6; 13:10; Acts 13:14-15; 14:1; 17:1-2, 17), put the Pharisees' doctrine of the resurrection to use (Lk 14:14; 20:27-40; Acts 17:18, 32; 23:6-8) and affirm that life is lived "in God" (Lk 20:38; Acts 17:28).

- Both Jesus and Paul are recognized by demons (Lk 4:34-35, 41; 8:28; Acts 16:17; 19:15) and a demon sees the link between them (Acts 19:15).

- Their ministry is first revealed to men who lay hands on them and speak of their ministry to the Gentiles and to Israel (Lk 2:25-32; Acts 9:15-17).

- Paul and Jesus are charged with four offenses: leading the people astray (Lk 23:1; Acts 24:5), opposing Caesar (Lk 23:2; Acts 17:7), stirring up sedition (Lk 23:5; Acts 24:5) and claiming sovereignty for Christ against Caesar (Lk 23:2; Acts 17:7).

- Like Jesus, Paul has four trials (Lk 22–23; Acts 23–26) and is seized by a mob after going to the temple and being welcomed by the people (Lk 19:37-48; 22:54; Acts 21). Both are exonerated—but not released—by Roman authorities (Lk 23:4; Acts 13:28; 23:29); Pilate and Agrippa both try to release them (Lk 23:16, 20; Acts 26:32); and Roman governors note that neither is worthy of death (Pilate in Luke 23:15; Festus in Acts 25:25).

There are many other possible connections besides those listed here, but the general trend should be clear.[14] Many of these links seem unique and unrepeatable, and at least part of Luke's purpose is to emphasize the authority of the apostles, an authority not fully shared by other believers. But Luke's emphasis on the links between the identity and mission of Jesus and the apostles is also applied more broadly.

In Luke-Acts, Jesus' ministry and that of the apostles is characterized by the little Greek word *dei*, usually translated "it is necessary" and often tied to divine compulsion or command. The suffering work of Jesus, the apostles and every other Christian are intertwined: "It is through many persecutions that we *must* enter the kingdom of God" (Acts 14:22). Remarkably, this word is said to "strengthen" believers.

Acts also links the imitation of the Son and the imitation of the saints as the early church illustrates obedience to Jesus' teaching. The church rejoices in suffering (Acts 5:41) just as Jesus commanded (Lk 6:23) and models joy at repentance and the boundary-breaking power of the gospel, taught by Jesus in Luke 15 (Acts 8:39; 11:23; 13:48; 15:31). Commanded by Jesus to pray without ceasing (Lk 18:1), the disciples model obedience: Prayer appears almost once per chapter in Acts. "The place of prayer in the life of the church finds a parallel in the place of prayer in the life of Jesus, just as there is a parallelism between the work of the Spirit in relation to Jesus and in relation to the church."[15]

Throughout Acts the disciples imitate the divine hospitality that Jesus himself extended in Luke to the hungry, hurting and lost. "Every Lazarus was sharing food in the house of someone better off ([Acts] 2,46)."[16]

---

[14]See especially the farewell speeches (Lk 21–22; Acts 20). It should be noted that the observation that Luke shaped his stories in this way does not fictionalize his accounts. Mattill notes parallels that could have been employed, but were not, most likely due to Luke's restraint; "Jesus-Paul Parallels," pp. 36, 40 n. 49.

[15]I. Howard Marshall, *Luke: Historian and Theologian* (Exeter, UK: Paternoster, 1989), p. 204 n. 2.

[16]David Seccombe, *Possessions and the Poor in Luke-Acts* (Linz, Austria: SNTU, 1983), p. 220,

Table fellowship is modeled and required by Jesus (Lk 5:29-30; 14:12-14; 15:1-2; 19:1-10) and enacted by his disciples (Acts 2:42, 46; 10:1-48). In Acts the disciples imitate the content of Jesus' proclamation in Luke: the kingdom, forgiveness of sins and the Scriptures point to him and his death, resurrection and enthronement.[17] The church's preaching illustrates Jesus' teaching that every corner of the Scriptures (Moses, Prophets, Psalms)[18] testifies to the life, death, resurrection, enthronement and final victory of the Messiah (Lk 24).

In these ways and many others, the early church participated in and extended the ministry of her master and modeled obedience to his teaching (Acts 20:33-35). In fact, the church becomes a corporate demonstration of the ministry of Jesus. In her prayers, preaching, suffering, forgiveness and Spirit-led problem-solving (Acts 15), the church in Acts is a model for the church to imitate. Luke records its "Acts" not just for history's sake but to provide a book of models exhibiting obedience to Jesus.[19]

To be sure, there are also negative examples like Ananias and Sapphira; the response of the church (Acts 5:11) suggests that they were effective in that role! Acts also tells readers about actions that are not necessarily to be imitated, such as drawing lots. But between Jerusalem in chapter 1 and Rome in chapter 28, the thrust of the story is one of Jesus working through and in (not just despite) his disciples. They are not perfect, but they are a great cloud of witnesses who become a template of the work of Jesus. During Paul and Barnabas's miraculous ministry in Lystra, the locals respond by exclaiming, "The gods have come down to us in human form!" (Acts 14:11). Paul and Barnabas quickly and loudly insist that they are merely men.

---

cited by Dennis J. Ireland, *Stewardship and the Kingdom of God: An Historical, Exegetical, and Contextual Study of the Parable of the Unjust Steward in Luke 16:1-13* (Leiden, Netherlands: Brill, 1992), p. 194. Ireland adds on p. 193, "The charitable use of possessions called for in Luke's Gospel is illustrated in the life of the early church in the book of Acts."

[17]Jerram Barrs, *The Heart of Evangelism* (Wheaton, IL: Crossway, 2005), explores aspects of contemporary evangelism that should echo Jesus' approach to unbelievers.

[18]See Mattill, "Jesus-Paul Parallels," p. 24, for fuller reflections.

[19]"The authors of the New Testament plumbed the life of Jesus for nuggets of theological and moral insight . . . pertinent to their own ministry contexts." Michael Allen, *The Christ's Faith: A Dogmatic Account* (New York: T & T Clark, 2009), p. 359.

But the pagans were not far from the truth. Like their master, the apostles displayed the living God to the world.

IMITATION OF SACRIFICE: HEBREWS AND PETER

Across the New Testament the imitation of Jesus appears as one of the primary applications of the message of the cross. If Christians are destined for affliction (1 Thess 3:3-4), if cross-bearing and co-suffering with Christ are required (Mk 8:34; Rom 8:17), then one would expect to find a considerable amount of such teaching. That emphasis must not be overlooked or diminished.[20]

The author of Hebrews uses Jesus as an example at the conclusion of a long line of Old Testament characters. These characters model endurance and the rejection of sin to New Testament believers (Heb 12:1). In this list of examples, Jesus is present as a reminder of the access and inheritance he has secured for sojourners—described in detail earlier in Hebrews—but also because he models endurance in the face of shame and suffering. That same endurance is required of those who would follow him. As Michael Allen has recently argued, Jesus models faith: trust in the Father that leads to obedience. Our imitation of Jesus starts with the imitation of his faith in the God who raises the dead (even if our faith is not precisely like his).[21]

The objective of Jesus' suffering, that we might be holy like Father and Son, is also the objective of our suffering and endurance: "[God] disciplines us for our good, in order that we may share his holiness" (Heb 12:10). Jesus' motivation—"the joy that was set before him" (Heb 12:2)—can be ours as well. Hebrews applies sacrificial language both to believers and to Jesus. The sacrifices are not equal in weight: all is nothing without Jesus, the great high priest and the final sacrifice for sins (Heb 10:12). But through him believers make sacrifices to God that consist of praise, do-gooding and generosity (Heb 13:15-16).

The author of Hebrews does not think that the imitation of Jesus

---

[20]Much of what follows is adapted from Jason Hood, "The Cross in the New Testament: Two Theses in Conversation with Recent Studies (2000–2007)," *Westminster Theological Journal* 71, no. 2 (2009): 281-95, with the permission of the editors.

[21]Michael Allen, *The Christ's Faith*.

threatens the uniqueness of Jesus' suffering. Certainly there is a focus on the uniqueness of Jesus and the superiority of his sacrifice to Old Testament sacrifices (and, by implication, our sacrifices as well). But having established Jesus' uniqueness, he draws the comparison so closely that Jesus' abuse is said to be ours: we go outside the camp "and bear the abuse he endured" (Heb 13:13).[22] The author uses the location of Jesus' suffering outside Jerusalem as a metaphor for the sort of abuse Christians receive for failing to reflect the culture around them: Jesus suffered "outside the city gate in order to sanctify the people by his own blood. Let us then go to him outside the camp. . . . For here we have no lasting city, but we are looking for the city that is to come" (Heb 13:12-14).

Like Hebrews, 1 Peter is one of the New Testament books most closely focused on the cross. As Dan McCartney explains, "The comments in this letter on the redemptive work of Christ in his suffering and death all take place in the context of ethical discussions about the behavior of servants, or the Christian response to undeserved suffering, or general exhortations regarding the Christian life."[23] Bruce Demarest claims that imitation is less important in 1 Peter than the atonement.[24] While Jesus' death as a substitute for sin is of fundamental importance for Peter, Demarest's claim is difficult to square with the content and rhetoric of the letter as noted by McCartney and could lead readers and preachers to downplay Peter's pastoral application of the cross (1 Pet 2:18-25; 3:16-18; 4:1-2, 12-19).

Peter presents Jesus as the ultimate example of a life lived in sub-

---

[22]Geerhardus Vos, *The Teaching of Jesus Concerning the Kingdom of God and the Church* (Cambridge, MA: American Tract Society, 1903), pp. 67-68, notes the connection to Moses in Heb 11:25-26, who suffered for the Messiah by suffering *with God's people*; the two verses must go together. The Christian's "reproach is thus to be seen a reproach which Christ Himself first bore and which we now bear together with Him. . . . Back of all the reproaches and sufferings which God's people have endured" throughout the ages "stood Christ." Cited by S. M. Baugh, "The Cloud of Witnesses in Hebrews 11," *Westminster Theological Journal* 68, no. 1 (2006): 130-31 n. 69.

[23]Dan G. McCartney, "Atonement in James, Peter and Jude: 'Because Christ Suffered for You,'" in *The Glory of the Atonement* (Downers Grove, IL: IVP Academic, 2004), p. 180. Note the subtitle of Edmund Clowney's exposition of 1 Peter: *The Message of 1 Peter: The Way of the Cross*, The Bible Speaks Today (Downers Grove, IL: InterVarsity Press, 1989).

[24]Bruce Demarest, *Cross and Salvation: The Doctrine of Salvation* (Wheaton, IL: Crossway, 1997), p. 182. The observation is partially explained by the focus of Demarest's text.

mission to God in a broken world resolutely opposed to God and his people: "Christ also suffered for you, leaving you an example, so that you should follow in his steps" (1 Pet 2:21). The term *hypogrammos*, usually translated "example," can refer to a metal plate on which the alphabet was engraved. Students used such a template when learning to write letters. Karen Jobes notes the inability of English terms to convey this sense: "'Example,' 'model,' or 'copy' are too weak, for Jesus' suffering is not simply an example or pattern or model, as if one of many; he is the paradigm by which Christians write large the letters of his gospel in their heart." She concludes her analysis by recalling the death-then-glorification pattern throughout the New Testament: "This is a strong image associating the Christian's life with the life of Christ. For one cannot step into the footsteps of Jesus and head off in any other direction than the direction he took, and his footsteps lead to the cross, through the grave, and onward to glory."[25]

IMITATING CROSS-SHAPED VICTORY: REVELATION

In the book of Revelation, John draws links between the priestly, prophetic and royal roles of the Lamb and his flock. Jesus played a priestly role through his sacrificial death and faithful witness without compromise (Rev 1:5). The church is then introduced as a kingdom of priests (Rev 1:6). Jesus "reigned as king ironically by conquering death and sin through the defeat at the cross and subsequent resurrection (Rev 1:5)." Those who follow the Lamb "fulfill the same offices . . . by following his model." In so doing, they overcome as he overcame (Rev 2:7, 17, 26; 3:5, 12, 21; 15:2). Their faithful witness mediates the authority of the Messiah to the world. Sharing in Jesus' royal victory and priestly witness are not isolated themes with no connection to the rest of Revelation.[26] The rest of this book unpacks this theme. Disciples "follow the Lamb wherever he goes," and they are blameless and holy, free from lies and dedicated to purity of

---

[25]Karen Jobes, *1 Peter,* Baker Exegetical Commentary on the New Testament (Grand Rapids: Baker, 2005), p. 195.

[26]Gregory Beale, *The Book of Revelation: A Commentary on the Greek Text,* New International Greek Testament Commentary (Grand Rapids: Eerdmans, 1999), p. 193.

witness after the pattern of Jesus (Rev 14:4-5).

The Lamb's followers are to recapitulate the model of his ironic victory in their own lives; by means of enduring through tribulation they reign in the invisible kingdom of the Messiah (see Rev 1:6, 9). They exercise kingship in the midst of their suffering just as Christ did from the cross; Christians are called to be conquerors by emulating in their own lives the archetypal messianic triumph of Jesus.[27]

John sees "under the altar the souls of those who had been slaughtered for the word of God and for the testimony they had given" (Rev 6:9). The portrayal of death on an altar depicts these witnesses as a priestly sacrifice, an offering after the pattern of Jesus' sacrificial death and witness. Not all believers will die for the faith. Yet all must witness faithfully as Jesus did in life and death.[28]

New Paternity Brings New Power

In previous chapters we have seen the importance of moral genetic testing in Matthew, John and Paul. Our paternity is reflected in our behavior, and a change in paternity (adoption) should produce a change in character. Peter similarly describes what "obedient [spiritual] children" should look like by pointing to God's character. He quotes the great slogan of Leviticus, "You shall be holy, for I am holy." In the same context Peter calls for impartiality, and that is another divine trait (1 Pet 1:14-17). Peter does not think that believers have earned a new status but that they are called to illustrate a new God-given character and power. They have been transformed by new birth (1 Pet 1:23; compare Jas 1:18), God's mercy (1 Pet 2:10) and Christ's precious self-sacrifice (1 Pet 2:24-25). "His divine power has given us everything needed for life and godliness" (2 Pet 1:3). Not yet fully transformed, they are not now what they once were, and they grow in their reflection of God.

Transformed behavior is a function of new nature. Sinners respond

---

[27]G. Beale, "Revelation, Book of," in *New Dictionary of Biblical Theology*, ed. T. D. Alexander and B. S. Rosner (Downers Grove, IL: InterVarsity Press, 2000), p. 356.
[28]On the imitation of Jesus and witness language in Revelation, see Michael Allen, *The Christ's Faith*, p. 361.

to the good news so that "they might live in the spirit as God does" (1 Pet 4:6). Peter even goes so far as to say that believers partake of the divine nature (2 Pet 1:4). First John 3:2 describes Christian destiny in similar terms: "We will be like him, for we will see him as he is." Believers become godly (godlike), responding to God's promises by cleansing themselves from dishonorable and youthful passions. They pursue God's character traits—"righteousness, faith, love and peace"—in community with others (2 Tim 2:22; see also Jas 1:21-22). The godly character pursued by believers (2 Peter 1:3, 7; 3:11, 14) stands in sharp contrast to godless character that must be actively rejected (2 Pet 3:7; Jas 1:21; 4:8).

The alternative to imitating Jesus and his Father is not neutrality. As Dylan said, we have to serve somebody. And as Beale advances the refrain, we are all imitators, for good or for ill. To reject cross-bearing— for ourselves or for Jesus—is to move in the direction of Satan, which is why Jesus confronts Peter's cross denial by calling him Satan. The alternative to godliness and the imitation of the self-giving love of God in Jesus is satanic self-centeredness that leaves humans looking demonic, rejecting Jesus' cross and the need for his work (Mt 16:21-26).

CONCLUSION

The New Testament picks up the call to imitate the Father by showing us the Son. The Son displays the character of the Father in human form: holiness, impartiality, godliness, the divine nature, righteousness, reliance on the Father, love, faithfulness and peace. To the extent Jesus' followers reflect his imitation of the Father, they are earthly mirrors of heavenly character, just as he mirrored the Father on earth as "the image of the invisible God" (Col 1:15). By his Spirit, Jesus is now at work creating what he requires in his disciples, cloning a cross-shaped image, so to speak, in the humans in whom he lives. He molds their patterns of desire and deeds so they reflect him. As he does so, his imprint can be seen in the saints whose lives imperfectly yet tangibly mirror his perfect template.

The result is a great deal of overlap in the imitation of the Father, the Son and the saints. As Jesus' representatives, his body and temple in his world, Paul and other New Testament writers regularly hold out themselves, their associates, church leaders, Old Testament characters and other congregations for imitation. To examine these features of the New Testament, we'll begin the third section of this book, an investigation of the ways believers should imitate those who reflect the Father and the Son.

PART THREE

Imitating the Saints

12

A Community of Imitation

A true Christian pastor will be one who can dare to say to his people:
"Follow me, as I am following Jesus." That is a terrible test for any pastor.
A true pastor must have such a relation with Jesus and with his
people that he follows Jesus and they follow him.

LESSLIE NEWBIGIN

We all know that if you just dig a little deeper, you'll probably find the dirt. Sooner or later, it seems that good behavior turns out to be a façade, a game played by politicians, celebrities and religious people for social, spiritual or economic profit. There is no black and white; at best, we're all a shade of gray.[1] The Bible is sympathetic to our skepticism. It dissects its characters and ruthlessly exposes their flaws. If you want to pray as Jesus taught, you have to ask for mercy. If you want to take Paul as a model, you must acknowledge sin and a need for redemption. It's in his state as a sinner in need of mercy that Paul becomes "an example to those who would come to believe in [Jesus] for eternal life" (1 Tim 1:16).

Of course, as we saw in the introduction, Paul's exemplary role does

---

[1]See especially Thornton Wilder's 1927 novel, *The Bridge of San Luis Rey* (London: Longmans, Green, 1927), and the 1959 film *They Came to Cordura*, starring Gary Cooper and Rita Hayworth.

not end there, nor is the Bible content to shine a light on the flaws of its characters. The New Testament presents a community across the ages, a great cloud of witnesses (Heb 12:1) past and present who can and should be imitated. If humans are to imitate God, they are also to emulate those who reflect his character. If believers imitate Jesus as God's perfect image, they are also to imitate those who stumble along after him, growing into the shape of Jesus by his Spirit. A maturing believer in Jesus can present herself as a model for others to imitate. In fact, if she is faithful to her identity in Christ, she must become a model.

A COMMUNITY OF IMITATION: 1 THESSALONIANS TO TITUS

When Paul holds himself out as a model, he reveals a belief that disciples of Jesus can experience success in imitating the Messiah. He intends for his model of Christian life and ministry to be passed on to others. The pattern is intended to be self-duplicating: Because Paul and his companions imitate the Lord (1 Thess 1:6), they serve as initial models for disciples (1 Thess 1:5-6) who are then an example for others (1 Thess 1:7).

Paul wants pastors to be conservationists, following faithfully in the footsteps of those who were faithful with the message and way of life they received. Those ministers then pass the message and the way of life to others, both as teachers and models. Elders and shepherds are conduits of the community's beliefs and behavior, which is why Paul insists that all who lead must be "an example in speech and conduct, in love, in faith, in purity" (1 Tim 4:12). These requirements for overseers and deacons are not just for leaders alone (1 Tim 3:1-13).

Paul himself models a life that departs from the desire (common both then and now) to be idle, engaged in gossip and living off others (1 Thess 2:1-12; 2 Thess 3:6-12). "Just as Paul worked with his hands in order not to burden the converts . . . so the Thessalonians are to work with their hands and contribute to the common good (rather than unnecessarily tax the charity of the community). . . . Paul's example is to be replicated in the lives of the disciples, then and now."[2]

Timothy's life shows that this process is never-ending. He was an excellent example for believers in Corinth (1 Cor 4:7-18). Some years later, in the letter we call 2 Timothy, Paul commands him to continue setting a standard for others to emulate. The basic framework for Timothy's ministry is to keep what Paul has given him and pass it to others, who will imitate Timothy, faithfully holding the truth and teaching others (1 Tim 6:11-14; 2 Tim 2:2). Timothy and other readers are invited to wade ever more deeply into a life of co-suffering with Paul (2 Tim 1:8; 2:3; 3:10-13; 4:5-8). Titus is similarly to be "in all respects a model of good works" (Titus 2:7). Because these pastors imitate Paul's faithful mindset and deeds, they are Paul's "loyal child[ren] in the faith," reflecting the cross-shaped character of their "father" (1 Tim 1:2; Titus 1:4; see also 1 Cor 4:15-16).

A similar view of leadership is provided in Acts. Paul summarizes his ministry during his time in Ephesus: bold evangelism, faithful ministry, humility in manual labor and generous giving (Acts 20:28-31, 33-35). The goal of this litany is not self-congratulation but imitation. As in his letters to Corinth, Paul is not afraid to list what he has done and suffered in order to urge the elders to imitate him: "Remember what you saw and heard from me? Stick to that pattern," he is saying. Scott Hafemann helpfully summarizes Paul's approach and its implications for contemporary pastoral ministry:

> Paul's message in 2 Corinthians reminds us that just as redemption took place through the coming of Christ, so too God's plan for strengthening the faith of his people is not ultimately a program, but a person. The life and proclamation of the pastor, replicated in the faith of his people in the midst of their own sufferings, is the primary way God grows his church. . . . At the heart of the pastoral office is the suffering of the pastor, even as Christ came as the suffering servant who was obedient to the point of death.
>
> In an age when pastors are being increasingly reconfigured as professional therapists, business managers, and "coaches in the game of

[2]David deSilva, *An Introduction to the New Testament: Contexts, Methods and Ministry Formation* (Downers Grove, IL: InterVarsity Press, 2004), p. 541.

life," such an understanding seems as strange as it is needed.

"Virtually all the trouble that the best, and most talented pastors get into comes from not following the Way of the Cross. . . . Sexual sin gets the press, but ego sin kills the church."[3]

Hafemann and David Hansen use 2 Corinthians 4:10-11 to summarize the power of a life of Christian sacrifice: "[We are] always carrying in the body the death of Jesus, so that the life of Jesus may also be made visible in our bodies. For while we live, we are always being given up to death for Jesus' sake, so that the life of Jesus may be made visible in our mortal flesh." If time spent with Paul and the unspeakable blessing of having Scripture written directly to a congregation did not remove the need to have flesh-and-blood models, following someone on Twitter and faithfully listening to sermon series on the Web will not suffice for discipleship.

Paul and his associates are not just a model for church leaders. All mature believers are expected to walk in a way that can be imitated by others. The love believers show one another should mirror the love Paul and his associates have shown them (1 Thess 3:11-13). By choosing a quiet life focused on their own affairs, they imitate Paul (1 Thess 4:9-12; 2:4-11; 2 Thess 3:6-15). Learning to tell oneself "no" with respect to idleness and gossip is often more difficult and more counterintuitive than resisting more obvious sins, and it requires flesh-and-blood models and constant repetition to get such a message home.

Peter also teaches shepherds to live as examples (1 Pet 5:2-4), just as Jesus was a model for his own flock (1 Pet 2:21, 25). The author of Hebrews assumes that leaders will be models worth emulating, both in their faith and in the way of life that accompanies faith (Heb 13:7). It is too much to suggest that our leaders will be perfect or that we will never need to forgive them, but it is not too much to require that they be worth following.

---

[3]Scott Hafemann, "A Call to Pastoral Suffering: The Need for Recovering Paul's Model of Ministry in 2 Corinthians," *Southern Baptist Journal of Theology* 4, no. 2 (2000): 34, citing in the last paragraph David Hansen, *The Art of Pastoring: Ministry Without All the Answers* (Downers Grove, IL: InterVarsity Press, 1994), p. 27.

GLOBALIZING IMITATION

While Paul gives priority to local imitation of pastors and other mature believers, the New Testament writers as a whole globalize imitation chronologically and geographically—Christians are not simply to imitate local leaders and congregations. Congregations in distant places also need to be imitated, not least since we often become desensitized to the sins of our own culture. Peter encourages his readers to follow the example of other "brothers and sisters" who resist satanic opposition (1 Pet 5:9-10). The Thessalonians are commended for becoming imitators of Judean churches who suffer at the hands of those opposed to Christianity (1 Thess 2:14-17), which in turn makes the Thessalonian believers an example for others (1 Thess 1:7). Since churches are influenced by the values and habits of the culture in which they live, the imitation of believers on other continents and from other traditions can provide invaluable help with the diagnosis of unhealthy cultural influences.

If the community we are to imitate is not limited geographically, it is also not bound by time. The New Testament's most famous use of characters as models is found in Hebrews 11. The author extends imitation deep into the chronology of biblical history and then forward for the audience of his day and beyond. This list of characters to imitate builds on an earlier admonition to avoid laziness and to imitate those who inherited promises through faith(fulness) and patience (Heb 6:12). The author runs out of time (Heb 11:32) to include all the characters who acted by faith in response to the eternal goodness of the unseen God. The similarity between the sacrifice of Jesus and the sacrifice of Old Testament saints makes them, like Jesus, models for perseverance and faithfulness in suffering and trial.

> The most striking aspect of [Hebrews 11:1–12:2] is the elaboration of the relationship between faith and suffering. It is an arresting fact that the individuals mentioned in this well-known digest of the history of Israel are those who exercised faith in the face of death. Almost without exception, the context links each of the examples in some way or another to the experience of death (11:4, 5, 7, 11-12, 13, 17-19, 20, 21, 22, 23, 25-26, 29, 30, 31, 33-34, 35-38; 12:1-2). Those for whom death is not spec-

ified in the context were exposed to severe trials or peril because they were faithful to God.[4]

Hebrews 12 makes it clear that these examples are valuable because of the role suffering plays in the Christian life for those who persevere in faith (Heb 12:3-12). But the author of Hebrews extends imitation to small details, commanding the emulation of Abraham and Sarah's hospitality to strangers (Heb 13:1-2). These characters are imperfect, of course. There are differences between life in the old covenant and life in the new covenant (Heb 8:13; 12:18-27), and appropriating the hospitality of Abraham's era and the first century requires some hermeneutical effort.

But sinners and saints new and old can still be compared and contrasted. "The good news came to us just as to them" (Heb 4:2), the author says of Israel's wilderness generation, and this link allows him to contrast the wilderness generation's unbelief and disobedience with the belief and obedience expected of his audience. Esau lost his inheritance because he failed to desire it more than momentary satisfaction, and the author of Hebrews wants his readers to see the consequences and respond appropriately. Those who have an even greater appreciation of God's goodness should not fail to obtain the gift (or grace, *charis*) of God because of bitterness, sexual immorality or despising God's blessings for temporary gain (Heb 12:15-17; contrast Abraham, Sarah and Moses in Heb 11:8-12, 24-26).

James refers to Old Testament characters five times in five chapters. Abraham, Rahab, Elijah, Job and "the prophets" are all used as examples for New Testament–era believers (Jas 2:14-26; 5:10-18). All five characters responded to the work and promises of God. James notes that Elijah "was a human being like us" whose prayers worked powerfully (Jas 5:17). I suspect that many Christians today would not make such a connection as they read 1 Kings. Many leaders would never think to encourage their congregations to see themselves in Elijah's story so that they gain confidence in prayer. Only my charismatic friends seem to teach such things.

---

[4]William Lane, *Hebrews: A Call to Commitment* (Peabody, MA: Hendrickson, 1985), p. 159.

The letters of Peter, Jude and John also provide numerous examples for their readers. Sarah is a model for wives in their relationship to husbands (1 Pet 3:3-6). Even if it is not entirely clear what portion of Genesis Peter has in mind, it is clear that Peter thinks that Sarah is a model to be imitated. In a study of 2 Peter and Jude, Daryl Charles notes that even angels "are illustrative" and can be used "to warn the reader" (2 Pet 2:4) or instruct in appropriate behavior (2 Pet 2:11; Jude 8-9). The use of humans and angels as examples is "well established in the history of Jewish interpretation" and "integral to the Christian moral tradition." The use of characters for moral instruction—a pattern so ingrained in New Testament authors that they even used angels as examples—is virtually absent from some contemporary interpretation.[5]

CONCLUSION

The New Testament provides a standard, a master who provides a perfect paradigm; it also provides accessible models.[6] As they use Old Testament characters, the New Testament writers show believers how to read the Old Testament, drawing out lessons about God, his work, his people and their opponents. The use of characters—even entire nations—as patterns teaches readers to see themselves in the drama of redemption. The Bible provides a portrait of real humans who wrestle with believing God's promises and walking in his ways in the face of a real world, sometimes succeeding, sometimes failing and sometimes throwing God's promises away like trash.

While this chapter has shown how characters function as examples, it also prompts questions about the source of such interpretation. What led New Testament authors to put the Old Testament to use in this way? The next chapter will consider this question and more.

---

[5]Daryl Charles, "The Angels Under Reserve in 2 Peter and Jude," *Bulletin for Biblical Research* 15, no. 1 (2005): 39-48, especially 39 and n. cited. "These paradigms . . . are proverbial in character and part of moral-typological tradition."

[6]Michael Allen describes this as "ethical triangulation" in *The Christ's Faith*, pp. 359-64. See especially Graham Tomlin, *Spiritual Fitness: Christian Character in a Consumer Society* (London: Continuum, 2006), pp. 69, 138-39, 142-43, for reflections on the role of community in discipleship. In Bonhoeffer-speak, we cannot have "cost of discipleship" without "life together."

13

Objections, Obstacles and Presuppositions for Interpretation

If the Scriptures speak about Jesus,
and if Jesus is the head of all things for the church,
then the Scriptures speak about everything.

PETER LEITHART

The best way to learn how the Old Testament books
apply to us is gradually to absorb the way in
which the New Testament uses the Old.

SIMON GATHERCOLE

My heart almost stopped. The email read, in part, "Can you shoot Jason . . . ?" It was exactly the proof I needed. But I wasn't out to catch a would-be murderer. I simply needed a good illustration for an undergraduate course later that day. (It's possible that I get a little too excited about good examples. After all, I'm writing a book on the subject.) The difference between the fragment alone and the fragment in its context helped flesh out a vital lesson in interpretation. The rest of the sentence read, "Can you shoot Jason and me an email?"

In order to understand this sentence (as with most communication), you need to have a grasp of cultural context on understanding of American slang, contemporary technology and English grammar (direct versus indirect object). Above all, you need the full literary context, the whole sentence, the story in which the statement is going to make sense.

In the same way, the use of characters by biblical authors is the result of pre-understandings (or presuppositions) that guided interpretation. But these presuppositions are often not spelled out, and we find ourselves substituting other presuppositions. It is tempting to suppose that we share Scripture's take on the way it uses itself. But if we do not fully share the presuppositions of New Testament writers regarding how Scripture should be used, we may find ourselves with a shrunken hermeneutical toolbox.

First let's consider some of the presuppositions at work in the biblical writers' interpretation of Scripture. These six presuppositions overlap with and mutually inform one another, as well as contribute in some way to a framework for understanding God, Messiah and biblical characters as models for imitation.

THE SCRIPTURES REVEAL GOD'S CHARACTER

Early Jews and Christians believed that the biblical books revealed God's character. This presupposition makes every text relevant. Even challenging texts (such as the slaughter of Canaanites, Psalm 110 and Psalm 137) taught readers about God. And if a text speaks of God, it will often address his image-bearers, since human character should conform to his character and ways. In the face of wickedness that was destroying Israel, Phinehas kills an idolatrous man and woman. God describes him as "jealous with my jealousy" (Num 25:1-13 ESV), and Phinehas imitates God by killing the wicked and preserving the holiness of Israel (Num 16). Disturbing as he might be to modern readers, a biblical character like Phinehas emulates God's own character and action. As my understated British friends might say, he shows readers that God doesn't much care for unfettered sin in his covenant people. Phinehas becomes a model for later generations

(1 Chron 9:20; Ps 106:28-31), not necessarily for them to imitate his violent response but to imitate his commitment to share God's concern for the holiness and fame of God's name. From a New Testament perspective, the imitation of God's zeal for his fame is now mediated not simply through Phinehas but through a Messiah who perfectly demonstrated the pursuit of God's holiness and fame by piercing himself and letting the guilty go free.

THE SCRIPTURES REVEAL THE MESSIAH AND HIS MISSION

Luke 24 teaches us that Jesus is something of a "skeleton key" for interpreting the Old Testament. "It appears that Jesus is giving the disciples the key to understanding the Old Testament as a whole."[1] Such an assertion is backed up by other passages (Jn 5:39-40). When Luke says, "Then beginning with Moses and all the prophets, he interpreted to them the things about himself in all the scriptures" (Lk 24:27), Jesus probably does not teach that every single Old Testament passage points directly to him and his work. Rather, Jesus teaches that his identity and mission can be found in many passages from every area of Scripture and function as the grand conclusion for the whole of the Old Testament's unfinished narrative. His point is clarified both in extent (Jesus can be preached from the Law, Prophets and Psalter) and in content (Jesus' suffering, death, resurrection on the third day and reception in glory; repentance and forgiveness being proclaimed everywhere, beginning in Jerusalem) in several verses in the immediate context (Lk 24:25-26, 44-47).[2] And as we have seen, if the Scriptures speak of Jesus, they also surely speak of those who now have their identity in him and those through whom Jesus is working.

---

[1]Don McCartney, "The New Testament's Use of the Old Testament," in *Inerrancy and Hermeneutic: A Tradition, a Challenge, a Debate*, ed. Harvie M. Conn (Grand Rapids: Baker, 1988), pp. 109, 113-14, 116. D. Ralph Davis identifies some concerns regarding the use of Luke 24 and a "Christ-centered only" methodology in *Word Became Fresh: How to Preach from Old Testament Narrative Texts* (Fearn, UK: Christian Focus, 2006), pp. 134-38.

[2]I have heard many a lament that the lessons in Luke 24 were not written down. There is no need for this lament: the sermons in Acts model the sort of interpretation that Jesus used with his disciples in Luke 24.

THE SCRIPTURES REVEAL GOD'S PEOPLE
IN RELATIONSHIP WITH HIM

Biblical interpreters presupposed that the Scriptures revealed appropriate and inappropriate responses to the unchanging nature of God's character. Old Testament texts tell us of people who respond to God's promises, character and actions, and biblical writers believed their audiences had the same God, lived in the same world, experienced the same opposition and had similar tasks required of them as earlier saints.[3] By drawing parallels between Old Testament characters and New Testament readers, the New Testament writers teach us that a new relationship with God through Jesus makes the ancients more valuable as examples, not less so. Yahweh promised Abraham a place, a family and his presence, and the same promises are given to new covenant believers (Jn 14:2-3; Mt 5:5; Rom 4:13). Abraham's "free" children are not just genetic descendants from his union with Sarah but all those who share his faith in Yahweh (Rom 4; Gal 4). Abraham's response of faith and obedience become a standard for New Testament believers, who are Abraham and Sarah's spiritual descendants (Gen 15:6; Lk 3:8; Jn 8:39; Rom 4:3; Gal 3:6; Jas 2:14-23; 1 Pet 3:6). God's people in the Old and New Testament "are part of the one people of God sharing in one story of salvation. That is why the achievements of the Israelites of the past should inspire the Christians of the first century."[4]

The saints in the Old Testament and New Testament were on the way to the same destination (Heb 11:8-10, 13-16), and the writers be-

---

[3]On this point and what follows, see Richard Pratt, *He Gave Us Stories: The Bible Student's Guide to Interpreting Old Testament Narrative* (Phillipsburg, NJ: P&R, 1990), especially pp. 321-33; Harvie Conn, *Eternal Word, Changing Worlds: Theology, Anthropology, and Mission in Trialog* (Grand Rapids: Zondervan, 1984), especially p. 228; and Gordon Wenham, *Story as Torah: Reading Old Testament Narrative Ethically* (Grand Rapids: Baker Academic, 2004), p. 134 and especially 154-55: "The coming of the kingdom may be more apparent in the Christian era than it was before Christ, but it is still partial. The Church today, like Israel of old, still hopes and prays for the consummation. It still has to live in a world distorted by hardness of heart and not as it was in the beginning. It still lives in a world where sin and violence are endemic. Individual Christians and the Church are afflicted by both. They need the laws and narratives of the Old Testament to remind them of the creator's ideals and how to handle situations which fall short of these ideals. In this way the experience of the saints of the Old Testament has much to teach those of the New."
[4]Wenham, *Story as Torah*, p. 134.

lieved that they could encourage readers to see themselves on the pages of Scripture in the life, trials, success, faithfulness and failure of those characters. Hebrews 3–4 and 11 are particularly instructive examples: Abraham and the Israelites were on the way not just to Canaan but to New Jerusalem and new creation (a heavenly city and country). Their pursuit of this destination by faith and faithfulness became a pattern in which later believers were to walk, while other characters who despised promises and inheritance became examples to avoid (Esau, Heb 12:16; first generation of Israelites, Heb 3–4). Yahweh's promise to be with Joshua (Josh 1:5) can be read in the pages of the Old Testament and applied to believers in the first century (Heb 13:5) or the twenty-first and can lead others to courageous action like the courage displayed by Joshua. Details are clarified, but the destination and requirements for God's people are the same: they are still called to hope, humility, faith and repentance, obedience and faithfulness.

THE SCRIPTURES ADDRESS THE MESSIAH'S PEOPLE AND THEIR MISSION

A number of studies of Paul's use of the Old Testament move us one step beyond the previous point by summarizing his belief that the church could be found in the Old Testament: "When Paul looks in the Bible to understand the church he finds his understanding in what the Bible says about Israel."[5] "When Paul goes to the Old Testament he finds there, above all else, 'a prefiguration of the church as the people of God.'" Richard Hays calls this an ecclesiocentric ("church-centered," or "people of God–centered") approach to interpretation.[6]

Paul charges Timothy, "You have known the holy Scriptures, which are able to make you wise for salvation through faith in Christ Jesus" (2 Tim 3:15 NIV). Like Luke 24:27, this verse is sometimes cited

---

[5]Roy Ciampa, *The Presence and Function of Scripture in Galatians 1 and 2*, vol. 2, no. 102, Wissenshftliche Untersuchungen Zum Neuen Testament (Tübingen: Mohr Siebeck, 1998), p. 231.

[6]Richard Hays, *Echoes of Scripture in the Letters of Paul* (New Haven, CT: Yale University Press, 1989), pp. 86, 162; see also G. K. Beale, "The Old Testament Background of Paul's Reference to 'the Fruit of the Spirit' in Galatians 5:22," *Bulletin for Biblical Research* 15, no. 1 (2005): 28.

as a passport to the interpretation of Christ in all the Scriptures.[7] But wisdom for the initiation of a salvific relationship with Jesus is not the limit nor always the goal of Christian interpretation. Christian interpretation should always be organically connected to this salvation and must never stand opposed to it. But according to the two verses following (2 Tim 3:16-17), good works are the *telos*, and all Scripture is to be used to this end in "teaching, rebuking, correcting and training in righteousness." These tasks—not merely the articulation of "wisdom for salvation in Christ" apart from sanctification and moral transformation—explicitly describe the utility of every Scripture.

First Corinthians 10 illustrates that moral instruction is not contrary to finding Jesus in the Old Testament. In that passage Paul finds Jesus in the Old Testament: "the rock" in the wilderness that nourished Israel "was Christ" (1 Cor 10:4). He then explains the relevance of the Old Testament passage he mines for Christian moral admonition, telling the Corinthians not to commit idolatry (1 Cor 10:7) or sexual immorality (1 Cor 10:8), not to test Christ (1 Cor 10:9) and not to grumble (1 Cor 10:10). These lessons come from Paul's use of the Old Testament, and he finds these lessons because he believes that "these things occurred as examples for us, that we might not desire evil as they did" (1 Cor 10:6).

Other passages similarly indicate a moral use for Scripture that fits hand-in-glove with an emphasis on Christocentric interpretation or the revelation of God's character. For instance, Romans 15:4 draws from God's character and the mission of the Messiah when it teaches that "whatever was written in former days was written for our instruction." In context Paul exhorts the believers to draw encouragement from God's character and Jesus' salvation, and to pursue virtues like humility, hospitality and love of neighbor.

In each of these passages, church-centered interpretation is not opposed to Christ-centered interpretation; rather, it may be connected to it.

[7]Graeme Goldsworthy, *Preaching the Whole Bible as Christian Scripture* (Grand Rapids: Eerdmans, 2000), pp. 84-85.

THE SCRIPTURES WERE WRITTEN FOR MORAL INSTRUCTION

Biblical and other ancient authors did not write and shape texts merely for amusement. When later interpreters put the Bible to use for moral instruction, they did so because the original function of biblical books invited or even required such application. Biblical authors wrote books and told stories in order to provide moral direction and give shape to a community. Therefore, God's promises and faithfulness to earlier generations of Israelites as they worshiped, prayed and warred were still relevant for Israel after the exile. Consider the implications for Daniel: "The book [of Daniel] presents Daniel as a model for behavior during periods of oppression and persecution. He is a historical embodiment of righteousness."[8] His three companions are examples who show that faithfulness is the appropriate response to the fact that God himself is with his people in their trials.

As we have seen, the application of messianic interpretation to an Old Testament text does not rule out moral interpretation. Ruth sheds light on the messianic line, and the acts of Ruth and Boaz foreshadow the redemptive work of Jesus. The book also points powerfully to God's care for his people.[9] But Ruth also provides valuable moral instruction. In the order of the canon in Hebrew, Ruth follows the description of the ideal woman in Proverbs 31. Ruth and the woman of Proverbs 31 are both praised as "valiant" or "noble" in answer to the question, "A wife of noble character who can find?" (Prov 31:10 NIV; see Ruth 3:11; Prov 31:29).[10] Ruth and Boaz model the blessing that comes to the faithful who "trust God, serve the community and aid the poor," as depicted in the Law, Psalms, Proverbs and Job, while also taking pains (literally) to embody the pain and sorrow found in those same books.[11] Ruth and Boaz "demonstrate how the laws found in Leviticus and Deuteronomy ought to be obeyed."[12] Christians do not

---

[8]Tremper Longman III and Ray Dillard, *An Introduction to the Old Testament* (Grand Rapids: Zondervan, 1994), p. 380.

[9]Paul House, *Old Testament Theology* (Downers Grove, IL: InterVarsity Press, 1998), pp. 455-62.

[10]Al Wolters, *Song of the Valiant Woman: Studies in the Interpretation of Proverbs 31:10-31* (Carlisle, UK: Paternoster, 2001).

[11]House, *Old Testament Theology*, p. 455.

[12]Ibid., p. 462.

imitate obedience to levirate laws, but it would be foolish to ignore Ruth and Boaz as examples of the sort of faithfulness and mercy that God requires from those who have received redemption.

In 1 and 2 Kings as in Ruth, christological interpretation and moral interpretation are not mutually exclusive. Iain Provan provides helpful balance in his commentary on 1 and 2 Kings: "Christians must read a book like Kings in light of the whole biblical story as it has unfolded to its end. We must, in particular, read it in the light of the words and actions of the central character of that story, Jesus Christ." Old Testament stories point typologically to Christ, but also to readers: Kings "invites us to read our own lives into the lives of its characters—to attach our story to its larger narrative whole—and it gains its full significance for us only as we begin to understand ourselves in its context."[13] Provan offers several examples to that end.

The Chronicler's stories directed the reestablishment of Jewish life in their homeland. They are also capable of anticipating and directing life in the age of the already-but-not-yet kingdom. Granted, adjustments may need to be made as interpreters move from the Old Testament era to the New Testament era, but such adjustments do not make the original function irrelevant for interpretation. Provan's comments on the use of Kings also apply to Chronicles, notwithstanding the differences in emphasis in the two books: Kings is generally more negative in its portrayal of characters (as if to say, "Avoid these examples"), while Chronicles is often more positive. Some commentators point out 1 and 2 Chronicles' connections to the inauguration of the kingdom in Christ and the continuation of kingdom work by New Testament saints.[14] The Chronicler's concern for land acquisition, the participation of "all Israel" in important tasks and the inclusion of Gentiles can reflect New Testament emphases: the unity of the church, the work of the saints in "conquering" through evangelism, and the need to participate zealously in the expansion of God's kingdom so that more humans move from the kingdom of darkness to light (Col 1) and find a foretaste of future inheritance in the family of God

---

[13]Iain Provan, 1 and 2 Kings (Peabody, MA: Hendrickson, 1995), p. 14.
[14]Richard Pratt, 1 and 2 Chronicles (Fearn, UK: Mentor, 1999).

(1 Chron 5). The Chronicler's message points to the expansion of God's kingdom, which usually does not occur apart from human participation, and this is certainly a New Testament concern as well (Mt 28:16-20). Abandoning Yahweh and his ways will have negative consequences for this mission in the Old Testament and in the New Testament (1 Chron 5:23-26). The author of Chronicles believed that David had the same God as the Chronicler's audience. Readers see on the Chronicler's pages that God answers prayers of repentance and petition, whether for forgiveness and restoration (2 Chron 33:11-13) or for victory in warfare (1 Chron 5:18-22). They should find in these models encouragement to pray and knowledge that God will forgive and provide victory in new covenant warfare.

THE SCRIPTURES ARE FOR CONTEMPORARY MORAL INSTRUCTION

As a result, New Testament authors can use Old Testament characters for moral instruction because they see paradigms or patterns of belief and behavior in its pages that formed earlier generations of believers. This use of characters to identify patterns is one aspect of biblical interpretation commonly called typology:

> The Greek *tupos* [type] as used in the Bible means "example" or "pattern." A type may be understood as an event, person or institution in the biblical history which serves as an example or pattern for other events, persons or institutions. . . . Sometimes a particular figure in the Bible becomes a type of how believers should live, such as David . . . whereas Cain . . . and the stubborn Israelites in the wilderness are examples not to be imitated.[15]

In fact, this use of characters is simply part of how literature works:

> Stories about wicked stepmothers, lost children, good but misguided kings, wolves that suckle twin boys . . . children learn or mislearn both what a child and what a parent is, what the cast of characters may be in the drama into which they have been born, and what the ways of the

---

[15]David Baker, "Interpreting Texts in the Context of the Whole Bible," *Themelios* 5, no. 2 (1980): 251-53.

world are. Deprive children of stories and you leave them unscripted, anxious stutterers in their actions as in their words.[16]

We have already seen Abraham presented as a paradigm of the righteous believer whose faith works. Conversely, the opponents of God's people are compared to Cain and those who participated in Korah's rebellion (1 Jn 3:12; Jude 11). Second Peter cites the "world of the ungodly," including Noah's contemporaries and Sodom and Gomorrah, as "an example of what is coming to the ungodly" (2 Pet 2:5-6; see also Jude 7). False prophets like Balaam arose in the past; that pattern will be repeated as others rise with similar motives (2 Pet 2:1, 15; Jude 11). The judgment of the wicked throughout history reminds readers not to imitate their errors of lawlessness and greed (2 Pet 2:2, 3, 7, 10, 18). Comparing the wicked in the Old Testament to contemporary opponents of the church provides comfort for saints under pressure, encouraging them to imitate more righteous characters whose obedience led to their rescue, such as Noah and Lot (2 Pet 2:5, 7).

The church in Smyrna is encouraged to see itself in the story of Daniel and his friends, who are evoked by the use of "ten days" of testing (compare Dan 1:12-15 with Rev 2:10). The church in Thyatira has its imagination fueled when those troubling her are characterized as New Testament versions of Jezebel, who enticed God's people to sexual immorality and idolatry and got what she earned (2 Kings 9; Rev 2:23). Later in Revelation Babylon appears as the great opponent of God's people (compare 1 Pet 5:13). Comparing theological opponents to Balak and Balaam (Rev 2:14) or painting theological opponents in Jerusalem and Rome as Babylon is not as straightforward a use of imitation as Hebrews 11. But the effect is similar, for one should avoid imitating someone who drank a double shot of payback from Yahweh (Rev 18:6).

John gives believers and their opponents roles in a drama reaching back through salvation history. Old Testament characters are part of

---

[16]Alasdair MacIntyre, *After Virtue: A Study in Moral Theory*, 3rd ed. (South Bend, IN: University of Notre Dame Press, 2007), p. 216.

John's arsenal for ministry to his congregations because he sees them as paradigms that fuel believers' imaginations and guide their mindsets and behaviors.[17]

The New Testament's use of such patterns may strike some as harsh, political or prejudicial. But Jesus himself (Rev 2-3) ties readers or their opponents to Jezebel, Balak and Balaam. This observation does not make it easy to determine when such negative labels are appropriate, and there are many examples throughout church history of rhetoric gone overboard. One important way forward is not to reject paradigms and examples but to consider carefully their context and application: permitting or practicing unbelief, idolatry, sexual immorality, greed, hardheartedness, lovelessness (often exemplified by a failure to take care of the poor and marginalized) and sloth are particularly problematic.

Interpreters of sacred Jewish texts in the ancient world, including New Testament authors, had an irrepressible belief—sometimes explicit, sometimes implicit[18]—that Scripture could speak directly to their audiences (again, see 2 Tim 3:16-17). "Despite the great variety of motives and methods evinced in this vast body of material, one principle seems to underlie the practical results of the interpretive activity of this period. These interpreters shared a general attitude: biblical interpretation meant bringing the Scriptures to bear on their present circumstances."[19] James Kugel observes, "It was precisely the inter-

---

[17]"Because examples are personal, they possess an element of concrete reality that is missing from instructions, which, despite their specificity, are still unrealized theory." Examples are "things within the realm of human experience and possibility." "Examples provide a pattern to follow and a person to emulate; in so doing, they define duties and invite action." Jeff Dryden, *Theology and Ethics in 1 Peter: Paraenetic Strategies for Christian Character Formation* (Tübingen: Mohr Siebeck, 2006), p. 164. Versions of this practice can be found throughout church history. Kevin Vanhoozer, *The Drama of Doctrine: A Canonical-Linguistic Approach to Christian Theology* (Louisville, KY: Westminster John Knox, 2005), p. 430, cites Brad Gregory, *Salvation at Stake* (Cambridge, MA: Harvard University Press, 1999), p. 121: "Sixteenth century martyrs were encouraged to identify with specific biblical martyrs after the particular form of their execution (e.g., Jonah for drowning, Stephen for stoning, John the Baptist for beheading, Daniel's three friends for burning)."

[18]Craig Evans cites the implicit use of Scripture in this fashion, "The Genesis Apocryphon and the Rewritten Bible," *Revue de Qumran* 13 (1988): 161-66.

[19]Peter Enns, "Biblical Interpretation, Jewish," in *Dictionary of New Testament Background*, ed. Craig A. Evans and Stanley E. Porter (Downers Grove, IL: InterVarsity Press, 2000), p. 162.

mittent obsession with past events and the necessity of having them bear on the present that gave interpretation of all kinds its urgency." The one constant in all forms of biblical interpretation is "the belief that sacred texts have a bearing on the present."[20] Such scholarly observations on the basic nature of the use of Scripture could be multiplied many times over.[21] Thus, one of the "fundamental assumptions that characterize all ancient biblical interpretation," including the interpretation done by New Testament authors, was that biblical texts were written down in order to be "*relevant*."[22] The belief in Scripture's applicability opened doors to all manner of use of Scripture, not all of it followed by New Testament authors and other early Christians.

New Testament writers learned to create patterns in part from their reliance on the Old Testament. Psalm 78 summarizes Israel's history, recalling the tendency of Israel to rebel and God's pattern of judging and trimming his people. The lengthy song serves as a warning for those who would flaunt grace and election as the Israelites tended to do: their paradigm was not to be imitated.[23]

---

[20]James Kugel and Rowan Greer, *Early Biblical Interpretation* (Philadelphia: Westminster, 1986), p. 38.

[21]Howard Clark Kee, "Appropriating the History of Israel: A Survey of Interpretations of the History of God's People," in *The Pseudepigrapha and Early Biblical Interpretation*, ed. J. Charlesworth and C. Evans (Sheffield, UK: JSOT Press, 1993), p. 64; Willard Swartley, "Intertextuality," *Dictionary of the Later New Testament and Its Developments*, ed. R. P. Martin and P. H. Davids (Downers Grove, IL: InterVarsity Press, 1997), p. 536; Joachim Jeska, *Die Geschichte Israels in der Sicht des Lukas*, vol. 195, Forschungen zur Religion und Literatur des Alten und Neuen Testaments (Göttingen, Germany: Vandenhoeck & Ruprecht, 2001), p. 19; Jacob Neusner, *Judaism When Christianity Began: A Survey of Belief and Practice* (Louisville: Westminster John Knox, 2002), pp. 186-87.

[22]James Kugel, *Traditions of the Bible: A Guide to the Bible as It Was at the Start of the Common Era* (Cambridge, MA: Harvard University Press, 1998), p. 15, emphasis original; repeated with emphasis on p. 16; also emphasized in the parallel material in *The Bible as It Was* (Cambridge, MA: Harvard University Press, 1997), p. 19.

[23]On ethical instruction in summaries of Israel's story such as Deut 32, Neh 9, Ps 78 and Acts 7, see Brian Rosner, "'Written for Us': Paul's View of Scripture," in *A Pathway into the Holy Scripture*, ed. P Satterthwaite and D. F. Wright (Grand Rapids: Eerdmans, 1994), p. 98. Against postmodern emphases on the ambiguity of characters in literature, when characters are put to use for moral instruction, the result is not ambiguity but clarity via repetition, as Rosner notes (1 Chron 1–9; Ps 106:30-31; Heb 11; Acts 7). Biblical authors have no obligation to point out how sinful these characters are at every turn. Characters can be mentioned as examples without giving the full picture. Authors are not being deceptive or ignorant in such characterization, for no one can say everything.

OBJECTIONS AND OBSTACLES

In contemporary discussion these presuppositions are not uncontroversial.[24] Attempts to find Jesus in the Old Testament have commonly been ridiculed and ignored. More recently, the practice of using characters for moral instruction is often downplayed or even rejected by scholars and pastors. Homiletics scholar Sidney Greidanus has charted this opposition.[25] Although writing as an evangelical, Greidanus also cites recent interpreters outside evangelicalism, a helpful reminder that the debate over the use of characters as examples is not a liberal-versus-conservative issue. Donald Gowan, Ernest Best and Karl Barth are all cited as purveyors of an explicitly Christocentric (as opposed to theocentric or anthropocentric) approach to preaching and interpretation.[26] Leander Keck challenges the notion that the historical-cultural gap between Scripture and contemporary audiences should be bridged by moralizing, "drawing moral inferences, usually things to do or become."[27] William Willimon states that such moralizing is "perhaps the most frequent modern interpretive pitfall" into which interpreters stumble as a result of their desire to "be relevant."[28]

Greidanus denigrates "biographical preaching, character preaching and the use of human 'examples' for imitation."[29] "Imitating Bible characters, though popular and superficially easy, is a dead-end road

---

[24]The following analysis derives from an earlier article, Jason B. Hood, "Christ-Centered Interpretation Only? Moral Interpretation as a Caveat and Guide," *Scottish Bulletin of Evangelical Theology* 27, no. 1 (2009): 50-69, and appears here with permission from the editors.

[25]Greidanus originally explored interpretive method in an extensive study of a major debate over the content of preaching in the Dutch Reformed Church in the 1920s and 1930s. Sidney Greidanus, *Sola Scriptura: Problems and Principles in Preaching Historical Texts* (Toronto: Wedge, 1970). More recently he has articulated and defended the practice of Christ-centered preaching; Sidney Greidanus, *Preaching Christ from the Old Testament* (Grand Rapids: Eerdmans, 1999), and most recently *Preaching Christ from Genesis: Foundations for Expository Sermons* (Grand Rapids: Eerdmans, 2007).

[26]Sidney Greidanus, *The Modern Preacher and the Ancient Text: Interpreting and Preaching Biblical Literature* (Grand Rapids: Eerdmans, 1988), p. 117. For Barth, see especially *Homiletics* and *Church Dogmatics* 1.2.

[27]Leander Keck, *The Bible in the Pulpit: The Renewal of Biblical Preaching* (Nashville: Abingdon, 1978) p. 101, cited by Greidanus, *Modern Preacher*, p. 163.

[28]William H. Willimon, *Preaching and Leading Worship* (Philadelphia: Westminster, 1984), p. 71, cited by Greidanus, *Modern Preacher*, p. 164. See also pp. 178-79 in the latter text.

[29]Greidanus, *Modern Preacher*, pp. 117, 163.

for true biblical preaching," he says.[30] He cites scholarly heavyweights from across the theological spectrum, including Martin Noth: "A legitimate 're-presentation' cannot use the individual human figures of biblical history as its subjects, either as ethical 'models', which in fact they never are, or as exemplary 'heroes of faith' since in the biblical narratives they are never so presented." Characters are not present, Noth and Greidanus contend, to "be imitated."[31] Other scholars are similarly forceful, including John Goldingay: "To concentrate on the human deed" as opposed to the divine act, which more often than not works despite human effort not through it, "is often to miss the point" of the text. "Indeed, it is not merely to misuse it: it is to bring a message that is its opposite."[32]

These scholars, working within movements that insist on redemptive-historical or theological interpretation, have worked for years to overturn both the resistance to Christian interpretation of the Old Testament in the guild and the glut of legalist sermons in our churches. To cite but one vital observation, for the purpose of Christian interpretation, the context of a passage is not just the biblical book in which the passage is located or the paragraphs surrounding it, but the whole of Scripture. I am sympathetic to these efforts and have learned much from them myself.

But in some instances these efforts lead practitioners to downplay moral aspects of interpretation. Goldsworthy believes that many such approaches to the text too often substitute for "more fundamental aspects of biblical teaching. Paradoxically, they may even lead us away from the basic foundations of the gospel." If characters become examples, such as "what response Elijah made to the threats of Jezebel, or where Saul showed chinks in his moral armour, as examples to avoid or follow, then we have reduced the significance of these people to the lowest common denominator."[33] Goldsworthy elsewhere allows

[30]Ibid., p. 163. Greidanus references his *Sola Scriptura*, pp. 56-120.
[31]Greidanus, *Modern Preacher*, p. 163, citing M. Noth, "'Re-presentation' of the Old Testament in Proclamation," in *Essays on Old Testament Hermeneutics*, ed. C. Westermann (Richmond, VA: John Knox, 1962), p. 86.
[32]J. Goldingay, *Models for Interpretation of Scripture* (Grand Rapids: Eerdmans, 1995), p. 39.
[33]Graeme Goldsworthy, *Gospel and Kingdom* (Exeter, UK: Paternoster, 1981), p. 25.

that characters can sometimes serve as examples and cites the New Testament's example. But it is difficult to grasp how a preacher or lay person could not have the wind utterly taken out of his or her sails by Goldsworthy's cautions, or at least walk away very confused about how we are to use characters. Who wants to engage in an interpretive practice that undermines "the foundations of the gospel" or distracts from "more fundamental aspects of biblical teaching"? Who wants to spend any time at all on topics representing a "lowest common denominator" approach to Scripture?

Like Noth, Michael Horton so wants his readers to focus on Christ instead of imitation that he encourages an emphasis on the wickedness of characters, running them through Romans 3. This is an important aspect of Christian interpretation, but it is not the only way in which the New Testament uses characters (indeed, a majority of references are not concerned to show "all have sinned"). To fit the biblical data to his interpretation, Horton tries to downplay this emphasis in his interpretation of the more famous passages illustrating the use of characters as examples: "The so-called 'Hall of Heroes' in Hebrews 11 is misnamed. The writer consistently mentions that they overcame by faith in Christ, not by their works."[34] But faith is never pitted against works. Rather, Abraham and Rahab (to take two) are commendable because they had the sort of faith that worked. Their appearance in Hebrews parallels their appearance in James, where they are commended neither simply for what they believed, nor for what they did apart from faith, but for what was done on the basis of belief (Jas 2:14-16), since faith without works is worthless. Contra Horton, the heroes are held out as examples precisely because they acted in obedience and faithfulness on the basis of God's character and in response to his promises and commands. These characters overcame and persevered by faith and by works.

---

[34]Michael Horton, *Christless Christianity: The Alternative Gospel of the American Church* (Grand Rapids: Baker, 2008), pp. 149-50. He adds on pp. 142-43, "The Old Testament saints were not heroes of faith and obedience but sinners who, despite their own wavering, were given the faith to cling to God's promise." Faith is a gift, but Horton's approach veers in the direction of a monergistic approach to interpretation, where God's work is all that counts and human work is downplayed, irrelevant or entirely negative.

We can contrast the biblical emphasis on finding Jesus and examples within Scripture with Horton's puzzling comments that appear to limit the imitation of Old Testament characters to mere belief in Jesus and God's promises. "[Abraham's] willingness to sacrifice Isaac was not an example for us, but was an occasion for God to foreshadow Christ as the ram caught in the thicket so that Isaac—and the rest of us—could go free."[35] Horton sets up a false dichotomy between two approaches to interpretation: the passage either points to Christ, or the passage shows us a faithful model. But what if the New Testament takes Genesis 22 in both directions? Should we not follow the New Testament's approach? We certainly do not imitate Abraham by sacrificing our children. But as we have seen, imitation is not rote, indiscriminate mimicry, but "creative imitation" informed by Scripture.[36] The New Testament authors use Abraham as a model of faith and obedience (not least in Gen 18:17-19; 22:1-24; Heb 11:17; Jas 2:14-26). Abraham does not merely believe. Trusting God to raise the dead, he acts in obedience (Heb 11:19).[37] What's more, Abraham's obedience is crucial to the original meaning of the text, given the role that it plays in describing the covenant relationship between himself and God (Gen 22:1, 16-17).

These scholars are not tilting at windmills. There has been, and still is, a crisis in contemporary preaching of moralistic sermons and church-based education for children and adults that present characters—and even Jesus—merely as behavioral models. I am grateful for the recovery of God-centered, Christ-centered, gospel-centered

---

[35]Ibid., p. 149.

[36]Vanhoozer, *Drama of Doctrine*, and Jimmy Agan, "Toward a Hermeneutic of Imitation: The Imitation of Christ in the *Didascalia Apostolorum*," *Presbyterion* 37 (2011): 42-43.

[37]Michael Allen, "Imitating Jesus," *Modern Reformation* 18, no. 2 (2009): 27-30, correctly sees that in Heb 11, saints from Abel to Jesus have their obedience "described in multiple ways. They are to be imitated as those whose belief impelled radical obedience (11:6)." Both Horton and his Westminster Seminary California colleague S. M. Baugh deny that characters in Heb 11 function as exemplars in any respect save for faith in a saving God; see Baugh, "The Cloud of Witnesses in Hebrews 11," *Westminster Theological Journal* 68, no. 1 (2002): 132. Contrast Calvin on Hebrews 11, *Epistle of Paul the Apostle to the Hebrews*, trans. William B. Johnston (Grand Rapids: Eerdmans, 1963), p. 187. I owe the Baugh and Calvin references and analysis to R. Michael Allen, *The Christ's Faith: A Dogmatic Account* (New York: T & T Clark, 2009), p. 324 n. 794, who identifies Baugh's argument as a "reductionistic" account that "creates fissures where none need exist."

and canonwide emphases in interpretation. Many of the solutions modeled by Goldsworthy, Greidanus and others are vitally important for the recovery of healthy interpretation and preaching. I hasten to note that scholars are fighting a commendable uphill battle in placing Jesus on the map of Old Testament interpretation at all. Goldsworthy, Horton, Willimon and others have placed grace back into the landscape of contemporary preaching, playing an invaluable role in overturning the "gospel amnesia" in twentieth century moralistic and legalistic preaching. I cannot stress too much the degree of sympathy I have for such efforts.

Yet it is possible to cast a vision that does not exclude or marginalize important aspects of biblical interpretation and preaching. Consider the story of David and Goliath, which, some would say, should not be used as a source for the moral instruction of believers. I have taught this passage a number of times. I always bring out the Christ typology in David's work as a messianic conqueror who defeats invincible enemies, particularly the greater enemies of sin and death. But I do not think this is the only thing to be learned from the text. Believers should learn from David's confidence in God and God's victory and the way in which that confidence enabled him to act when all around him were paralyzed. Like David, we fight because God has secured the victory. Just as other Israelites were inspired by David's victory and proceeded to win a great victory in that light (1 Sam 17:51-54), New Testament writers teach that those who have been liberated by Christ's victory will conquer as God himself works through them: "The God of peace will shortly crush Satan under your feet" (Rom 16:20; see also Rev 2–3; 15:2). Paul, using the plural "your feet," puts Christ followers into action in the battle of the ages (Gen 3:15). We imitate the greater victories of both David and his greater Son.

CONCLUSION

For the New Testament writers, the Old Testament characters stood in the text ready to affirm or challenge contemporary believers. Abel's sacrifice by faith still speaks. Jesus' sacrifice is greater than Abel's and remains our supreme sacrifice. But because the Christian life requires sacrifice (Heb 13), holiness and faithfulness in the face of shame and trials (Heb 11–12), believers need all the examples we can get. Failing to see that the faith and obedience of Old Testament characters can be imitated robs new covenant disciples of important instruments in Christian sanctification. The Old Testament is a tool chest full of resources, and faithful interpreters should learn to use them all.

If we overlook the Bible's presuppositions for interpretation, we contribute to a reluctance to use Old Testament characters or we use characters as models in unhealthy ways. A commitment to reading the Bible like the ancients requires a commitment to share their web of presuppositions. Peter Leithart aptly summarizes the contemporary dilemma in the reluctant right and muddled middle, respectively.

> If the Bible is about Christ, some preachers and interpreters conclude, then any direct application of Scripture to the life of the believer introduces works and threatens to collapse into moralism. Other preachers insist that the Bible be made practical, so that the stories of David are read not as foreshadowings of Christ but as stories that teach us courage, faith, and tricks for dealing with oppressive fathers-in-law and kings. The first has the head, the second has the body. Neither has the whole Christ.[38]

---

[38]Peter Leithart, *Deep Exegesis: The Mystery of Reading Scripture* (Waco, TX: Baylor University Press, 2009), p. 174.

PART FOUR

Imitation
Yesterday and Today

Imitation for Today's Left, Right and Center

Our sufferings are consistently set in the context of Christ's sufferings;
Christ's sufferings placed insistently alongside ours.

EUGENE PETERSON

The imitation of God, Jesus and the saints is prevalent in the Bible. But on the left, center and right side of contemporary Christianity, a biblical approach to the imitation of Jesus and the saints is often nowhere to be found. We briefly discussed these three spheres in the introduction. In this chapter, we return to these contemporary approaches to imitation and attempt to summarize the message of this book for the three different audiences.

A LATITUDINAL LEFT

For more than two centuries the imitation of Jesus has been a favorite "kernel" for post-orthodox theologians interested in jettisoning the indigestible, inconvenient, unpalatable "husk" of orthodox Christianity, such as supernaturalism, exclusive claims and stringent sexual ethics.[1] Several notable historical characters exemplify this approach, including Thomas Jefferson and UN secretary general and Nobel

---

[1]Notable examples include Friedrich Schleiermacher and Adolf von Harnack.

Peace Prize winner Dag Hammarskjöld. Mahatma Gandhi famously used the imitation of Jesus' nonviolence without adopting the religious beliefs on which it is grounded.

Writing recently at popular and academic levels, authors like Brian McLaren, Jay Bakker, Gary Wills and Richard Burridge employ imitation and downplay or dismiss some orthodox teachings. They point out crucial (and sometimes overlooked) aspects of Christian praxis modeled by Jesus, such as his radical embrace of sinners. Yet in their writings, the imitation of Jesus is at times no longer a countercultural activity but a tool for charting a path away from the imitation of biblical religion. These authors sometimes imitate cultural norms in areas such as sexuality, exiting the death-inducing journey that is foolishness to the world (1 Cor 1:20-31; 3:18-19; 4:10).

As we have seen, the imitation of Jesus does not arise *de nouveau* in the New Testament. It is rooted in the Old Testament, which describes humanity as God's image-bearers and imitators. In both testaments God requires that the people who bear his name and receive his redemption share his character: "Be holy as I am holy." Paul neatly summarizes the task of sanctification by linking the imitation of Jesus to the pursuit of the likeness of God: Christian discipleship is the work of growing into "the full stature of Christ" (Eph 4:13), putting on "the new self [Christ], created according to the likeness of God in true righteousness and holiness" (Eph 4:24). If the imitation of Jesus involves the imitation of divine righteousness and holiness, it cannot be used to push past biblical moral instruction that contemporary persons find difficult.

In some versions of left-leaning Christianity there is a long tradition of downplaying traditional theological commitments in favor of ethics. But this approach fails to follow the New Testament habit of relying on theological facts to inform ethics. Jesus' work on the cross as ransom and sin bearer (Mk 10:31-45; 1 Pet 2:21-24); his resurrection, which ushers in new life and new reality (Rom 6); and his pre-existence and incarnation (Phil 2) are not optional or incidental pillars for a life of sacrificial Christian love. Rather, they are foundational.[2]

[2]See John Webster, "The Imitation of Christ," *Tyndale Bulletin* 37 (1986): 111; Jason Hood, "The Cross in the New Testament: Two Theses in Conversation with Recent Studies (2000-2007),"

A MUDDLED MIDDLE

Imitation is common in discipleship and preaching across the evangelical spectrum: megachurches, seeker-sensitives, fundamentalists, Pentecostals, evangelical social activists and the evangelical sectors of mainline denominations freely use the imitation of Jesus and biblical characters. But just as the horde of music stations in my city proves that ubiquity does not guarantee quality, the omnipresence of imitation in evangelicalism does not always ensure that the contemporary emphasis on imitation is helpful.

No doubt there are many in the muddled middle striking a helpful balance in their use of Scripture. But critics from the Reformed right and radical left point with ease to the poor nature of much contemporary preaching and discipleship, not least when it features imitation. It is not hard to find pulpits mired in moralism and congregations whose ministries seem to focus largely if not entirely on what those churches are doing for God, with a near-total loss of the proclamation of what God has done, is doing and will do in the Messiah. Critics rightly pan the all-too-common failure to feature any sort of gospel motive for imitating Jesus and the saints. WWJD-oriented kitsch and an emphasis on practical application can eclipse redemption. We see Nehemiah mined within an inch of its life for leadership principles or an inspired diet ripped out of Daniel 1.[3] In contrast, Paul's description of his own Jesus imitation often sounds impractical. His imitation of Jesus produced scars (Gal 6:17) and chains, not wristbands.

Imitation in evangelical circles often dies the death of a thousand trivializations. It is typically neither as robust nor as challenging as the Bible's message, and it is frequently presented in isolation from a gospel foundation for motivation. Without gospel motivation—a steady diet of God's work for us rather than our work for him—imitation is an exercise in bankruptcy. On the other hand, despite the difficulties and dangers, there is something profoundly right about

---

Westminster Theological Journal 71, no. 2 (2009): 281-95.
[3]Nehemiah certainly does teach us things about leadership. I am referring to the hermeneutical tendency to invest in vastly inflated analogical allegories.

efforts to put imitation into play in the church, including the effort to make imitation practical (Eph 5:25; 2 Cor 8:9; Heb 13:2). In other instances, the imitation of Jesus is applied only in extreme fashion—going to the ends of the earth to evangelize or fight human trafficking; Paul addresses mundane areas such as selfishness in marriage (Eph 5).

When the uniqueness of Jesus is recognized and celebrated, writers and preachers in "the middle" note difficulties: for instance, that we are not at present able to imitate him perfectly.[4] This difficulty can result in a crippling stalemate, with imitation left stranded in no man's land. Essential tasks—and imitation is certainly essential—are often difficult, but that does not make them unimportant. If one encounters trivial or misleading gospel presentations, it is a major mistake to downplay evangelism altogether. So with imitation: faced with shortcomings and errors in the muddled middle of evangelicalism, a pastor should not conclude that imitation is a dead end.

A RELUCTANT OR RESISTANT RIGHT

A third phenomenon, chiefly arising in the "Reformation Nation" in which I was trained (and which I call home), is a backlash against the other two camps. If Paul says that he teaches something "everywhere in every church," one would think that the contemporary Reformed community claiming Paul's mantle would be familiar with this teaching, unleashing it without reluctance "everywhere in every church." But caution, concern and objections from Reformed voices can sometimes leave young pastors and laity with the impression that imitation is relatively unimportant for investigation and instruction. If imitation is mentioned at all, a protective wall of caveats is immediately erected to guard against semi-Pelagianism, moralism and bootstrap religion.[5]

Such caveats can be helpful, but it is notable that New Testament

---

[4]N. T. Wright simultaneously addresses and exemplifies the problem when he identifies following Jesus as a key discipleship concept, stresses Jesus' uniqueness, and hedges on imitation rather than embracing it, in *After You Believe: Why Christian Character Matters* (New York: HarperOne, 2010), pp. 14-16, 126-27.

[5]Michael Allen, *The Christ's Faith*, pp. 317-18 nn. 780-82, charts some of the unease and its impact, then builds a case for imitation within a Reformed framework.

authors do not feel the need to erect such walls every time they employ imitation. The previous chapter charted discomfort with the imitation of biblical characters (and for good reason), and there is also in Reformed circles some reluctance to focus on the imitation of Jesus. As one Reformed New Testament scholar puts it, "The topic of the imitation of Christ—the shaping of Christian character and conduct according to patterns observed in the life of Christ—has largely been neglected among Protestant and Reformed scholars."[6]

Michael Horton exemplifies a critical or cautious approach to imitation. His target is usually not liberalism so much as the muddled middle of evangelicalism:

> Like the liberals of yesteryear, a growing number of evangelical leaders are fond of setting Jesus' teaching on the kingdom—especially the Sermon on the Mount—over against the more doctrinal emphasis found especially in Paul's epistles. Many celebrate this emphasis on Christ-as-example rather than Christ-as-Redeemer as the harbinger of a new kind of Christian, but is it really an old kind of moralist? . . .
>
> I'm not saying that these brothers and sisters are liberals but that there is no discernable difference for our witness whether we ignore or deny the message of Christ and his cross. When the focus becomes "What would Jesus do?" instead of "What has Jesus done?" the labels no long matter.[7]

As I have noted, there is certainly much that needs correction in the moralistic, me-centered, muddled middle. Horton's laudable efforts to exalt the unique work of Jesus in redeeming unworthy sinners are an important contribution, and I share many of his concerns. While Horton knows that imitation is part of New Testament Christianity, one part of his solution to the contemporary crisis seems to be downplaying imitation because of the abuses or misguided approaches in the left and the middle. One finds far more hesitation than affirmation (indeed, almost nothing positive) on the imitation of

---

[6]Jimmy Agan, "Toward a Hermeneutic of Imitation: The Imitation of Christ in the *Didascalia Apostolorum*," *Presbyterion* 37 (2011): 31. I have charted the lack of interest in Hood, "Cross in the New Testament."

[7]Michael Horton, *Christless Christianity: The Alternative Gospel of the American Church* (Grand Rapids: Baker, 2008), pp. 25-26.

Jesus in his recent books and in an essay titled "Following Jesus: What's Wrong and Right About the Imitation of Christ." He states, "With the exception of a few important passages in which we are told to follow Christ's example of suffering love on behalf of others, the New Testament makes it clear that Jesus is unique in every way." Horton's readers are left with the impression that imitation in Scripture is only found in a "few important passages," and that it is an "exception" to Jesus' uniqueness, a more central aspect of Christianity.[8]

If imitation is ignored, affirmed only on rare occasion, or always accompanied by heaps of reservations and cautions, a posture of suspicion and reticence toward imitation becomes the order of the day. Significant numbers of young pastors and laity have been exposed only to a cautious or critical approach to imitation—if they are familiar with the theme at all. Some even abandon it entirely (either formally or practically) in favor of more palatable concepts. Some propose that conformity is helpful and biblical imitation is not, because conformity implies God's work and passive transformation.[9] But this approach reflects the assumption that God might not be working in the pursuit of sanctification—and as we have seen, Paul assumes that God's Spirit is at work in believers as they work.

Such skepticism produces an atmosphere in which criticism is levied at healthy biblical interpretation. Horton would prefer that we focus on our imperfection and God's work for us rather than on our work for God. But our imperfection makes focusing on both God's work for us and our task of imitation more necessary, not less so. We have been given the Holy Spirit so that we will properly respond to calls to imitate, not that we will regard such teaching as secondary or unnecessary.

The trickle-down effect of a less-than-positive approach to imitation appears in the popular best-selling text for children by Sally

---

[8]Ibid., p. 106.

[9]Contrast Kevin Vanhoozer, *The Drama of Doctrine: A Canonical-Linguistic Approach to Christian Theology* (Louisville, KY: Westminster John Knox, 2005); and Michael Allen, "Imitating Jesus," *Modern Reformation* 18, no. 2 (2009): 27-30. Allen charts and critiques opposition to imitation in *The Christ's Faith*, pp. 337-40. As we noted earlier, conformity and imitation are overlapping concepts.

Lloyd-Jones, *The Jesus Storybook Bible*.[10] Influenced by the Reformed backlash against a moralistic muddle, the author radically departs from previous generations of children's Bible story books, which often focused solely on deriving messages of virtue or morality from biblical stories. Lloyd-Jones casts the stories so that redemption in Jesus is essentially the sum of what every story is intended to say.

I gratefully use this book with my children; we appreciate the focus on Jesus in the Old Testament as well as the way in which fuller aspects of biblical salvation such as the promise of new creation appear. It is refreshing to find a text capable of helping my children see how "every story whispers his name." But we have seen that finding Jesus in an Old Testament passage may make the characters more useful as positive or negative examples, not less so. If we find Jesus in the compassion, fidelity and courage displayed by Boaz and Ruth, should we not conclude that we are to act with compassion, fidelity and courage?

In light of the contemporary conundrum, perhaps church history could come to our aid. In the following chapter, we'll see that imitation has played a major role in the church throughout the centuries, and while we will barely scratch the surface in the glimpse that follows, the sample will indicate the richness of the endless meals on offer—and the possibility of food poisoning along the way.

CONTEMPORARY CULTURE

Contemporary Western people enjoy celebrating their independence and uniqueness. Peer pressure famously afflicts adolescents, but it doesn't go away after, say, high school or college graduation. We are enmeshed and constrained by the world we live in, which provides plausibility structures and opens up new ways of viewing the world and new ways of acting. We mimic models and adopt patterns (often without conscious effort or knowledge), repeatedly proving that we are profoundly influenced by others. Our habits of consumption, speech and thought are formed by playgrounds and malls, office com-

---

[10]*The Jesus Storybook Bible: Every Story Whispers His Name* (Grand Rapids: Zondervan, 2007).

plexes and nightclubs. Fashion, mindsets and habits are crafted by subtle and overt examples in urban, suburban and rural settings. Few of us try sushi, social media or facial hairstyles unless we are introduced to them by a flesh-and-blood model. Humans do not learn to speak, read, write, tie shoes or perform a vocation without steady doses of imitation.

Fields of study ranging from neurology to sociology tell us that imitation is an essential and inextricable part of human life. Imitation remains a fundamental aspect of human reality when one becomes a believer in Jesus. The question is not whether we will imitate, but who and to what end. As a result, the failure to attend to the imitation of Jesus and the godly is catastrophic. The loss of imitation is the loss of a vital resource for combating theological heresies and destructive practices. To cite but one, the prosperity or health-and-wealth gospel is probably North America's greatest theological export. In the global church it is arguably the greatest threat to Christian faithfulness. Crusades against health-and-wealth distortions of Christianity sometimes miss the opportunity to bring Scripture's greatest offensive weapon against such teachings: the sacrificial imitation of Jesus and the saints.[11] The global challenge presented by materialism and a theology of glory and comfort are nothing new. Paul, Chrysostom, Augustine, Luther, Calvin, Wesley, Bonhoeffer and many others dealt with similar crises by putting to use the imitation of Jesus, biblical characters and faithful believers.[12] Life as a child of God looks like the cross-shaped Son, not luxury vehicles: "We are children of God, and if children, then heirs, heirs of God and joint heirs with Christ—if, in fact, we suffer with him so that we may also be glorified with him" (Rom 8:16-17).

But the good news is that the recovery of imitation can bring with it significant benefits.

---

[11]Horton rightly critiques the health-and-wealth approach as a false gospel, but to my knowledge does not bring the imitation of Jesus to bear against it.

[12]For Augustine, see J. N. D. Kelly, *Early Christian Doctrines* (San Francisco: HarperCollins, 1978), p. 396; on Luther, see John C. Clark, "Martin Luther's View of Cross-Bearing," *Bibliotheca Sacra* 163 (October-December 2006): 335-47; on Calvin, *Institutes of the Christian Religion* 2.10.11.

CONCLUSION

Biblical discipleship and a biblical approach to ministry require a robust commitment to dive into all that Scripture teaches, including imitation. New Testament authors and early church fathers were surely aware of potential problems like moralism. They certainly faced pressure to make Christianity more practical or more like the surrounding culture. Yet as we shall see in the next chapter, they did not minimize, downplay or avoid imitation in response to such threats. Nor did they use the imitation of Jesus as a vehicle for departure from orthodoxy and orthopraxy in order to accommodate the culture. A nicer-than-thou Jesus may make Christians more endearing in Europe and North America, but he may not be true to Scripture or church history. As Richard Hays puts it, "Jesus is not only friend of sinners but also prophetic nemesis of the wicked."[13]

Contractions of the New Testament message based on fear, pragmatism and theological innovation should be rejected as subbiblical betrayals of the heritage bequeathed from the apostles and (as we shall see in the next chapter) church history. Proclaiming God's perfection, holiness and redemptive work for sinners, we respond to these awesome truths by pursuing the imitation of God, the imitation of Jesus and the imitation of faithful siblings past and present.

---

[13]Richard Hays, "Response to Richard Burridge's *Imitating Jesus*," *Scottish Journal of Theology* 63, no. 3 (2010): 331-35.

15

A History of Imitation

By loving him you will be an imitator of his goodness. Don't be surprised
that a person can become his imitator. One can, if God is willing.

EPISTLE TO DIOGNETUS 10:4

I have long admired C. S. Lewis's rich portrayals of the theological
significance of human beings.

> It is a serious thing to remember that the dullest and most uninter-
> esting person you talk to may one day be a creature which, if you saw
> it now, you would be strongly tempted to worship, or else a horror and
> a corruption such as you now meet, if at all, only in a nightmare. All
> day long we are, in some degree, helping each other to one or other of
> these destinations. It is in the light of these overwhelming possibilities,
> it is with the awe and the circumspection proper to them, that we
> should conduct all our dealings with one another, all friendships, all
> loves, all play, all politics. There are no ordinary people. You have never
> talked to a mere mortal.[1]

Lewis's fiction and nonfiction works contain striking portraits of erst-
while and future glory, not least in the restoration of godlikeness and

---

[1] C. S. Lewis, *The Weight of Glory* (San Francisco: HarperSanFrancisco, 1980), pp. 45-46.

the healing of the image of God. Many modern fans almost seem to regard Lewis as *sui generis*, a theological savant whose work may inspire mere mortals but ultimately belongs to an inaccessible intellectual sphere. But while his writer's touch is truly special, I have discovered part of the equation for Lewis's theology. In fact, a major part of Lewis's secret is readily available and in the public domain. In an introduction that he wrote for Athanasius's *On the Incarnation*, Lewis invites readers to consider the value of primary sources, for it is the keys of Scripture and tradition that unlock Lewis's theological treasure chest. Familiarity with these resources led Lewis to places oft-forgotten by the contemporary church, and they can do the same for pastors, teachers and believers today.

Early in the church's history, the themes of Scripture as seen in this book are put into play: imitation begins with the God who created image-bearers to be like him. In other words, this book turns out to be not just an exercise in biblical theology but an exercise in theological retrieval, a recovery of what our great tradition believes and says. When we listen to Augustine, Athanasius, Chrysostom, Ignatius of Antioch and many others, we find that "from the first the idea of image [bearing] is linked with the idea of imitation." Thus, "the doctrine of the image is a practical doctrine."[2] The imitation of God is concentrated in Jesus, and believers are to imitate him and those who share their character.

Interest in image-bearing and imitation was based on orthodox theology and praxis. In fact, this connection contributed to the development of orthodox doctrine and was a motivation for the fight for orthodoxy. "For Athanasius, as for many other Christians, the whole point of God becoming human was that we might be reformed into likeness to God, so that we might become images of God and imitators of Christ."[3] Unlike the use of imitation by theological revisionists, the

[2]Augustine, *On the Trinity* 7.3.5, ed. J. Rotelle and trans. Edmund Hill (Hyde Park, NY: New City, 1991), p. 225 n. 23.
[3]Imitation and image-bearing were part of Athanasius's motivation for defending *homoousisos*. Graham Tomlin, *Spiritual Fitness: Christian Character in a Consumer Society* (London: Continuum, 2006), pp. 108-10, who concludes his summary of Athanasius, trinitarian and christological doctrine, and Christian formation with this line (p. 110). He cites Rowan Williams,

imitation of Jesus is never used as a tool for avoiding difficult aspects of biblical religion or orthodox doctrine. Instead, the imitation of Jesus helped the early church bravely face consequences like death, ridicule and deprivation when they did not join pagans in their worship or sexual practices.

In this chapter, we will buttress the exploration of imitation in the Bible by considering the significance of imitation in church history. From the *Epistle to Diognetus* to Augustine, from Clement of Rome to Calvin, the imitation themes present in this book appear with some frequency. Such writers helped shape Lewis's approach to humanity and discipleship. To cite but one example:

> Our imitation of God in this life . . . must be an imitation of God incarnate: our model is the Jesus, not only of Calvary, but of the workshop, the roads, the crowds, the clamorous demands and surly oppositions, the lack of all peace and privacy, the interruptions. For this, so strangely unlike anything we can attribute to the Divine life in itself, is apparently not only like, but is, the Divine life operating under human conditions.[4]

From the Fathers and the Scriptures Lewis learned that doctrines like the incarnation and the creation of humans in the image of God are tightly bound to the imitation of God. And the Fathers regarded the imitation of Jesus as the pinnacle of religious practice. They regularly employed the imitation of saints past and present as a vital tool for discipleship. These three forms of imitation laid the groundwork for Christian mission.

For those on the left, the middle or the right of the contemporary church, the testimony of church history is an invitation to recalibrate our approach to imitation. Historical figures are fallible sources, not least when it comes to imitation. But too often the contemporary evangelical approach has been to reject the bad—and reject the good. At their best, however, these figures reflect the Bible's own emphases and provide a guide for the church's use of imitation.

Arius: Heresy and Tradition (London: Darton Longman and Todd, 1987), p. 240, and Alvyn Pettersen, *Athanasius*, Outstanding Christian Thinkers (London: Geoffrey Chapman, 1995), pp. 80-82.
[4]C. S. Lewis, *The Four Loves* (San Diego: Harvest, 1960), p. 6.

THE FATHERS, THE GOSPEL AND IMITATION

Evangelical ignorance of the church fathers is well documented.[5]
When modern-day evangelicals do address the Fathers, one common
point of criticism is the emphasis on morality found in their writings.
One can certainly find an unhelpful emphasis on imitating roles reserved for Jesus alone.[6] Greidanus critiques "anthropocentric interpretation" and moralism in church history, attributing an early moralizing "slide" to Clement of Rome and his use of Old Testament
characters as exemplars.[7] Blame for Clement is also found in Goldsworthy, who decries in early Christianity the "concentration on the
exemplary and ethical Christ, rather than on the substitutionary and
redemptive Christ."[8]

But whatever the flaws of the Fathers, Clement is not guilty of works
righteousness. Note the gospel context he creates for Old Testament
characters: "All [the Old Testament saints] therefore were glorified and
magnified, not through themselves or their own works or the righteous
actions that they did, but through His will. And so we, having been
called through His will in Christ Jesus, are not justified through ourselves or through our own wisdom or understanding or piety, or works
that we have done in holiness of heart, but through faith, by which the
Almighty God has justified all who have existed from the beginning."[9]

---

[5]See Michael Haykin, *Rediscovering the Church Fathers: Who They Were and How They Shaped
the Church* (Wheaton, IL: Crossway, 2011); Bryan Litfin, *Getting to Know the Church Fathers:
An Evangelical Introduction* (Grand Rapids: Brazos, 2007), pp. 11-17; and note D. H. William's subtitle, *Retrieving the Tradition and Renewing Evangelicalism: A Primer for Suspicious
Protestants* (Grand Rapids: Eerdmans, 1999).
[6]See also Perpetua's role as mediator, *The Martyrdom of Perpetua and Felicitas* 7-8.
[7]S. Greidanus, *The Modern Preacher and the Ancient Text: Interpreting and Preaching Biblical
Literature* (Grand Rapids: Eerdmans, 1988), p. 116; R. Scott Clark adds a historian's nuance
to his concerns, citing various social and theological factors that, he contends, contributed
to a loss of pure gospel presentation (he contrasts 1 Cor 1-2) in the early church fathers:
"Letter and Spirit: Law and Gospel in Reformed Preaching," in *Covenant, Justification, and
Pastoral Ministry: Essays by the Faculty of Westminster Seminary California*, ed. R. Scott Clark
(Phillipsburg, NJ: P&R, 2006), pp. 331-63, especially 333-37. For similar charges from a
very different perspective (Adolf von Harnack and others) and an important response, see
Michael Green, *Evangelism in the Early Church*, rev. ed. (Grand Rapids: Eerdmans, 2003),
pp. 188-205.
[8]Graeme Goldsworthy, *Gospel-Centered Hermeneutics: Foundations and Principles of Evangelical
Biblical Interpretation* (Downers Grove, IL: InterVarsity Press, 2007), pp. 92-93. See especially 1 *Clement* 4:1–12:8 for the offending passages.
[9]1 *Clement* 32:3-4.

A few decades after Clement wrote, Justin Martyr described a typical church service in the middle of the second century. Moral instruction and imitation feature prominently: "On the day called Sunday, all who live in cities or in the country gather together in one place, and the memoirs of the apostles and the writings of the prophets are read, as long as time permits. Then, when the reader has finished, the president speaks, instructing and exhorting the people to imitate these good things."[10] Given that such services also included liturgy, Eucharist, songs and rudimentary confessions—almost all of which contained gospel content—it is difficult to levy the charge that there is no gospel context for the sermon described by Justin.

In fact, there is often in the Fathers an emphasis on gospel and theological grounding that is absent in contemporary uses of imitation. While there are shifts in emphasis from the New Testament to the Fathers, the use of Jesus and biblical characters for moral instruction is already prominent in the New Testament and early Jewish interpretation. In light of the Bible's use of characters for moral instruction, it is difficult to make the case that Clement has fallen from the heights of a purely Christ-centered interpretation of the Old Testament from the apostolic era.[11] Moreover, Christ-centered interpretation (some of it allegorical and strained, some of it healthy and invaluable) can be found in the Fathers, proving that gospel-centered interpretation can sit in harmony with the use of characters as positive or negative examples, as seen in 1 Corinthians 10:1-11.[12]

Horton reminds those in the middle and the left that "the early Christians were not fed to wild beasts or dipped in wax and set ablaze as lamps in Nero's garden because they thought Jesus was a helpful life coach or role model but because they witnessed to him as the

[10]*First Apology* 67, trans. A. W. Blunt, Cambridge Patristic Texts (Cambridge: Cambridge University Press, 1911).

[11]Nor can interest in characters as exemplars among early Jewish and Christian authors be attributed to Hellenization, according to Michael Crosby, *Rhetorical Composition and Function of Hebrews 11 in Light of Example Lists in Antiquity* (Macon, GA: Mercer University Press, 1988), p. 109.

[12]See especially *Epistle to Diognetus* 9-10. David Aune, "Justin Martyr's Use of the Old Testament," *Bulletin of the Evangelical Theological Society* 9 (1966): 179-97.

only Lord and Savior of the world."[13] Horton is right: it is Jesus as
Savior and resurrected, enthroned Lord that roused Rome's wrath
and cost our ancestors so dearly. But the apostles and the martyrs of
the first few centuries did not think that Jesus' example was incidental. When faced with the decision to "burn or turn," many of the
earliest Christians looked to the one who modeled a faithful witness
in his death, resurrection and enthronement. He was a role model in
the truest and best sense of the term, faithfully performing the role
of witness (*martyria*).

During the church's infancy, some Fathers were guilty of pursuing
imitation in a rote fashion, to the point of desiring death. As we have
seen, Jesus himself did not pursue or wish for his own death. The
imitation of Jesus was considered something of a suicide cult by some
Gnostic and Roman observers, who were appalled at the degree of
willingness—and even outright desire—to die as Jesus died as a
faithful witness. Ignatius of Antioch links the image of God and the
imitation of God, Jesus and the saints. We find these elements in the
opening salutation and first chapter of his letter to the Ephesians. His
favorite designation for himself is "Ignatius the image-bearer," a line
he uses to open his letters. In his letter to the Magnesians, he describes believers as stamped images on a coin: those who are "the
coinage of God" are believers who are "faithful in love, who bear the
stamp of God the Father through Jesus Christ, whose life is not in us
unless we voluntarily choose to die into his suffering" (5:2).[14] Ignatius
elsewhere urges the church to imitate the unity of God (*Ep* 5). Ignatius had a profound impact on other early believers' willingness to
undergo martyrdom, even leading them to pursue martyrdom fer-
vently. This gross misunderstanding of the imitation of Jesus aside, he
at least understands the restoration of image-bearing through Jesus.

In contrast with Ignatius's literal approach, a number of early writers
highlight "creative imitation" rather than precise copying. When

---

[13]Michael Horton, *The Gospel Commission: Recovering God's Strategy for Making Disciples*
(Grand Rapids: Baker, 2011), pp. 32-33.
[14]Michael W. Holmes, *The Apostolic Fathers in English*, 3rd ed. (Grand Rapids: Baker Academic, 2006), p. 104.

Clement says, "Let us be imitators also of those who went about in goatskins and sheepskins, preaching the coming of Christ" (*1 Clement* 17:1)[15], he does not mean for his audience to wear goatskins and sheepskins. Mathetes (as the author of *Diognetus* identifies himself) likewise notes that there are ways in which we do not imitate God.

As with imitation in *1 Clement*, the emphasis on imitation in the *Epistle to Diognetus* is not anti-gospel. "But one who takes up a neighbor's burden, one who wishes to benefit someone who is worse off in something in which one is oneself better off, one who provides to those in need things that one has received from God, and thus becomes a god to those who receive them—this one is an imitator of God."[16] Mathetes describes the purity of belief and action that comes from this imitation of God. The preceding paragraph in the letter contains one of the most beautiful descriptions of the gospel exchange in church history.[17] Like Paul, the author ascribes any success to God's transforming grace. This juxtaposition reminds all three spheres of Christianity that orthodox doctrine is not optional, but rather the framework imitation requires.

REFORMATION IMITATION: LUTHER AND CALVIN

Space and competency prevent a full treatment of important thinkers and influential texts such as Thomas à Kempis's *Imitation of Christ* and Bonhoeffer's *Cost of Discipleship*.[18] Calvin and Luther deserve some exploration, as their heirs have sometimes struggled to duplicate their approach to imitation.

Concerned about the eclipse of supernatural Christianity by merely ethical Christianity in the nineteenth and twentieth centuries, Alister McGrath says, "Imitation brings in its wake a whole range of ideas and attitudes that are profoundly hostile to the gospel

---

[15]Ibid., p. 50.

[16]*Epistle to Diognetus* 10.2-6; see also *Didache* 1.5.

[17]*Epistle to Diognetus* 9.

[18]For a survey, see Colothet volume; Jimmy Agan's study of imitation in 3rd century *Didascalia Apostlorum*, "hermeneutic for imitation": "Toward a Hermeneutic of Imitation: The Imitation of Christ in the *Didascalia Apostolorum*," *Presbyterion* 37 (2011): 31-48.

of grace."[19] McGrath elsewhere suggests two options, which are in his
view entirely distinct: conformity to Christ (which he attributes to
Calvin and Luther) and imitation (which he links to Thomas à
Kempis and medieval traditions), with the former accomplished
"through the process of renewal and regeneration by the Holy Spirit"
and the latter a matter of questing for an "ideal," with emphasis laid
on "human responsibility."[20] McGrath gives the impression that one
must choose either evangelical belief that relies on God's work in
sinners, or imitation. But language of conformity and imitation are
both used in the Bible and by the Reformers, and in fact go hand in
hand, particularly once one sees that the Bible rarely employs "imitate" as "copy exactly" (an approach reflected by the best interpreters
in church history and careful contemporary interpreters).

LUTHER

While Luther is more well-known in the modern church for his work
on soteriology and the sacraments, Luther's writing contains no
small amount of attention to imitation.[21] Luther's stances and emphases shifted over time in some areas, making him difficult to
systematize, and some of his rhetoric has been taken in antinomian
directions. He certainly had sharp words for those who treated Jesus
merely as a model to imitate, but I am not aware of any negative
remark by Luther on imitation as Scripture describes it.[22] Luther
shared many of the ancient presuppositions addressed earlier in this
book, and thus he saw the Old Testament saints as participants in the
Christian drama of redemption and faith, just as the New Testament
saints and later Christians did. He interprets the "women of the pa-
triarchal households" in the Old Testament as Christians, "models of

---

[19]Alister McGrath, "In What Way Can Jesus Be a Moral Example for Christians?" *Journal of the Evangelical Theological Society* 34, no. 3 (1991): 297. I owe this reference and others to Justin Borger.

[20]Alister McGrath, *Christian Theology: An Introduction*, 4th ed. (Oxford: Blackwell, 2006), p. 329; see also "In What Way Can Jesus Be a Moral Example," p. 297.

[21]See Agan, "Hermeneutic of Imitation," p. 32 n. 4.

[22]For an example of Luther's opposition to suffering as imitation as practiced by some Roman Catholic and Anabaptist opponents, see his "Sermon on Cross and Suffering, Preached at Coburg."

the virtues whose examples had the power to inspire the Christian to faithfulness."[23] Luther imitates New Testament texts such as Hebrews and James when he uses characters as examples of faith and faithfulness throughout his lectures on Genesis: "In short, the heroes and heroines of Genesis were saints, people whose heroic virtues were to be admired and imitated."[24] Perhaps Luther would affirm Gordon Wenham's summary: "In its biographical sketches, character change is what Genesis is all about."[25]

Luther's theology of the cross is justly famous. Yet "there remains a correlative aspect of the 'theology of the Cross' that attracts somewhat less attention in the secondary literature of Luther scholarship, namely, the Reformer's understanding of cross-bearing." For Luther, "just as Christians cannot bear Christ's cross, so He will not bear theirs. In other words Luther thought that to view Jesus Christ correctly is to view him as both bearer and bestower of the Cross."[26]

Luther is certainly concerned to get the order of indicative (fact and free offer of salvation) and imperative (the life God then requires) correct, so that imitation is a response: "Imitation does not make a son; sonship makes an imitator," he tells us in his commentary on Galatians.[27] Consider Luther's "Brief Instruction on What to Look for and Expect in the Gospels," which mirrors what we uncovered in the exploration of the Gospels in earlier chapters:

> The chief article and foundation of the gospel is that before you take Christ as an example, you accept and recognize him as a gift, as a present that God has given you and that is your own. . . . Now when you have Christ as the foundation and chief blessing of your salvation, then the other part follows: that you take him as your example, giving yourself in service to your neighbor just as you see that Christ has

[23]M. L. Mattox, *"Defender of the Most Holy Matriarchs": Martin Luther's Interpretation of the Women of Genesis in the* Enarrationes in Genesin (Leiden, Netherlands: Brill, 2003), p. 249. I am grateful to Doug Sweeney for this reference.
[24]Ibid., p. 252.
[25]Gordon Wenham, *Genesis 16-50*, WBC 2 (Waco, TX: Word, 1994), p. 364.
[26]John C. Clark, "Martin Luther's View of Cross-Bearing," *Bibliotheca Sacra* 163 (October-December 2006): 335-47.
[27]This is similar to another saying of Luther's: "Good works do not make a good man, but a good man does good works." *Luther's Works* 31.361.

given himself for you. . . . Christ is yours, presented to you as a gift. After that it is necessary that you turn this into an example and deal with your neighbor in the very same way, be given to him also as a gift and an example. . . . This double kindness is the twofold aspect of Christ: gift and example.[28]

CALVIN

Calvin without hesitation employs biblical characters as examples for moral instruction in his theologizing, commentating and preaching. In his study of Calvin's preaching on Job, Derek Thomas notes the way in which Calvin freely departs from a rigid requirement among many Reformed interpreters "in Old Testament interpretation and homiletics: that the text should come to Christ."[29] "Calvin, in many instances, preached entire sermons, even successive sermons, without ever seeing a need to focus on Christ as the fulfillment and scope of Scripture. Over a third of these sermons fail to mention Christ at all. Barely a fifth of the sermons find Calvin concluding his message with a christological focus. Seventeen sermons, just over a tenth, allude to passages of Scripture cited by Jesus in the Gospels. In fact, only a handful of sermons have what we might term an extensive christological focus." Calvin shares the presupposition of the biblical writers noted previously, that the text is relevant for his audience: "His concern throughout is to adhere rigidly to the text before him, applying what he finds to the needs of folk who hear him as he deems it relevant."[30]

---

[28]Martin Luther, "Brief Instruction on What to Look for and Expect in the Gospels," in *Martin Luther's Basic Theological Writings*, ed. Timothy F. Lull (Minneapolis: Fortress, 1989), pp. 106-8. I owe this reference to Justin Borger. See similarly the twofold gift in Calvin, articulated by J. Todd Billings, *Union with Christ: Reframing Theology and Ministry for the Church* (Grand Rapids: Baker Academic, 2011).

[29]According to Thomas, only twenty-seven of Calvin's 159 sermons close with a christological focus (*Proclaiming the Incomprehensible God: Calvin's Teaching on Job* [Fearn, UK: Mentor, 2004], p. 314).

[30]Thomas places Calvin on the "*Jewish* end of any Jewish-Christian exegetical continuum" (p. 308) and cites others who share this perspective on Calvin's work (see esp. p. 307); Calvin was, according to some, carving a middle path between strictly Lutheran Christocentric interpretation and Jewish interpretation; see Ford Lewis Battles, *Calculus Fidei: Some Ruminations on the Structure of the Theology of John Calvin* (Grand Rapids: Calvin Theological Seminary, 1978). As a result Calvin was labeled a "Judaizer" by both Servetus (see *Inst.* 2.10.11) and some Lutherans; p. 337 n. 13.

Greidanus levies criticisms at Calvin for using David and other characters as examples in sermons.[31] In his first sermon on Job 1:1, Calvin states, "It is good that we have examples who show us that there are men frail like us, who nevertheless have resisted temptations, and have persevered constantly in obeying God, although He afflicted them to the limit. Now we have here an excellent example of it." Calvin treats Job as an important example for Christians who should be preached accordingly (see also Jas 5:7-11).[32] He describes Abraham in Genesis 22 as an exemplar "entirely devoted to God," concluding that Scripture's depiction of the patriarch is an "example proposed for our imitation." "As Abraham was for Clement the ideal for obedience, so Abraham for Calvin is the ideal for perseverance under fire."[33] But Greidanus calls Calvin's interpretation of Genesis into question and especially critiques his use of Abraham as an exemplar in passages such as Genesis 22.[34] For Greidanus, even if Abraham is an illustration of faithfulness and faith that works appropriately, such texts (he cites Jas 2 and Heb 11) should never be preached without elevating Christ.[35]

Calvin certainly believed that the interpreter's task included interpreting Christ from the Old Testament. But rather than making this approach an inviolable law for every sermon, he instead practiced variegated interpretation, or a "middle way": he did all kinds of things with the Bible in an attempt to interpret in the footsteps of the church fathers and the New Testament. His willingness to preach other than Christ may have owed something to the fact that he was never preaching in a gospel-free environment. The regular use of the Eucharist served to proclaim the Lord's saving work. But in Calvin's thought even the gospel message of the Eucharist is not opposed to imitation. Rather, it feeds it:

---

[31]S. Greidanus, *Preaching Christ from the Old Testament* (Grand Rapids: Eerdmans, 1999), pp. 150-51.

[32]Cited by Greidanus, *Preaching Christ from the Old Testament*, p. 150 n. 58, who disapproves of this use.

[33]Paul Borgman, "Abraham and Sarah: Literary Text and the Rhetoric of Reflection," in *The Function of Scripture in Early Jewish and Christian Tradition*, ed. Craig Evans and James Sanders (Sheffield, UK: Sheffield Academic Press, 1998), pp. 45-77, especially 63.

[34]Greidanus, *Preaching Christ from the Old Testament*, pp. 292-318, especially 303 n. 49.

[35]Ibid., p. 305. Something of a healthier impulse is found in pp. 227-28.

Paul enjoins that a man examine himself before eating of this bread or drinking of this cup [1 Cor 11:28]. By this (as I interpret), he meant that each man descend into himself, and ponder with himself whether he rests with inward assurance of heart upon the salvation purchased by Christ; whether he acknowledges it by the confession of his mouth; then, whether he aspires to the imitation of Christ with zeal of innocence and holiness; whether, after Christ's example, he is prepared to give himself for his brethren and to communicate himself to those with whom he shares Christ in common; whether, as he is counted a member by Christ, he in turn so holds all his brethren as members of his body as his Christ did.[36]

Such an approach shows that, for Calvin, categories such as union, participation, mission and imitation are tightly linked. A eucharistic context for the imitation of Jesus was not original to Calvin but something he found in the Fathers and in Scripture.[37] Calvin strove to be faithful to them, and as a result he emphasized both the vertical and horizontal dimensions of Eucharist.[38]

Calvin also emphasized the importance of imitation for cross-shaped ministry. His autobiographical comments are sometimes panned as dour, joyless and pessimistic. But Calvin's self-understanding and autobiographical comments were influenced by the catalog of sufferings found in Paul (1 Cor 4:9-13; 2 Cor 4:8-9; 6:4-10).[39] As someone who was persecuted and rejected while suffering intense personal loss (including the loss of his job, his home country and three children), Calvin identified with the remarkable degree of sacrifice he found in the Bible—for instance, in the life of Abraham.[40] Self-denial and cross-bearing were a crucial point of training for Calvin since many of the church planters he trained and sent from

[36]Calvin, *Institutes of the Christian Religion* 4.17.40.
[37]Note Augustine's imitation-heavy depiction of the night of the Last Supper in John's Gospel: "And this also is the sacrifice of the church celebrated in the sacrament of the altar, known to the faithful, in which she teaches that she herself is offered in the offering she makes to God." *City of God* 10.6. I owe this reference to Gerald Hiestand.
[38]See Billings, *Union with Christ*, pp. 95-122.
[39]Alister McGrath, *A Life of John Calvin: A Study in the Shaping of Western Culture* (Oxford: Blackwell, 1990), pp. 195-96; see also "The Discipline of the Cross" in *Institutes* 3.9.1, among other places.
[40]Calvin, *Instititues* 2.10.11.

Geneva were on their way to an early grave. The model for the ministry of a Christian is the whole life of the Messiah, not by "exact reduplication of the details of his outward life," but by "acting according to the Spirit that moved Jesus."[41]

Later Protestant heirs of Luther and Calvin and their Anabaptist opponents would sometimes employ imitation in profound ways. During the cold Dutch winter of 1569, an Anabaptist named Dirk Willems was convicted by Reformers of heresy and sentenced to death. After he fled from authorities, a bounty hunter tracked him down. As the lightweight Willems glided over a frozen body of water, his heavy pursuer broke through a narrow patch of ice and began to drown.

One might expect Willems to regard this event as providential interference for his liberation. But he regarded it as an opportunity to adhere to what Jesus taught, that he should imitate the self-sacrificial love that had been shown to him. He turned back and at great risk returned to the ice and saved his pursuer's life. The bounty hunter was still compelled to arrest him, and Willems was brought to trial, condemned and burned until he died.

Such stories are not incidental or unimportant for the Christian life. In the opening paragraph of his biography of David Brainerd, Jonathan Edwards lays out a brief theology of two modes of instruction in true religion, which mutually reinforce one another: "There are two ways of representing and recommending true religion and virtue to the world, which God hath made us of: the one is by doctrine and precept; the other is by instance and example: Both are abundantly used in the holy Scriptures." Edwards goes on to describe the two ways of instruction. In the Bible,

> we have many excellent examples of religion, in its power and practice, set before us, in the histories both of the Old Testament and New. Jesus Christ, the great prophet of God, when he came into the world to be

---

[41]Ronald Wallace, *Calvin's Doctrine of the Christian Life* (Grand Rapids: Eerdmans, 1959), p. 43; he adds that for Calvin, "the life of Jesus from His infancy was marked by crossbearing." Wallace is summarizing Calvin's teaching as represented by his commentary on Mt 16:24. Calvin frequently associated union and imitation; see his commentary on 1 Jn 2:6.

"the light of the world" [Jn 8:12; 9:5; Mt 5:14], to teach and enforce true religion, in a greater degree than ever had been before, made use of both these methods. . . . In his own practice [he] gave a most perfect example of the virtue he taught. He exhibited to the world such an illustrious pattern of humility, divine love, discreet zeal, self-denial, obedience, patience, resignation, fortitude, meekness, forgiveness, compassion, benevolence, and universal holiness, as neither men nor angels ever saw before.

God also in his Providence has been wont to make use of both these methods to hold forth light to mankind, and inducement to their duty, in all ages: He has . . . from age to age, raised up some eminent persons that have set bright examples of that religion that is taught and prescribed in the Word of God; whole examples have in divine providence been set forth to public view.

These have a great tendency to engage the attention of men to the doctrines and rules that are taught, and greatly to confirm and enforce them; and especially when these bright examples have been exhibited in the same persons that have been eminent teachers, so that the world has had opportunity to see such a confirmation of the truth, efficacy, and amiableness of the religion taught, in the practice of the same persons that have most clearly and forcibly taught it.[42]

Edwards goes on to celebrate the way in which these "bright examples" can be used both by God and human teachers to great effect.

CONCLUSION

The imitation of Jesus and the saints can be vividly captured in stories from church history, and such stories can still be found today.[43] If we distilled these stories into headlines, they would range from "Family packs possessions in coffins as it heads to Pacific Island missionary work" to "Man faithfully gives and forgives in local congregation" and

---

[42]*An Account of the Life of the Late Reverend Mr. David Brainerd* (Boston: 1749), vol. 7 in The Works of Jonathan Edwards, ed. Norman Pettit (New Haven, CT: Yale University Press, 1984).
[43]See short biographies compiled by John Piper, Desiring God: God-Centered Resources from the Ministry of John Piper, www.desiringgod.org/resource-library/biographies/by-title; and his *Filling Up the Afflictions of Christ: The Cost of Bringing the Gospel to the Nations in the Lives of William Tyndale, Adoniram Judson, and John Paton*, vol. 5, The Swans Are Not Silent (Wheaton, IL: Crossway, 2009).

"Family befriends down-and-out, dysfunctional family." The vast majority of Jesus imitation is frankly unremarkable, closer in nature to the second and third headline than the first. But the spectacular and the mundane are related. "The overarching theme of Thomas à Kempis's *Imitation of Christ* [is] that martyrdom is simply the most spectacular display of the Christian's everyday life of humility and endurance of suffering."[44]

Our brief review suggests that church history can assist the three audiences of this book in the recovery of biblical imitation. Somewhere, a left-leaning Christian activist is appealing to the imitation of Jesus while denigrating those who do not share a radical, post-biblical inclusive agenda. But church history rejects "the imitation of Jesus" as a battle cry that leads believers away from biblical teaching. He has much to learn from the connection between imitation and orthodox doctrine. And the imitation of holiness in Diognetus or Calvin echoes the scriptural emphasis on imitation (Eph 4:23-24).

Somewhere, a pastor from the muddled middle is looking down at his pastoral peers for not being practical. Perhaps he is publishing a how-to blog post with lots of helpful tips—but where the gospel and biblical exegesis are nowhere to be found. We can't tell if he's a preacher or the next Oprah Winfrey or Dale Carnegie. But the text-centered approach of Clement, Justin and Calvin suggests that he may have something to learn from the "impractical" pastor down the street. Teachers like Clement and Augustine offer a gospel context for moral instruction, showing the muddled middle and latitudinal left that a healthy focus involves not just "what to do" but "what has been done."

On the other hand, perhaps some in the reluctant right should learn that sermons are not just gospel delivery operations. Somewhere, a lay leader influenced by the reluctant right is critiquing her pastor—probably behind his back—for not having enough gospel content in every single sermon. Perhaps it would help her to realize

---

[44]Kevin Vanhoozer, *The Drama of Doctrine: A Canonical-Linguistic Approach to Christian Theology* (Louisville, KY: Westminster John Knox, 2005), p. 429.

that her criticisms could stamp Calvin and Luther as sub-Christian. J. Gresham Machen carefully distinguished between biblical imitation, which he thought vital, and the liberal imitation of a pseudo-Jesus invented by scholars: "The imitation of the real Jesus will never lead a man astray."[45]

---

[45]J. Gresham Machen, *Christianity and Liberalism* (New York: Macmillan, 1923), p. 95.

Conclusion

The good God has given them a share in His own Image, that is,
in our Lord Jesus Christ, and has made even themselves
after the same Image and Likeness.

ATHANASIUS

We will be like him.

1 JOHN 3:2

In this book we've explored three forms of imitation in the Bible. Humans were created in the image of God to reflect his character and his actions. They imitate God's perfect image-bearer, Jesus, and look to saints past and present as models for faith and action as these human models reflect the character of God and Jesus.

We've also seen that this theme permeates all corners of the Bible. Jesus presents himself as an example on a number of occasions, and each of the four Gospels includes the theme or was crafted to elevate Jesus as a standard. Paul tells the Corinthians that he teaches his Christ-imitating ways as a model "everywhere in every church" (1 Cor 4:8-17). His letters routinely feature imitation, and of the books appearing after Paul's letters in the canon, only tiny 2 John fails to teach the imitation of Jesus or use characters as positive or negative examples. We have also seen that imitation does not start in the New

Testament. Old Testament texts require the imitation of God, and a number of Old Testament books guide their original audiences with positive and negative models. (According to the New Testament, they continue to serve this purpose for new covenant believers.)

We will conclude our investigation of imitation by using a question and answer format to sum up the message of this book, answering questions by referencing the only New Testament books that have not yet been addressed: John's letters.

Question: What is biblical imitation?

Answer: Biblical imitation is a matter of aligning character, belief, mindset or action with a pattern or template so that the copy reflects the original. The biblical concept of the imitation of Jesus is never described as a matter of rote, precise copying.[1] His followers did not normally baptize in the Jordan, choose twelve disciples, fast for forty days and nights or die on Roman crosses. The goal of a cross-shaped life is not literal crucifixion. As Augustine put it in his first sermon on 1 John, "What is walking as Jesus walked? Walking upon the sea? No, it is walking in the way of righteousness. . . . Nailed onto the cross, he was walking in the way—the way of charity."[2]

In the same way, when John and other authors say that we will be "like God" (1 Jn 3:2; 4:16-17), they do not mean that we will be precisely like him in every respect. We will share God's character, do tasks that are similar to his (but far less spectacular) and walk in his ways.

Q: What is the biblical framework for imitation?

A: There are three forms of biblical imitation: the imitation of God, the imitation of Jesus and the imitation of the saints. These are linked, and we see these links again in John's letters. Imitation begins not with Jesus but with the creation of humans made in the image of God. The destiny of redeemed human beings is the renewal of God's original design, so that humans are like God, even

---

[1]We have seen similar comments in Clement of Rome, Augustine, Vanhoozer, Allen, Hays, Agan and others.
[2]"First Homily on 1 John," in *Augustine: Later Works*, ed. John Burnaby, Library of Christian Classics (Philadelphia: Westminster, 1955), p. 266.

if not in every respect. We are like him because we live in him by the Spirit: "As he is, so are we in this world" (1 Jn 4:17).

God wants orthodox belief "that reflects the loving, just, and holy character of the divine Parent in real-life interactions within the community of faith. . . . This reflection of God is refined and given more precise content as the 'imitation of Jesus.'" Jesus' followers "'ought to walk just as he walked' (1 Jn 2:6 NRSV)." This emphasis on the imitation of the Son is "a shift of subject from the unseen God-as-Father to the observable God-made-flesh. And most prominently, the 'love' of the God who 'is love' (1 Jn 4:18) is demonstrated precisely in the self-giving act of Jesus on the cross."[3]

Because the Spirit is at work in humans who reflect the Father and Son, we also imitate the saints. Divine or satanic parenthood is revealed by sin or righteousness, evil or love. Cain provides a negative example ("of the devil"), and Jesus is a positive example ("of God," 1 Jn 3:8). Disciples prove their parenthood by their imitation of God's love in the self-giving of his Son (1 Jn 3:17; 4:7-11, 16, 17, 19). John expects that the community will model godlikeness and Christlikeness for one another: "Beloved, do not imitate what is evil but imitate what is good. Whoever does good is from God; whoever does evil has not seen God" (3 Jn 11). Believers imitate these "do-gooders" because they illustrate the character exhibited by and required by the Father and the Son.

Q: In what areas are we supposed to be imitators?

A: Many different areas of imitation have been addressed in this book. John's letters contain a few comprehensive, all-embracing aspects of imitation. It doesn't get more comprehensive than the call to love, and we are to imitate the love of Father and Son (1 Jn 3:16-18; 4:7-11, 16, 17, 19). Nothing is more sweeping than the command, "Do not imitate what is evil but imitate what is good" (3 Jn 11), a command applicable to the imitation of God, the Son and the saints in every sphere of life.

---

[3]David deSilva, *An Introduction to the New Testament: Contexts, Methods and Ministry Formation* (Downers Grove, IL: InterVarsity Press, 2004), p. 459.

Q: Where does the power for imitation come from?

A: John's books contain two phrases—"born again" and "abiding in Christ" ("living in Christ")—that sometimes function as clichés in Christian subcultures. For John and other New Testament writers, these truths were about the beginning of the fulfillment of God's promises to restore humans and the whole world. In the Son, God raises humans from death and gives them new life by putting his own Spirit in them (1 Jn 3:23; 4:13).

John sees these aspects of salvation as part of the new identity and new reality that changes sinful humans. John agrees with Paul and the rest: salvation realities must have an impact if they are to be taken seriously. The result of being born again by God is a life lived in God (1 Jn 2:24-28), so that what appears to be an artificial identity begins to become a new reality. Divine identity means that a divine power is at work: "If you know that he is righteous, you may be sure that everyone who does right has been born of him" (1 Jn 2:29; see also 1 Jn 1:7). Conversely, patterns of life that depart from Jesus' pattern of life show that someone claiming to be a believer is not alive in God (1 Jn 3:17; 4:8).

Two implications of new birth follow. First, when John reaches back to the Old Testament promises of resurrection, new birth and the Spirit, it is not a new vision for humans that he sees but the restoration and fulfillment of God's original design. Second, humans are newly empowered by the Spirit for moral renovation that reflects this new identity in the Messiah, the "true vine." As a result, there is a distinction but no radical separation between God's work and human work in sanctification and discipleship.

Q: What is the goal of imitation?

A: John describes two objectives for our imitation and discipleship: perfection in love and purity, and witness to the world, the church and one's self. John takes seriously the sinful state of humans, the change that happens when they are joined to Christ by the Spirit, and the continuing reality of sin. Believers are born of God (1 Jn 5:1; Jn 1:13; 3:3-5). As these newly born children of God live ("abide") in the Father and the Son, the presence of God is revealed by the presence of a love that is like God's love: "Since God loved us so much [sending his Son to be a propitiation for our sins], we also ought to love one another. No one has ever seen God; if we love one another, God lives in us, and his love is perfected in us. . . . Love has been perfected among us in this: . . . As he is, so are we in this world" (1 Jn 4:11-12, 17; see also Jn 14:20-21). The goal of imitation is godlikeness.

John does not mean "perfection" in the sense of sinless perfection: "If we say that we have no sin, we deceive ourselves, and the truth is not in us. . . . We make him a liar" (1 Jn 1:8, 10). But he believes that we must take seriously the requirement to model change and to pursue the perfection of love. Believers are never at rest with sin (1 Jn 3:8-9).

The invisible God makes himself known through living images that reflect him to the world. In the Gospel of John, God is in a sense unknown: "No one has ever seen God," but the only Son reveals him to the world (Jn 1:18). Jesus' opponents haven't heard (Jn 5:37) or seen the Father (Jn 6:46). They cannot recognize that Jesus reflects the Father's character (Jn 8:38). However, as the Father has empowered Jesus with the Spirit and sent him to show God to the world, Jesus now sends his disciples for the same purpose with the same power (Jn 20:21-22). The world will see the love of the disciples, a love that reflects the love the disciples have received from the perfect image of God (Jn 13:34-35). Even if the world's recognition of the source of this love is not always an accurate measure of faithful witness (1 Jn 3:1), our witness of love is not just seen by the world but by other believers.

Picking up the refrain of John 1:18, John's letters teach that God is revealed through his people's godlike and Christlike love: "No one has ever seen God; if we love one another, God lives in us, and his love is perfected in us" (1 Jn 4:12). There may be no more powerful witness to the gospel than the love of God expressed through creative imitation of God himself. For John, such actions combine with orthodox belief to serve as the ultimate evidence of the identity and destiny of the family in faith (1 Jn 2:3; 3:10, 16-24; 4:2-3, 6, 8, 13; 5:2, 18). Godlikeness, righteousness and love illustrate our new nature and provide evidence that we may have "boldness on the day of judgment" (1 Jn 4:17; see also 1 Jn 2:29).

Q: What is the motivation for imitation?

A: There are many answers to this question. Many of them revolve around God's graciousness in creation, sustenance and salvation. In 1 John several aspects of salvation—incarnation, regeneration (rebirth), atonement and glorification—are all relevant for imitation. Nowhere is this more clear than in 1 John 3:15-18, where God's love in Christ's cross becomes both a standard and a motivation for action. Even something as small as the label for believers in 3 John 11 provides motivation: John tells them to be good, yet not before he calls them "beloved," a title that is gloriously evocative of their relationship with a God who is love (1 Jn 4:8, 16). Knowing that I am loved is a powerful motivation to live as this verse teaches. Goodness is not a means of earning God's favor but a reflection of that favor.

Q: Where in life do we put imitation to work?

A: While the practical aspects and implications of imitation have not been a major focus for this text, they are relevant in areas as diverse as ministry, marriage, hospitality and generosity, to name a few (Eph 5; 1 Pet 3; 1 John 3; Heb 13). The most dramatic and obvious use of the imitation of Jesus comes in martyrdom. But John does not address spectacular forms of imitation like martyrdom. Instead, he emphasizes aspects of imitation that are basic yet sweeping in their applicability.

John requires the imitation of God's purity (1 Jn 3:3) and goodness (3 Jn 11). He puts the cross to use in contexts outside of martyrdom, requiring disciples to love like the Father and Son have loved. Jesus' sin-bearing atonement can be compared to the thousand crosses we might bear, from forgiveness to generosity to martyrdom.

Purity, holiness, goodness and love are applicable for every Christian, every day, in every area of life. John connects the dots by applying these sweeping aspects of imitation to very specific problems: believers can imitate Jesus' atonement love by meeting the needs of members of the covenant community (1 Jn 3:16-18). "The doctrine of atonement provides crucial direction to the church for dying well daily. Performing the doctrine of atonement involves living well and dying well for the truth in creative imitation of Christ."[4]

Consider just one area of application. A leading scholar of mission notes the degree of sacrifice necessary to prevent our absorption into the monolithic Leviathan of contemporary culture:

> The remarkable power of technology to shape worldview along with the enormous amount of time young people spend with its many forms makes the small amount of time they spend in Christian nurture seem almost negligible by comparison. The best preaching, worship, and education programs of a church simply cannot compete with television, movies, the internet, cell phones, Facebook, Twitter, and the ever-expanding list of technologies that shape our vision of the world. If families are not taught to make radical, costly, and time-consuming commitments to nurturing their children, the future of the church as a missional community in the West will be bleak.[5]

Our cross-shaped mission is a mission in the shape of the true human, who died to the world, for the world. Faithfulness to our mission requires that we resist the cultural forces that would shape us into something other than the shape of Jesus, the true human.

Q: How prevalent or important is the idea of imitation?

A: Even in a very short letter, John puts imitation to use. He identifies those who are of God and teaches that the good works of God's do-gooders are to be imitated. He identifies several good examples and one bad example, then states, "Beloved, do not imitate what is evil but imitate what is good. Whoever does good is from God; whoever does evil has not seen God" (3 Jn 11). Even where

---

[4]Kevin Vanhoozer, *The Drama of Doctrine: A Canonical-Linguistic Approach to Christian Theology* (Louisville, KY: Westminster John Knox, 2005), p. 429.
[5]Michael Goheen, *Light to the Nations: A Missional Church and the Biblical Story* (Grand Rapids: Baker Academic, 2011), p. 221.

imitation is not as explicit (as with 2 Jn), it is not irrelevant for the application of the book's message. Future readers need not only 2 John and other biblical books but disciples and communities who model the belief and behavior required by John and other New Testament writers.

Imitation is a fundamental task of discipleship and a fundamental part of being human. In 1 John, the response to the promise that "we will be like him" (1 Jn 3:2) is that "all who have this hope in him purify themselves, just as he is pure" (1 Jn 3:3). Imitation informs our original design, our future destiny and our present duty.

Q: Is it dangerous to focus on imitation?

A: One might assume that John's answer would be "no," but let's not jump the gun. The imitation of Jesus is "a theme long out of favour in much Protestant writing."[6] It is often viewed as a threat to orthodoxy because it has been pressed into service as a substitute for the gospel.

But doctrines are inherently dangerous. As Luther put it, "Forgiveness of sins is at the very heart of Christian doctrine, yet it is a mighty dangerous thing to preach."[7] Allowing believers to read the Bible for themselves is dangerous.[8] Most heresies start with exegesis and a grain of truth.

The imitation of God, Jesus and the saints is also dangerous. But faithful interpreters do not shrink from dangerous ideas. They put them to work with care and craft. "Moderation in all things is good advice for drink, but not necessarily for doctrine."[9] So it is with imitation. May we drink up to become God-shaped, Jesus-shaped and saint-shaped by the work of God's Spirit and all the effort and energy he provides.

---

[6]Richard Hays, "Response to Richard Burridge's *Imitating Jesus*," *Scottish Journal of Thelogy* 63, no. 3 (2010): 331.

[7]Martin Luther, *D. Martin Luthers Werke: Kritische Gesamtausgabe*, 27 band (Weimar: Hermann Böhlau Nachfolger, 1903), p. 378: "Hoc est caput doctrinae Christianae, et tamen periculosissima praedicatio."

[8]Alistair McGrath's history of the Reformation plays on such ideas with the title *Christianity's Dangerous Idea: A History from the Sixteenth Century to the Twenty-First* (New York: Harper-Collins, 2007).

[9]Vanhoozer, *Drama of Doctrine*, p. 451.

Q: What should the three spheres of Christianity learn about imitation?
A: Many of John's emphases, such as the radical vision he presents for the imitation of Jesus' sacrificial love, speak to all who would follow Jesus. But to generalize one last time about the three sectors of contemporary Christianity (and keeping in mind the caveats on such generalization in the introduction), one can discern what John has to say to each branch.

For the muddled middle, John features orthodox theology and the gospel, particularly Christology, atonement and forgiveness. Imitation is not allowed to eclipse other vital aspects of biblical truth. John majors on the imitation of big picture items such as holiness and love rather than on incidentals such as Jesus' singleness (a medieval favorite) or modern obsessions such as self-help techniques and diet advice. He also avoids an emphasis on literal death on a cross, which shows that imitation is a matter of patterns, not precise duplication.

For the latitudinal left, John does not sacrifice theological or ethical fundamentals of the faith for the sake of the imitation of Jesus, as some theological innovators urge. John insists that orthodox Christian beliefs, including orthodox Christology (1 Jn 4:2), sin and atonement (1 Jn 1:7–2:2) are essential. Imitation does not render these beliefs optional but is in fact based on them. John also features the new birth by the Spirit and the necessity of new birth and new belief (1 Jn 4:2). He teaches a radically new and different status for those alive in God but a status of judgment for those who are apart from the Father, Son and Spirit (1 Jn 1:10; 2:4; 4:1-3).

For the reluctant right, John models the imitation of the Father, the Son and the saints without a trace of fear or reluctance. He does not kill the rhetorical force of his demands with caveats and cautions. In circles where theology matters, discipleship can contract from the robust way of life taught by Paul and Jesus into something akin to information dumping (even good information), and the loss of imitation certainly contributes to this phenomenon. Young pastors imitate professors, writers and popular preachers rather than godly elders and faithful saints. If discipleship becomes the dispensation of knowledge, we are left with the impression that knowledge of the right things makes one a fully formed disciple. John disagrees: it is the presence or absence of godlike and Christlike behavior—not belief alone—that tells us who we are (1 Jn 2:3-4; 3:16-24; 5:2).

My hope is that this study raises interest in the theme of imitation in Scripture (especially for the reluctant right), its gospel context (for the muddled middle and latitudinal left) and the agenda of radical discipleship and holiness (for all three audiences). For all believers, this book is an invitation to explore Scripture's own teaching about the topic. Generally speaking, all three spheres of Christianity need a more robust and more biblical approach to imitation. If Scripture is a guide, the abandonment or mitigation of imitation is not the need of this or any other hour. The present need, and the burden of this book, is to recapture the biblical practice of imitation by carefully considering Scripture's teachings so that we may recalibrate our approach accordingly. As we do so, we will discover that imitation is a central aspect of discipleship, preaching, teaching and self-conception.

CONCLUSION

This book began with the simple question, "What does the Bible say about imitation?" A host of angles, connections and answers arose over the course of our study. Our examination also introduced a number of questions, many of which cannot be settled in this book: "What do I preach when?" "How much moral instruction is too much?" "What is the relative weight between God's work and our work in a sermon or Sunday school lesson?" I cannot answer these questions authoritatively. This is a "what" book, not a how-to book, and no one should mistake it for a full-scale theology of preaching, interpretation, sanctification or discipleship. The challenge for readers is to search out the implications through the study of God's Word, in community, in prayer, in sermons and in private counsel.

Mixing an imitation cocktail requires pastoral sensitivity, awareness of context and cultural tendencies, and the assistance of Scripture and church history. All cultures and listeners bring baggage with them to the text, and the shape of this baggage is unique to each of us and our contexts. Our personalities, experience, language and knowledge shape the way we hear biblical truth, for good and for ill. Not every person is a Luther, tormented by conscience and legalism and converted by a "gospel" passage (Rom 1:16-17). Not every person is an Augustine, saturated in immorality and licentiousness and converted by a "law" passage (Rom 13:13-14).

Coordinating a focus on imitation while prioritizing the gospel is no easy task. This is particularly true given that "too many sermons are written 'in the imperative mode' [i.e., what we are to do for God], whereas the religion of the Bible 'is written largely in the revealing language of the indicative mode,'" that is, what God has done for us.[10] There is grave danger in making Christianity a matter of what we do for God while mitigating what God has done for us. There is also grave danger in making Christianity a matter of what God has done for us and ignoring or downplaying what we are to do in response. First John seems to suggest that both of these tendencies are deadly.

Among many other implications, two particularly challenging points deserve closing comment. First, the frequency with which we encounter imitation in the New Testament suggests that a cautious sermon on imitation every few years or an occasional reference to being like Jesus or a worthy character is an inadequate diet. Second, the creativity required in our imitation of Jesus heightens the need to attend to imitation in Scripture, history and the lives of our contemporary brothers and sisters. Legislation may guide us in the right direction, but it cannot provide a blueprint for every single activity. "Cruciformity," being shaped by carrying one's cross, "cannot be inscribed or legislated; it cannot be codified or routinized."[11] Cross-

[10]John Stott, *Between Two Worlds: The Art of Preaching in the Twentieth Century* (Grand Rapids: Eerdmans, 1987), p. 57; he is citing Theodore Parker Ferris's 1950 George Craig Stewart Lectures, later published as *Go Tell the People* (New York: Scribner, 1951).
[11]Michael Gorman, *Cruciformity: Paul's Narrative Spirituality of the Cross* (Grand Rapids: Eerdmans, 2001), p. 383. See also Richard Hays, *The Moral Vision of the New Testament: Community, Cross, New Creation; A Contemporary Introduction to New Testament Ethics* (New York: HarperOne, 1996), p. 46.

bearing acts of mercy, forgiveness, witness and resistance to conformity to the world's patterns of thought and action can never be fully and finally legislated.

The Scriptures, the Savior and the saints around us and before us display godliness—godlikeness—that conforms to the character of the true human and his Father. And this means that imitation is not just a grueling duty; it is a glorious destiny.

We were made for nothing less.

Author and Subject Index

Abraham, 45-46, 50, 86, 91-92, 120, 160, 166-67, 172, 177-78, 190n12, 202-4

Agan, Jimmy, 12n5, 15, 80n16, 178n36, 187, 199n18, 200n21, 210n1

Allen, Michael, 146n19, 147, 150n28, 161n6, 178n37, 186n5, 188n9, 210n1

Allison, Dale, 69n14, 77n11

Anderson, Matthew Lee, 108n1

Athanasius, 194, 209

Augustine, 24, 38, 137, 190, 194-95, 204n37, 207, 210, 219

Aune, David, 69nn13-14, 73n5, 197n12

Baker, David, 171n15

Balthasar, Hans Urs von, 103n17

Bargerhuff, Eric, 88n9

Barrs, Jerram, 146n17

Barth, Karl, 175

Bartholomew, Craig C., 35nn17-18, 21

Battles, Ford Lewis, 202n30

Baugh, S. M., 148n22, 178n37

Bavinck, Herman, 19, 85nn5-6

Beale, Greg, 41n1, 43-45, 97nn4-5, 98nn7-8, 118n4, 119n5, 134-35n33, 139nn3-4,

149n26, 150n27, 151, 167n6

Berkhof, Louis, 103n15

Billings, J. Todd, 99n10, 118n1, 202n28, 204n38

Bird, Michael, 100n12, 103n14

Boaz. See Ruth

Bock, Darrell, 68n12, 98n6

Boice, James Montgomery, 101n13

Bonhoeffer, Dietrich, 119, 190, 199

Borger, Justin, 29n8, 200n19

Borgman, Paul, 203n32

Brainerd, David, 205

Brueggemann, Walter, 21-22

Bultmann, Rudolf, 101n13, 126n17

Burridge, Richard, 14n7, 69n14

Calvin, John, 29n8, 95, 105, 178n37, 190, 195, 199-200, 202-5

Campbell, Constantine, 99n9

Capes, David B., 69n14

Charles, Daryl, 161

Chesterton, G. K., 25

Ciampa, Roy, 122n9, 167n5

Clark, John C., 190n12, 201n26

Clark, R. Scott, 196n7

Clement, 195-99, 207, 210n1

Clowney, Edmund, 148n23

co-creators, 29

Cole, Graham, 99n10, 103n16

Conn, Harvie, 166n3

Cothenet, Edouard, 133n30w

Crosby, Michael, 197n11

Crouch, Andy, 29, 52n6

David, 171, 179-80, 203

Davies, W. D., 77n11

Davis, D. Ralph, 165n1

Davis, Philip G., 76n9

Demarest, Bruce, 148

Dempster, Stephen, 23n5

deSilva, David, 157n2, 211n3

Douglas, Mary, 46nn8-9

Driscoll, Mark, 108n3

Dryden, Jeff, 12n6, 173n17

Eastman, Susan Grove, 132n27

Edwards, James, 74n6

Edwards, Jonathan, 205-6

Enns, Peter, 173n19

Erickson, Millard, 114n11

Eswine, Zack, 83-84

Evans, Craig, 173n18

fatherhood (of God, the devil, Paul), 10, 83-94, 96, 130-31, 150-51

Fee, Gordon, 104n18, 105, 132-33

Ferguson, Sinclair, 107, 121n7

Ferris, Theodore Parker, 219n10

Fletcher-Louis, Crispin H. P., 42n1, 118nn1-3

forgiveness, 67-68, 87-88, 98n6, 115, 143, 146, 171

Fowl, Stephen E., 73n4, 132n28

France, R. T., 72n1, 79

Fredericks, Cathi, 39n29

Gaffin, Richard, 95, 100n11, 104n18

Gathercole, Simon, 163

Geismar, E. O., 125n15

Glover, Donald E., 29n7

Goldingay, John, 176

Goldsworthy, Graeme, 176-77, 179, 196, 196n8

Goheen, Michael, 215n5

Gordon, Cyrus, 51n2

Gorman, Michael J., 129n21, 219n11

gospel, 64, 68-69, 91, 96-100, 105n21, 107, 109, 126, 178-79, 185, 196-97, 199, 201-13, 217-19

Green, Joel, 85n4, 88n8

Green, Michael, 16n11, 196n7

Greer, Rowan, 174n20

Gregory, Brad, 173n17

Greidanus, Sidney, 175-76, 179, 196, 203

Grudem, Wayne, 114n11

Gunton, Colin, 33n13, 65n9

Hafemann, Scott, 109nn4-5, 124n14, 130n22, 157-58

Hansen, David, 158

Haykin, Michael, 196n5

Hays, Richard, 12, 14, 15n9, 117, 127, 167, 191, 210n1, 216n6, 219n11

Heidelberg Catechism, 68n11

Hess, Richard, 51n3

Hill, Edmund, 23n4

Hoekema, Anthony, 114n11

Hood, Jason, 43n3, 74n5, 121n8, 132n27, 147n20, 175n24, 184n2, 187n6

Holmes, Michael W., 198n14

Horton, Michael, 15n8, 177-79, 187-88, 190n11, 197-98

House, Paul, 52n5, 169n9, 169nn11-12

Howell, David, 75n7, 77n11

Hurtado, Larry, 69n13, 75-76

idolatry, 19-20, 43-45, 96-98, 117-19

Ignatius, 62n3, 194, 198

Ireland, Dennis J., 146n16

Irenaeus, 19, 112n9, 114n11

Jeska, Joachim, 174n21

Job, 169, 202-3

Jobes, Karen, 149

Johnson, Keith, 68n11

Jones, E. Stanley, 99n10

Justin Martyr, 197, 207

Kapic, Kelly, 29n8, 61n1

Keck, Leander, 175

Kee, Howard Clark, 174n21

Keller, Timothy, 68n11

Kelly, J. N. D., 190n12

Kidner, Derek, 35

Kierkegaard, Søren, 26, 124-25

Kline, Meredith, 22n3

Kugel, James, 173-74

Lane, William L., 74n6, 160n4

Larkin, William, 118n4

Leithart, Peter, 49, 56, 163, 180

Lewis, C. S., 29n7, 141, 193-95

Liftin, Bryan, 196n5

Lindars, Barnabas, 51n2

Lloyd-Jones, D. Martyn, 101n13

Lloyd-Jones, Sally, 188-89

Longman, Tremper, 35n22, 37n25, 169n8

Luther, Martin, 131n24, 190, 200-202, 216, 219

Machen, J. Gresham, 70, 207-8

MacIntyre, Alasdair, 172n16

Marcus, Joel, 64n8

Marshall, I. Howard, 90n12, 103n14, 145n15

Mattill, Andrew Jacob, 143n13, 145n14, 146n18

Mattox, M. L., 201nn23-24

McCall, Tom, 85n6

McCarthey, D. J., 38n28

McCartney, Dan G., 36n23, 63n7, 148, 165n1

McConville, Gordon, 33, 34n15

McGrath, Alister, 199-200, 204n39, 216n8

McKnight, Scot, 57n11
Meier, John P., 73n7
Menander, 134n32
Moessner, David, 142n12
Moo, Douglas J., 96n2
Moore, Russ, 70n16
Moran, William, 38n28
Moses, 50-51, 53, 120, 143n12, 148n22, 160
Mouw, Richard, 52n6
Merrill, Eugene H., 22n3
Meyer, Ben F., 101n13
Murray, John, 54, 99n10, 100n11
Naselli, Andy, 23-24n5
Neusner, Jacob, 174n21
Newbigin, Lesslie, 155
Noah, 50, 64, 172
Nolland, John, 81n18
Noth, Martin, 176-77
O'Brien, P. T., 129n21
O'Donnell, Doug, 37n25
O'Donovan, Oliver, 108n1
O'Dowd, Ryan P., 35nn17-18
Ortlund, Dane, 84n3, 108n3
Packer, J. I., 99-100n11, 108nn2-3, 112-13
participation (partaking), 12, 24, 39-40, 49-57, 99n9, 100, 109, 111, 119-24, 131, 133n30, 134, 141-47, 151, 203-4
paternity. *See* fatherhood of God
Pelikan, Jaroslav, 38n27
Pennington, Jonathan, 69n15

Peterson, David, 138n2, 140n7, 141n9
Peterson, Eugene, 141n10, 183
Pettersen, Alvyn, 194n3
Piper, John, 21, 206n43
Pratt, Richard, 20n1, 61, 62n4, 166n3, 170n14
Provan, Iain, 170
Quintilian, 80n17
Rad, Gerhard von, 28n4
Rahab, 160, 177
Reid, Dan, 129n21
resurrection, 24n6, Richter, Sandra, 22n3
Rosner, B., 122n9, 174n23
rule/rulers/ruling, 21-25, 29, 34, 39-40, 42-43, 46-48, 55, 57, 62-64, 66, 68, 68n11, 79, 102, 112, 122, 130, 149-50
Ruth, 32, 52, 169-70, 189
sacrifice, 10-11, 69, 74-75, 85, 87, 120, 123-35, 137, 147-50, 158-60, 178-80, 190, 204n37, 205, 215
Samra, James, 12n6, 72n1, 73n2, 73n4, 91n13, 92n15, 114n11
sanctification, 46-48, 54-57, 96-97, 104, 111-16, 128-31, 139n5, 184, 188, 212
Sarah, 50, 160-61
Sayers, Dorothy, 29
Schneider, John R., 33n14
Seccombe, David, 145-46n16
Seneca the Younger, 126n16

Sproul, R. C., 108n3, 139n5
Stein, Robert, 61-62
Stewart, James S., 99n10, 101n13
Stott, John, 135n34, 219n10
sub-creators, 29
Swartley, Willard, 174n21
Talbert, Charles, 142n12
Tannehill, Robert, 142-43n12
Taylor, Justin, 108n3
theology of the cross, 201
Thielman, Frank, 132n28
Thomas, Derek, 202
Tolkien, J. R. R., 29
Tomlin, Graham, 83n2, 114n12, 115n14, 131n25, 161n6, 194n3
Turner, David, 33n13
Turner, Max, 130n23
union with Christ, 54-55, 99-103, 108-9, 116, 138-39, 204-5
Vanhoozer, Kevin, 11n4, 76n10, 80n15, 92n14, 92n16, 108n2, 128n20, 131n26, 173n17, 178n36, 188n9, 207n44, 210n1, 215n4, 216n9
Van Leeuwen, Raymond C., 35n17
vice regency. *See* rule/rulers/ruling
Volf, Miroslav, 90n11
Vos, Geerhardus, 148n22
Wallace, Ronald, 122n10, 205n41

Waltke, Bruce, 35n20, 37, 39

Warfield, B. B., 27, 116, 127n19

(the) way, 36, 91-93, 158, 210

Webster, John, 103n17, 126n17, 184n2

Wenham, Gordon, 28n5, 30, 41, 46n8, 166nn3-4, 201

Westminster Shorter Catechism, 83, 104

Wilder, Thornton, 155n1

Wilder, William, 42n2

Willems, Dirk, 205

Williams, D. H., 196n5

Williams, Michael D., 62n5, 96n2

Williams, Rowan, 194n3

Willimon, William, 15n8, 175, 179

wisdom, 34-38, 55, 69, 80, 167-68, 196

Witherington, Ben, 24n5, 104n18, 104n20, 105n22, 140n6

Wolters, Al, 7, 169n10

Wright, Christopher J. H., 28, 30n9, 31nn11-12, 34, 38n28, 46n7, 124n13

Wright, N. T., 186n4

Scripture Index

OLD TESTAMENT

Genesis
1, *22, 53*
1–2, *63*
1:2, *105*
1:26-28, *20, 21,*
  100
1:27, *118*
1:28, *102*
1:31, *28*
2:2-3, *28*
2:7, *110*
2:15, *42*
2:18, *28*
2:19-20, *28*
2:23, *28*
3, *42*
3:5, *23, 42*
3:15, *123, 179*
3:22, *23*
3:22-23, *42, 50*
4:15, *42*
4:19-24, *42*
8–11, *52*
12:1-3, *46*
13:10, *42*
15:6, *166*
16–50, *201*
18:17-19, *45, 178*
18:18-19, *91*
22, *178, 203*
22:1, *178*
22:1-24, *178*
22:16-17, *178*
26:3-5, *45, 46*
26:4-5, *91*
49:8-11, *63*
50:20, *52, 56*

Exodus
4:17, *50*
4:22-23, *46*
6, *31*
7:1, *50*
15, *31*
16:18, *33*
18:19-20, *50*
19:6, *46*
20:8-11, *28*
21:6, *50*
22:28, *40, 51*
24:9-11, *36*
32:7-14, *50*
32:32, *120*
34, *91*
34:5-7, *91*
34:6, *92*

Leviticus
11:45, *46*
19:2, *46*
19:34, *30*
20:7-8, *48*
22:31-33, *46*
26:11-12, *47*

Numbers
16, *164*
25:1-13, *164*

Deuteronomy
6:20-24, *48*
9:22-25, *98*
10, *38*
10:12, *38*
10:15, *38*
10:18-19, *38*
15:11-15, *32*

17:14-20, *24*
24:17-22, *31*
25:4, *30*
29–30, *98*
30, *98*
32, *174*

Joshua
1:5, *167*
1:6, *51*
1:7, *51*
1:11, *51*
1:12-15, *51*
8:1-2, *51*
10:8-11, *51*
10:42, *51*
23–24, *51*

Judges
1–5, *51*
2:17, *91*
2:22, *91*
3:15, *51*
3:31, *51*
5:9, *51*
6:13, *51*
6:15, *51*
Ruth
2:11-12, *52*
2:20, *52*
3:11, *169*
4:14, *52*
4:15, *52*

1 Samuel
17:51-54, *179*

2 Samuel
7:14, *47*

1 Kings
16:19, *92*
16:26, *92*
22:52, *92*

2 Kings
9, *172*
21:22, *92*

1 Chronicles
1–9, *174*
5, *171*
5:18-22, *171*
5:23-26, *171*
9:20, *165*

2 Chronicles
20:17, *53*
33:11-13, *171*

Nehemiah
9, *174*

Job
1, *115*
1:1, *203*

Psalms
8, *100*
8:3-8, *22*
25:4, *92*
45:6, *50*
48, *52*
78, *174*
81:13, *91*
95:10, *91*
103:7-8, *91*
103:10, *91*
103:13, *91*

104:24-25, *34*
106:23, *50*
106:28-31, *165*
106:30-31, *174*
111, *30*
111:3, *30*
111:10, *31*
112:1, *31*
112:9, *30, 31*
113:5-6, *27*
119:2, *115*
119:10, *115*
119:34, *115*
135:18, *44*

Proverbs
1–15, *37*
3:7, *37*
3:11-12, *37*
3:12, *34*
3:19-20, *34*
4:11-14, *36*
8, *35*
8:15, *34*
8:22-32, *34*
8:30-31, *28*
8:31, *36*
14:1, *35*
23:19, *36*
24:3, *35*
25:21-22, *37*
26:11, *37*
31, *35, 169*
31:10, *169*
31:10-31, *169*
31:29, *169*

Isaiah
6:9-10, *144*
11:1-10, *63*
29, *97*
43:6, *47*
49:6, *98*

52:13–53:12, *122*
55, *25*
55:6-7, *26*
55:8-9, *25*
57:15, *24*
60:6-22, *52*

Jeremiah
31, *98*

Ezekiel
11:15-20, *98*
27, *52*
28, *39*
28:5-6, *39*
28:17, *39*
28:18, *39*
36–37, *98*
37, *98, 111*

Daniel
1, *185*
1:4, *36*
1:12-15, *172*
1:17, *36*
1:20, *36*
2:34, *52*
4:18, *36*
4:19-32, *40*
5:11, *36*
5:14, *36*
5:17-28, *53*
7, *24, 40, 57, 63,
66, 100, 143*

Hosea
6:6, *87*

Joel
2, *98*

Micah
6:8, *56*

New Testament

Matthew
3, *79*
3:7, *86*
3:9, *86*
3:15, *84*
4, *84*
4:1-11, *64*
4:8, *78, 79*
4:10, *77*
5:5, *77, 166*
5:7, *77*
5:9, *84, 88*
5:10, *77*
5:10-12, *67, 86*
5:13-16, *78*
5:14, *206*
5:17-20, *77*
5:37, *78*
5:39, *78*
5:43-48, *84*
5:44-45, *28*
5:45, *84*
5:48, *84, 114*
6, *84*
6:5-15, *78*
6:6, *78*
6:8-10, *139*
6:9-10, *84, 98*
6:10, *78*
6:12, *87*
6:14-15, *87*
6:19, *78*
6:24, *77*
6:33, *84, 98*
7, *36, 88*
7:1-2, *88*
7:3-6, *88*
7:6, *78*
7:24-27, *36*
8:4, *77*
8:20, *78*

9:8, *78*
9:13, *77, 87*
9:27, *77*
9:34, *79*
10:1, *65*
10:5-8, *65*
10:24-25, *71, 77,
81*
10:25, *79, 84*
11:3, *65*
11:19, *37*
11:29, *77*
12:1-8, *77*
12:7, *77, 87*
12:24, *79*
12:27, *40*
12:34, *86*
12:41, *40*
12:42, *37*
12:50, *84*
14:23, *78*
15:1-20, *77*
15:22, *77*
15:31, *78*
16:18, *53*
16:18-20, *40*
16:21-26, *151*
16:24, *78, 103, 205*
16:24-27, *79*
18, *88, 140*
18:4, *77*
18:10-14, *88*
18:15, *88*
18:15-20, *40, 88*
18:18-20, *66*
18:21-22, *87*
18:21-35, *88*
18:23-33, *77*
18:23-35, *87*
19–28, *77*
19:21, *114*
19:27-30, *79*
19:28, *40, 111*

19:28-30, *64, 66, 85*
20:23, *71*
20:26-28, *77*
20:28, *77*
20:30, *77*
21:5, *77*
21:33-46, *67, 79, 86*
23:1-2, *77*
23:2-3, *62*
23:5, *78*
23:12, *77*
23:23, *86*
23:29-36, *79, 86*
23:33, *86*
23:34, *67*
24:25, *36*
24:45-46, *77*
25:1-12, *36*
25:14-23, *77*
25:31-32, *79*
26:28, *87, 88*
26:37-39, *67*
26:37-44, *78*
26:64, *78*
26:67, *78*
27:19, *84*
27:23, *77*
27:26, *78*
27:30, *78*
27:54, *85, 88*
28, *79*
28:16-20, *64, 139, 171*
28:18, *64, 79*
28:18-20, *53, 65, 102*
28:20, *53, 55*

Mark
1–8, *64*
1:7, *75*
1:14, *75*
1:16, *72*
3:13-15, *73*
3:14, *75*
3:31-35, *73*
6:7-13, *73*
8:22-30, *75*
8:31-33, *74*
8:34, *74, 147*
8:34-38, *74*
9:3, *75*
9:9, *80*
9:12, *74*
9:13, *74*
9:30-32, *74*
9:32-35, *74*
10, *66*
10:30, *80*
10:31-45, *184*
10:32-34, *74*
10:33, *75*
10:34, *80*
10:35-44, *24*
10:35-45, *74*
10:37, *81*
10:40, *81*
10:46-52, *75*
13, *74*
13:9-13, *75*
14:14, *76*
14:49, *76*
15:26-27, *81*

Luke
1:6, *115*
2:10, *90*
2:21-24, *144*
2:25, *98*
2:25-32, *144*
2:36-38, *98*
2:41-42, *144*
3:7-14, *80*
3:8, *166*

3:21, *143*
4:16, *144*
4:16-30, *143*
4:22, *143*
4:27-28, *144*
4:34-35, *144*
4:38-39, *143*
4:41, *144*
4:43, *143*
5:20, *143*
5:24, *143*
5:26, *144*
5:29-30, *146*
6:6, *144*
6:23, *145*
6:40, *61*
7:11-16, *143*
8, *132*
8:1-3, *93*
8:2-3, *143*
8:10, *144*
8:13, *90*
8:19-21, *85*
8:28, *144*
8:44-48, *143*
8:52, *143*
9:2, *143*
9:23, *11*
9:46-48, *85*
9:57-62, *85*
9:58, *85*
10:1-20, *65*
10:18-19, *65*
10:20, *90*
10:20-21, *90*
10:38-42, *67, 85*
11:4, *80*
11:42, *86*
11:49, *67*
12:37, *93*
13:10, *144*
13:17, *90*
14, *89*

14:12-14, *89, 146*
14:14, *144*
14:25-27, *85*
15, *89, 90, 145*
15:1-2, *146*
15:2, *89, 90*
15:5, *90*
15:7, *90*
15:10, *90*
15:19, *89*
15:24, *90*
15:29, *89*
15:32, *90*
16:1-13, *146*
16:17, *144*
17:11-16, *143*
18:1, *145*
18:28-30, *85*
18:29-30, *85*
18:35–24:53, *81*
19:1-10, *146*
19:6, *90*
19:8, *80*
19:37-48, *144*
20:27-40, *144*
20:38, *144*
21–22, *145*
22–23, *144*
22:1-8, *144*
22:25-27, *93*
22:28-30, *93*
22:54, *144*
23:1, *144*
23:2, *144*
23:4, *145*
23:5, *144*
23:15, *145*
23:16, *145*
23:20, *145*
23:34, *143*
23:46, *143*
24, *146, 165*
24:25-26, *165*

24:27, *165, 167*
24:44-47, *165*
24:45-49, *143*
24:47, *142*
24:49, *105*
24:51-53, *90*

John
1:1-18, *36*
1:13, *212*
1:14, *57*
1:18, *213*
2:18-22, *110*
2:21, *138*
3, *111*
3:2, *151*
3:3-5, *212*
5:37, *213*
5:39-40, *165*
6:46, *213*
7:39, *110*
8:12, *206*
8:38, *213*
8:39, *166*
8:39-41, *86*
8:44-45, *86*
9:5, *206*
11, *86*
11:49-53, *86*
12:9-11, *86*
12:16, *110*
13:34-35, *213*
13:36-37, *110*
13:38, *110*
14:2-3, *166*
14:19, *111*
14:20-21, *213*
15:20, *67*
15:26, *110*
16:7, *110*
16:32, *85*
18:15-27, *110*
20:21, *67*

20:21-22, *110, 213*
20:21-23, *111*
20:22, *111*
20:23, *88*
21:19, *110*
21:22, *110*

Acts
1:1, *142*
1:5, *105*
1:8, *105, 143*
2, *143*
2:14-40, *143*
2:17, *97*
2:22-23, *52*
2:22-36, *68*
2:23, *142*
2:38, *143*
2:42, *146*
2:43, *144*
2:46, *146*
3:12-26, *68*
3:22, *143*
4:7-10, *142*
4:27-28, *52, 142*
5:11, *146*
5:28, *142*
5:41, *145*
6:14, *144*
7, *174*
7:22-39, *143*
7:59-60, *143*
8, *143*
8:39, *145*
9:4-5, *142*
9:13-16, *122*
9:15-17, *144*
9:36-41, *143*
10:1-48, *146*
10:36, *88*
10:38, *143*
10:43, *143*
11:23, *145*

13:14-15, *144*
13:28, *145*
13:38-39, *143*
13:47, *122*
13:47-50, *144*
13:48, *145*
14:1, *144*
14:3, *143*
14:11, *146*
14:22, *122, 145*
15, *146*
15:31, *145*
16:3-4, *144*
16:17, *144*
17, *52, 98, 134*
17:1-2, *144*
17:7, *144*
17:17, *144*
17:18, *144*
17:28, *55, 118, 142, 144*
17:30, *118*
17:31, *118*
17:32, *118, 144*
18:18, *144*
18:21, *144*
19:12, *143*
19:15, *144*
20, *132, 145*
20:6, *144*
20:9-12, *143*
20:16, *144*
20:28-31, *157*
20:32, *143*
20:33-35, *146, 157*
20:34, *125*
21, *13, 144*
21:21-24, *144*
21:25, *40*
22:3, *144*
22:7-8, *142*
22:21-22, *144*
23–26, *144*

23:3-5, *40*
23:6, *144*
23:6-8, *144*
23:13, *142*
23:29, *145*
24:5, *144*
24:14, *93*
25:25, *145*
26:4-5, *144*
26:14-15, *142*
26:32, *145*
27:9, *144*
28:1-30, *144*
28:10, *143*
28:17, *144*
28:26-27, *144*

Romans
1:2-4, *97*
1:3-4, *68*
1:16-17, *219*
1:18-27, *96*
1:23, *138*
3, *177*
3:23, *68, 96*
4, *166*
4:3, *166*
4:13, *120, 166*
5, *101, 102*
5:14, *102*
5:17, *63, 64, 99*
6, *62, 101, 103, 120, 184*
6:2, *103*
6:3-4, *103*
6:5, *103*
6:8-11, *103*
6:12-14, *103*
7:4-6, *103*
8:1-11, *103*
8:3, *68*
8:9, *95*
8:13, *103*

8:14-15, *112*
8:15, *119, 131*
8:15-25, *64*
8:16-17, *119, 123,*
  190
8:17, *12, 98, 104,*
  119, 120, 122, 147
8:18-25, *98*
8:19-23, *24*
8:21-23, *112*
8:23, *98, 120*
8:29, *44, 45, 64,*
  98, 104, 114
8:29-30, *96*
8:32, *98*
8:35-37, *123*
8:36, *123*
9:1-3, *120*
10:9, *97*
12, *135*
12:1-2, *45, 103,*
  120, 121, 140
12:2, *114*
12:20, *37*
12:21, *135*
13, *39*
13:13-14, *120, 219*
13:14, *12, 105*
14, *121*
15:1, *103*
15:1-3, *121*
15:1-7, *121*
15:1-17, *121*
15:4, *168*
15:7, *121*
15:8, *121*
15:9, *121*
15:15-16, *140*
15:21, *122*
15:23-27, *121*
16, *122*
16:20, *123, 179*
16:27, *34*

1 Corinthians
1–2, *196*
1:16, *53*
1:20-31, *184*
1:23-24, *37*
1:27, *125*
2:2, *9, 93, 126*
3:16-17, *140*
3:18-19, *184*
3:21-23, *40*
4:2, *10*
4:7-8, *40*
4:7-18, *157*
4:8-17, *119, 124,*
  209
4:9, *10*
4:9-13, *204*
4:10, *184*
4:10-13, *10*
4:12, *125*
4:15-16, *10, 157*
4:16, *10*
4:17, *9, 10, 125,*
  126
4:21–5:13, *40*
5:5, *88*
5:7, *122*
6:1-5, *40*
6:2, *40*
6:3, *40*
6:5-7, *124*
6:12-20, *140*
6:17, *109*
6:19, *138*
7, *11*
7:17, *9*
8:1–11:1, *127*
8:13, *124*
9:1-27, *124*
9:22, *127*
10:1-11, *197*
10:4, *168*
10:6, *168*

10:7, *168*
10:8, *168*
10:9, *168*
10:10, *168*
10:11, *97*
10:32–11:1, *124*
10:33, *127*
11:1, *11, 109, 125,*
  128
11:7, *113, 138*
11:28, *204*
13, *135*
13:4-7, *135*
14:20, *114*
14:33-34, *9*
14:40, *40*
15, *24, 64, 68, 101,*
  102
15:1-4, *68*
15:1-5, *97*
15:10, *54, 113*
15:22, *99*
15:30-35, *124*
15:33, *134*
15:45, *102*
15:49, *119, 128*
16:4, *53*

2 Corinthians
1:5, *104*
1:8-10, *103, 124*
2:14-16, *124, 127*
3:18, *104, 126, 128*
4:7-12, *124*
4:8-9, *204*
4:10-11, *158*
4:11, *103*
4:16, *103*
4:17, *128*
5:14, *100*
5:14-17, *103*
5:16-17, *100*
5:17, *102, 105*

5:17-20, *54, 67*
5:18, *54*
5:20, *54*
6:1, *54*
6:2-13, *54*
6:3-10, *124*
6:4-10, *204*
6:5, *129*
6:14–7:1, *47*
6:16, *47*
6:16–7:1, *140*
6:18, *47*
7, *88*
7:1, *47*
8:1-9, *127*
8:2, *127*
8:9, *33, 127, 186*
8:12, *37*
8:13-15, *33*
9, *30*
9:9, *30*
9:11-15, *31*
11:7–12:10, *124*
11:23, *129*
12:1-10, *24*
12:14-15, *124*
13:3-4, *124*
13:9-11, *88*

Galatians
1, *167*
2:19-20, *103*
2:19-21, *128*
2:20, *102, 103*
3:6, *166*
3:27, *128*
4, *166*
4:1-7, *129*
4:5-6, *131*
4:12, *129*
4:13, *109*
4:19, *108, 112, 114,*
  128, 131

5:1, *129*
5:22, *98, 131, 167*
5:22-23, *112, 131*
5:24, *103, 128*
6:1, *40*
6:14, *128*
6:15, *102, 105*
6:17, *129, 185*

Ephesians
1, *100*
1:4, *99*
1:5, *130*
1:7, *99*
1:10, *102, 113, 138, 139*
1:19-20, *101*
1:21-22, *101*
1:22, *64*
1:22-23, *105, 113*
1:23, *102, 138, 139*
2, *101, 139*
2:1, *109, 130*
2:1-5, *101*
2:1-10, *99, 101*
2:3, *130*
2:5, *101*
2:5-6, *128*
2:6, *100, 101, 130*
2:9, *102*
2:10, *54, 101, 102, 113*
2:11-16, *101*
2:11-22, *47, 53, 129, 138*
2:14-17, *88*
2:19-22, *138*
3:1, *129*
3:7, *129*
3:13, *129*
4, *53, 113, 131*
4:7-24, *131*
4:9, *129*

4:11-13, *131*
4:13, *113, 114, 138, 184*
4:13-16, *83, 102, 115, 138*
4:15, *138*
4:17-24, *39*
4:17-32, *102*
4:23-24, *83, 98, 102, 112, 207*
4:23–5:2, *131*
4:24, *44, 104, 138, 184*
4:28, *125*
4:31–5:2, *83*
4:32, *130*
5, *186, 214*
5:1, *28, 130*
5:1-33, *130*
5:2, *140*
5:5-6, *130*
5:6-8, *130*
5:8, *130*
5:15, *36*
5:20, *130*
5:20-21, *112*
5:25, *186*
5:25-31, *83*
5:25-32, *131*
6:19, *129*

Philippians
1, *134*
1:6, *54, 113, 132*
1:7, *129*
1:8, *54, 113, 132*
1:13, *129*
1:14, *129*
1:17, *129*
1:29-30, *133*
2, *133, 184*
2:1, *134*
2:1-3, *133*

2:3-11, *24, 132*
2:4-13, *133*
2:5-11, *64*
2:6, *24*
2:6-11, *132*
2:11-13, *132*
2:12-13, *48*
2:13, *54, 113, 115, 134*
2:14-18, *133*
2:15, *134*
2:17, *140*
2:25-30, *133*
2:29, *134*
3, *103, 113*
3:3-5, *133*
3:7-9, *133*
3:9, *134*
3:9-11, *133*
3:10, *104*
3:10-11, *104*
3:10-15, *114, 115*
3:10-16, *133*
3:11, *134*
3:14, *134*
3:15, *114, 115*
3:17, *117*
3:17-21, *133*
3:21, *96, 134*
4:2, *134*
4:2-3, *140*
4:3, *134*
4:4-7, *134*
4:7, *134*
4:8-9, *134*
4:9, *134*
4:9-13, *115*
4:10-13, *134*
4:11-16, *115*
4:13, *134*
4:14-19, *134*
4:17-19, *134*
4:18, *140*

Colossians
1, *170*
1:15, *114, 119, 151*
1:15-20, *36*
1:20, *88*
1:24, *103, 120, 129, 135*
1:28, *114*
1:29, *54, 113*
2:11-13, *103*
2:12, *100, 103*
2:12-15, *99*
3:1, *103*
3:1-11, *102*
3:1-17, *131*
3:3-4, *103*
3:9-10, *105, 128*
3:10, *119*
3:17, *36*
3:23, *36*
4:12, *114*
4:18, *129*

1 Thessalonians
1:5-6, *156*
1:6, *156*
1:7, *156, 159*
2:1-12, *156*
2:4-11, *158*
2:14-17, *159*
3:3-4, *147*
3:11-13, *158*
4:3-7, *141*
4:9-12, *158*
4:11, *125*
5:10, *103*
5:23, *114*

2 Thessalonians
3:6-12, *156*
3:6-15, *158*
3:14-15, *88*

1 Timothy
1:2, *157*
1:16, *155*
3:1-13, *156*
3:16, *62*
4:12, *156*
5:17, *40*
6:11-14, *157*

2 Timothy
1:8, *157*
2:2, *157*
2:3, *157*
2:8, *68, 97*
2:8-12, *103*
2:9, *129*
2:10, *135*
2:22, *151*
3:10-13, *157*
3:15, *167*
3:16-17, *115, 168,*
    173
4:5-8, *157*
4:6, *140*

Titus
1, *111*
1:2, *134*
1:4, *157*
1:8, *134*
1:12, *134*
2:7, *134, 157*
3:5, *111*

Philemon
10, *129*
13, *129*

Hebrews
1:2, *97*
3–4, *141, 167*
3:6, *141*
4:2, *160*

4:15, *70*
5:12–6:3, *72*
5:14–6:12, *115*
6:12, *159*
8:13, *160*
10:12, *147*
11, *148, 159, 172,*
    174, 177, 178,
    197, 203
11–12, *180*
11:1–12:2, *159*
11:8-10, *166*
11:8-12, *160*
11:13-16, *166*
11:17, *178*
11:19, *178*
11:24-26, *160*
11:25-26, *148*
11:32, *159*
12, *139, 160*
12:1, *147, 156*
12:2, *147*
12:3-12, *160*
12:5-7, *37*
12:7-8, *40*
12:10, *147*
12:14, *47, 141*
12:15-17, *160*
12:16, *167*
12:18-27, *160*
13, *180, 214*
13:1-2, *160*
13:2, *186*
13:5, *167*
13:7, *158*
13:12-14, *148*
13:13, *148*
13:15-16, *140,*
    147
13:21, *115*

James
1:4, *115*

1:18, *150*
1:21, *151*
1:21-22, *151*
1:27, *115*
2, *203*
2:14-16, *177*
2:14-23, *166*
2:14-26, *160,*
    178
3:13, *36*
3:13-17, *36*
4:5, *37*
4:8, *151*
4:10, *103*
5:7-11, *203*
5:10-18, *160*
5:17, *160*
5:19-20, *88*

1 Peter
1:6-9, *88*
1:14-17, *47, 150*
1:23, *150*
2:9, *140*
2:10, *150*
2:18-25, *148*
2:21, *149, 158*
2:21-24, *184*
2:24-25, *150*
2:25, *158*
3, *214*
3:3-6, *161*
3:6, *166*
3:16-18, *148*
4:1-2, *148*
4:6, *151*
4:9-11, *138*
4:12-19, *148*
4:13, *103*
5:2-4, *158*
5:5, *37*
5:9-10, *159*
5:13, *172*

2 Peter
1:3, *150, 151*
1:4, *105, 151*
1:7, *151*
2:1, *172*
2:2, *172*
2:3, *172*
2:4, *161*
2:5, *172*
2:5-6, *172*
2:7, *172*
2:10, *172*
2:11, *161*
2:13-14, *39*
2:15, *172*
2:18, *172*
2:22, *37*
3, *12*
3:7, *151*
3:11, *151*
3:14, *151*
3:15, *36*

1 John
1:7, *212*
1:7–2:2, *217*
1:8, *213*
1:10, *213, 217*
2:3, *214*
2:3-4, *218*
2:4, *217*
2:6, *205, 211*
2:24-28, *212*
2:29, *212, 214*
3, *214*
3:1, *213*
3:2, *45, 209, 210,*
    216
3:3, *214,*
    216
3:8, *211*
3:8-9, *213*
3:10, *214*

3:12, *172*
3:15-18, *214*
3:16-18, *211, 215*
3:16-24, *214, 218*
3:17, *211, 212*
3:23, *212*
4:1-3, *217*
4:2, *217*
4:2-3, *214*
4:6, *214*
4:7-11, *211*
4:8, *212, 214*
4:11-12, *213*
4:12, *213*
4:13, *212, 214*

4:16, *211, 214*
4:16-17, *210*
4:17, *211, 213, 214*
4:18, *211*
4:19, *211*
5:1, *212*
5:2, *214, 218*
5:18, *214*

2 John
7, *62*

3 John
11, *211, 214, 215*

Jude
7, *172*
8–9, *161*
11, *172*

Revelation
1:5, *149*
1:6, *149, 150*
1:9, *150*
2–3, *140, 173, 179*
2:4-5, *141*
2:7, *149*
2:10, *172*
2:14, *172*
2:16, *141*

2:17, *149*
2:21-23, *141*
2:23, *172*
2:26, *149*
3:1-3, *141*
3:5, *149*
3:12, *138, 149*
3:21, *149*
6:9, *150*
11:15, *52*
14:4-5, *150*
15:2, *149, 179*
18:6, *172*
19:7-8, *30*
20:4, *40*